Thomas Carlyle

History of Friedrich II. of Prussia, called Frederick the Great

Thomas Carlyle

History of Friedrich II. of Prussia, called Frederick the Great

ISBN/EAN: 9783742822154

Manufactured in Europe, USA, Canada, Australia, Japa

Cover: Foto ©ninafisch / pixelio.de

Manufactured and distributed by brebook publishing software (www.brebook.com)

Thomas Carlyle

History of Friedrich II. of Prussia, called Frederick the Great

COLLECTION
OF
BRITISH AUTHORS.
VOL. 764.

FREDERICK THE GREAT BY THOMAS CARLYLE.

VOL. X.

HISTORY

OF

FRIEDRICH II. OF PRUSSIA,

CALLED

FREDERICK THE GREAT.

BY

THOMAS CARLYLE.

COPYRIGHT EDITION.

VOL. X.

LEIPZIG

BERNHARD TAUCHNITZ

1865.

CONTENTS

OF VOLUME X.

BOOK XVIII.

SEVEN-YEARS WAR RISES TO A HEIGHT. 1757—1759.

CHAPTER	PAGE
I. THE CAMPAIGN OPENS	3

Reich's Thunder, slight Survey of it; with Question, Whitherward, if anywhither? p. 9.
Friedrich suddenly marches on Prag, 15.

II. BATTLE OF PRAG	25
III. PRAG CANNOT BE GOT AT ONCE	57

Colonel Mayer with his "Free-Corps" Party makes a Visit, of didactic Nature, to the Reich, p. 61.
Of the singular quasi-bewitched Condition of England; and what is to be hoped from it, for the Common Cause, if Prag go amiss, 66.
Phenomena of Prag Siege:—Prag Siege is interrupted, 79.

IV. BATTLE OF KOLIN	85

The Maria-Theresa Order, new Knighthood for Austria, p. 105.

V. FRIEDRICH AT LEITMERITZ, HIS WORLD OF ENEMIES COMING ON	108

Prince August Wilhelm finds a bad Problem at Jung-Bunzlau; and does it badly: Friedrich thereupon has to rise from Leitmeritz, and take the Field elsewhere, in bitter Haste and Impatience, with Outlooks worse than ever, p. 128.

CONTENTS OF VOLUME X.

CHAPTER	PAGE
VI. DEATH OF WINTERFELD	146
VII. FRIEDRICH IN THÜRINGEN, HIS WORLD OF ENEMIES ALL COME	153

    I. Friedrich's March to Erfurt from Dresden (31st August—13th September 1757), p. 156.

    II. The Soubise-Hildburghausen People take into the Hills; Friedrich in Erfurt Neighbourhood, hanging on, Week after Week, in an Agony of Inaction (13th September—10th October), 162.

    III. Rumour of an Inroad on Berlin suddenly sets Friedrich on March thither: Inroad takes Effect,—with important Results, chiefly in a left-hand Form, 180.

VIII. BATTLE OF ROSSBACH	201

    Catastrophe of Dauphiness (Saturday, 5th November 1757), p. 207.

    Ulterior Fate of Dauphiness; flies over the Rhine in bad Fashion: Dauphiness's Ways with the Saxon Populations in her Deliverance-Work, 225.

IX. FRIEDRICH MARCHES FOR SILESIA	239
X. BATTLE OF LEUTHEN	257
XI. WINTER IN BRESLAU: THIRD CAMPAIGN OPENS	286

    Of the English Subsidy, p. 297.

    Friedrich, as indeed Pitt's People and Others have done, takes the Field uncommonly early: Friedrich goes upon Schweidnitz, as the Preface to whatever his Campaign may be, 304.

XII. SIEGE OF OLMÜTZ	309

BOOK XVIII.
SEVEN-YEARS WAR RISES TO A HEIGHT.
1757-1759.

Jan. — April 1757

CHAPTER I.

THE CAMPAIGN OPENS.

SELDOM was there seen such a combination against any man as this against Friedrich, after his Saxon performances in 1756. The extent of his sin, which is now ascertained to have been what we saw, was at that time considered to transcend all computation, and to mark him out for partition, for suppression, and enchainment, as the general enemy of mankind. "Partition him, cut him down," said the Great Powers to one another; and are busy, as never before, in raising forces, inciting new alliances, and calling out the general *posse comitatus* of mankind, for that salutary object. What tempestuous fulminations in the Reichstag, and over all Europe, England alone excepted, against this man!

Latterly the Swedes, who at first had compunctions on the score of Protestantism, have agreed to join in the Partitioning adventure: "It brings us his Pommern, all Pommern ours!" cry the Swedish Parliamentary Eloquences (with French gold in their pocket): "At any rate," whisper they, "it spites the Queen his Sister!" — and drag the poor Swedish Nation into a series of disgraces and disastrous platitudes it was little anticipating. This precious French-Swedish Bargain ("Swedes to invade with 25,000; France to give fair subsidy," and bribe largely) was consummated in March;* but did

* "21st March 1757" (Stenzel, v. 35; &c.).

not become known to Friedrich for some months later; nor was it of the importance he then thought it, in the first moment of surprise and provocation. Not indeed of importance to anybody, except, in the reverse way, to poor Sweden itself, and to the French, who had spent a great deal of pains and money on it, and continued to spend, with as good as no result at all. For there never was such a War, before or since, not even by Sweden in the Captainless state! And the one profit the copartners reaped from it, was some discountenance it gave to the rumour which had risen, more extensively than we should now think, and even with some nucleus of fact in it as appears, That Austria, France and the Catholic part of the Reich were combining to put down Protestantism. To which they could now answer, "See, Protestant Sweden is with us!"—and so weaken a little what was pretty much Friedrich's last hold on the public sympathies at this time.

As to France itself,—to France, Austria, Russia,—bound by such earthly Treaties, and the call of very Heaven, shall they not, in united puissance and indignation, rise to the rescue? France, touched to the heart by such treatment of a Saxon Kurfürst, and bound by Treaty of Westphalia to protect all members of the Reich (which it has sometimes, to our own knowledge, so carefully done), is almost more ardent than Austria itself. France, Austria, Russia; to these add Polish Majesty himself; and latterly the very Swedes, by French bribery at Stockholm: these are the Partitioning Powers;—and their shares (let us spare one line to their shares) are as follows.

The Swedes are to have Pommern in whole; Polish-Saxon Majesty gets Magdeburg, Halle, and opulent slices thereabouts; Austria's share, we need not say, is that jewel of a Silesia. Czarish Majesty, on the extreme East, takes Preussen, Königsberg-Memel Country in whole; adds Preussen to her as yet too narrow Territories. Wesel-Cleve Country, from the other or Western extremity, France will take that clipping, and make much of it. These are quite serious business-engagements, engrossed on careful parchment, that Spring 1757, and I suppose not yet boiled down into glue, but still to be found in dusty corners, with the tape much faded. The high heads, making preparation on the due scale, think them not only executable, but indubitable, and almost as good as done. Push home upon him, as united Posse Comitatus of Mankind; in a sacred cause of Polish Majesty and Public Justice, how can one malefactor resist? "*Ah, ma très-chère Reine,*" and "Oh, my dearest Princess and Cousin," what a chance has turned up!

It is computed that there are arrayed against this one King, under their respective Kings, Empress-Queens, Swedish Senates, Catins and Pompadours, populations to the amount of above 100 millions, — in after stages, I remember to have seen "150 millions" loosely given as the exaggerative cipher. Of armed soldiers actually in the field against him (against Hanover and him), in 1757, there are, by strict count, 430,000. Friedrich's own Dominions at this time contain about Five Millions of Population; of Revenue somewhat less than Two Millions sterling. New taxes he cannot legally, and will not, lay on his People. His *Schatz* (ready-money Treasure, or Hoard yearly accumulating for such end) is, I doubt not, well filled, — express amount not mentioned. Of drilled men he has, this Year, 150,000 for the field; portioned out thriftily, — as well beseems, against Four Invasions coming on him from different points. In the field, 150,000 soldiers, probably the best that ever were; and in garrison, up and down (his Country being, by nature, the least defensible of all Countries), near 40,000, which he reckons of inferior quality. So stands the account.* These are, arithmetically precise, his resources, — *plus* only what may lie in his own head and heart, or funded in the other heads and hearts, especially in those 150,000, which he and his Fathers have been diligently disciplining, to good perfection, for four centuries come the time.

France, urged by Pompadour and the enthusiasms, was first in the field. The French Army, in superb equipment, though privately in poorish state of discipline, took the road early in March; "March 26th and 27th," it crossed the German Border, Cleve Country and Köln Country; had been rumoured of since January and February last, as terrifically grand; and here it now actually is, above 100,000 strong, — 110,405, as the Army-Lists, flaming through all the Newspapers, teach mankind.** Bent mainly upon Prussia, it would seem; such the will of Pompadour. Mainly upon Prussia; Maréchal d'Estrées, crossing at Köln, made offers even to his Britannic Majesty to be forgiven in comparison; "Yield us a road through your Hanover, merely a road to those Halberstadt-Magde-

---
* Stenzel, iv. 305, 306, v. 39; Ranke, III. 415; Preuss, II. 339, 43, 124; &c. &c., — substantially true, I doubt not; but little or nothing of it so definite and conclusively distinct as it ought, in all items, to have been, by this time, — had poor Dryasdust known what he was doing.
** Helden-Geschichte, iv. 591; III. 1073.

burg parts, your Hanover shall have neutrality!"
"Neutrality to Hanover?" sighed Britannic Majesty:
"Alas, am not I pledged by Treaty? And, alas, withal,
how is it possible, with that America hanging over
us?" and stood true. Nor is this all, on the part of
magnanimous France: there is a Soubise getting under
way withal, Soubise and 30,000, who will reinforce the
Reich's Armament, were it on foot, and be heard of by
and by! So high runs French enthusiasm at present.
A new sting of provocation to Most Christian Majesty,
it seems, has been Friedrich's conduct in that Damiens
matter (miserable attempt, by a poor mad creature, to
assassinate, or at least draw blood upon the Most
Christian Majesty*); about which Friedrich, busy and
oblivious, had never, in common politeness, been at
the pains to condole, compliment, or take any notice
whatever. And will now take the consequences, as
due! —

The Wesel-Cleve Countries these French find abandoned: Friedrich's garrisons have had orders to bring off the artillery and stores, blow up what of the works are suitable for blowing up; and join the "Britannic Army of Observation" which is getting itself together in those regions. Considerable Army, Britannic wholly in the money part: new Hanoverians so many, Brunswickers, Bückeburgers, Sachsen-Gothaers so many; add those precious Hanoverian-Hessian 20,000, whom we have had in England guarding our liberties so long, — who are now shipped over in a lot; fair wind and full sea to them. Army of 60,000 on paper; of

---

* "Evening of 5th January 1757" (exuberantly plentiful details of it, and of the horrible Law-procedures which followed on it: in Adelung, vii. 197-220; Barbier, &c. &c.).

effective, more than 50,000; Headquarters now at Bielefeld on the Weser; — where, "April 16th," or a few days later, Royal Highness of Cumberland comes to take command; likely to make a fine figure against Maréchal d'Estrées and his 100,000 French! But there was no helping it. Friedrich, through Winter, has had Schmettau earnestly flagitating the Hanoverian Officialities: "The Weser is wadeable in many places, you cannot defend the Weser!" and counselling and pleading to all lengths, — without the least effect. "Wants to save his own Halberstadt lands, at our expense!" Which was the idea in London, too: "Don't we, by Apocalyptic Newswriters and eyesight of our own, understand the man?" Pitt is by this time in Office, who perhaps might have judged a little otherwise. But Pitt's seat is altogether temporary, insecure; the ruling deities Newcastle and Royal Highness, who withal are in standing quarrel. So that Friedrich, Schmettau, Mitchell pleaded to the deaf. Nothing but "Defend the Weser," and ignorant Fatuity ready for the Impossible, is to be made out there. "Cannot help it, then," thinks Friedrich, often enough, in bad moments; "Army of Observation will have its fate. Happily there are only 5,000 Prussians in it, Wesel and the other garrisons given up!"

Only 5,000 Prussians: by original Engagement, there should have been 25,000; and Friedrich's intention is even 45,000 if he prosper otherwise. For in January 1757 (Anniversary, or nearly so, of that *Neutrality Convention* last year), there had been, — encouraged by Pitt, as I could surmise, who always likes Friedrich, — a definite, much closer *Treaty of Alliance*, with "Subsidy of a million sterling," Anti-

Russian "Squadron of Observation in the Baltic," "25,000 Prussians," and other items, which I forget. Forget the more readily, as, owing to the strange state of England (near suffocating in its Constitutional bedclothes), the Treaty could not be kept at all, or serve as rule to poor England's exertions for Friedrich this Year; exertions which were of the willing-minded but futile kind, going forward pellmell, not by plan, and could reach Friedrich only in the lump, — had there been any "lump" of them to sum together. But Pitt had gone out; — we shall see what, in Pitt's absence, there was! So that this Treaty 1757 fell quite into the waste-basket (not to say, far deeper, by way of "pavement" we know where!), — and is not mentioned in any English Book; nor was known to exist, till some Collector of such things printed it, in comparatively recent times."* A Treaty 1757, which, except as emblem of the then quasi-enchanted condition of England, and as Foreshadow of Pitt's new Treaty in January 1758, and of three others that followed and *were* kept to the letter, is not of moment farther.

Reich's Thunder, slight Survey of it; with Question, Whitherward, if anywhither!

The thunderous fulminations in the Reich's Diet, — an injured Saxony complaining, an insulted Kaiser, after vain *Dehortatoriums*, reporting and denouncing, "Horrors such as these: What say you, O Reich?" — have been going on since September last; and amount to boundless masses of the liveliest Parliamentary Elo-

---

* "M. Koch in 1802," not very perfectly (Schöll, III. 30n; who copies what Koch has given).

quence, now fallen extinct to all creatures.* The Kaisor, otherwise a solid pacific gentleman, intont on commercial operations (furnishes a good deal of our meal, says Friedrich), is Officially extremely violent in behalf of injured Saxony, — that is to say, in fact, of injured Austria, which is one's own. Kur-Mainz, Chairman of the Diet (we remember how he was got, and a Battle of Dettingen fought in consequence, long since); Kur-Mainz is admitted to have the most decided Austrian leanings: Britannic George, Austria being now in the opposite scale, finds him an unhandy Kur-Mainz, and what profit it was to introduce false weights into the Reich's balance that time! Not for long generations before, had the poor old semi-imaginary Reich's-Diet risen into such paroxysms; nor did it ever again after. Never again, in its terrestrial History, was there such agonistic parliamentary struggle, and terrific noise of parliamentary palaver, witnessed in the poor Reich's Diet. Noise and struggle, rising ever higher, peal after peal, from September 1756, when it started, till August 1757, when it had reached its acme (as perhaps we shall see), though it was far from ending then, or for years to come.

Contemporary bystanders remark, on the Austrian part, extraordinary rage and hatred against Prussia; which is now the one point memorable. Austria is used to speak loud in the Diet, as we have ourselves seen: and it is again (if you dive into those old Æolus'-Caves, at your peril) unpleasantly notable to what pitch of fixed rage, and hot sullen hatred, Austria has now gone; and how the tone has in it a potency of

* Given, to great lengths, in *Helden-Geschichte*, iii., iv. (and other easily avoidable Books).

world-wide squealing and droning, such as you nowhere heard before. Omnipotence of droning, edged with shrieky squealing, which fills the Universe, not at all in a melodious way. From the depths of the gamut to the shrieky top again, — a droning that has something of porcine or wild-boar character. Figure assembled the wild-boars of the world, all or mostly all got together, and each with a knife just stuck into its side, by a felonious individual too well known, — you will have some notion of the sound of these things. Friedrich sometimes remonstrates: "Cannot you spare such phraseology, unseemly to Kings? The quarrels of Kings have to be decided by the sword; what profit in unseemly language, Madam?" — but, for the first year and more, there was no abatement on the Austrian part.

Friedrich's own Delegate at Regensburg, a Baron von Plotho, come of old Brandenburg kindred, is a resolute, ready-tongued, very undaunted gentleman; learned in Diplomacies and Reich's Law; carries his head high, and always has his story at hand. Argument, grounded on Reich's Law and the nature of the case, Plotho never lacks, on spur of the hour: and is indeed a very commendable parliamentary mastiff; and honourable and melodious is the bark of him, compared with those enfuriated porcine specimens. He has Kur-Hanover for ally on common occasions, and generally from most Protestant members individually, or from the *Corpus Evangelicorum* in mass, some feeble whimper of support. Finds difficulty in getting his Reich's Pleadings printed; — dangerous, everywhere in those Southern Parts, to print anything whatever that is not Austrian: so that Plotho, at length, gets printers to himself, and sets up a Printing-Press in his own house at Regensburg. He did a great deal of sonorous pleading for Friedrich; proud, deep-voiced, ruggedly logical; fairly beyond the Austrian quality in many cases, — and always far briefer, which is another high merit. October coming, we purpose to look in upon Plotho for one minute; "October 14th, 1757;" which may be reckoned essentially the acme or turning-point of these unpleasant thunderings.*

What good he did to Friedrich, or could have done with the tongue of angels in such an audience, we do not accurately know. Some good he would do even in the Reich's-Diet there; and out of doors, over a German public, still more; and is worth his frugal wages, — say 1,000*l.* a year, printing and all other expense included! This is a mere guess of mine, Dryasdust having been incurious: but, to English readers, it is incredible for what sums Friedrich got his work done, no work ever better. Which is itself an appreciable advantage, computable in pounds sterling; and is the parent of innumerable others which no Arithmetic or Book-keeping by Double Entry will take hold of, and which are indeed priceless for Nations and for persons. But this poor old bed-ridden Reich, starting in agonistic spasm at such rate: is it not touching, in a Corpus moribund for so many Centuries past! The Reich is something; though it is not much, nothing like so much as even Kaiser Franz supposes it. Much or not so much, Kaiser Franz wishes to secure it for himself; Friedrich to hinder him, — and it must be a poor something, if not worth Plotho's wages on Friedrich's part.

It would insult the patience of every reader to go

* *Helden Geschichte,* iv. 745-9.

into these spasmodic tossings of the poor paralytic Reich; or to mention the least item of them beyond what had some result, or fraction of result, on the world's real affairs. We shall say only, therefore, that after tempests not a few of porcine squealing, answered always by counter-latration on the vigilant Plotho's part; — squealing, chiefly, from the Reichs-Hofrath at Vienna, the Head Tribunal of Imperial Majesty, which sits judging and denouncing there, touched to the soul, as if by a knife driven into its side, by those unheard-of treatments of Saxony and disregard to our *Dehortatoriums*, and which bursts out, peal after peal, filling the Universe, Plotho not unvigilant; — the poor old Reich's-Diet did at last get into an acting posture, and determine, by clear majority of 99 against 60, that there should be a "Reich's Execution Army" got on foot. Reich's Execution Army to coerce, by force of arms, this nefarious King of Prussia into making instant restitution to Saxony, with ample damages on the nail; that right be done to Kurfürsts of this Reich. To such height of vigour has the Reichs-Diet gone; — and was voting it at Regensburg, January 10th, 1757;* that very day when nefarious Friedrich at Berlin, case-hardened in iniquity to such a pitch, sat writing his *Instruction to Count Finck*, which we read not long since. Simultaneous movements, unknown to one another, in this big wrestle.

Reich's-Diet perfected its Vote; had it quite through, and sanctioned by the Kaiser's Majesty, January 29th: "Arming to be a *triplum*" (triple contingent required of you, this time); with Romish-months (*Römermonate*) of cash contribution from all and sundry (rigorously

* *Helden-Geschichte*, IV. 259-262-330; Stenzel, v. 62.

gathered, I should hope, where Austria has power), so many as will cover the expense. Army to be got on actual foot hastily, instantly if possible: an '*eilende Reichs-Executions-Armee;*' so it ran, but the word *eilende* (speedy) had a mischance in printing, and was struck off into *elende* (contemptibly wretched): so that on all Market-Squares and Public Places of poor Teutschland, you read flaming Placards summoning out, not a speedy or immediate, but 'a *miserable* Reich's Execution Army!' A word which, we need not say, was laughed at by the unfeeling part of the public; and was often called to mind by the Reich's Execution Army's performances, when said *speedy* Army did at last take the field.

For the Reich performed its Vote; actually had a Reich's Execution Army; the last it ever had in this world, not by any means the worst it ever had, for they used generally to be bad. Commanders, managers are named, Römermonate are gathered in, or the sure prospect of them; and, through May — June 1757, there is busy stir, of drumming, preparing, and enlisting, all over the Reich. End of July, we shall see the Reich's Army in Camp; end of August, actually in the field; and later on, a touch of its fighting withal. Many other things the Reich tried against unfortunate Friedrich, — gradual advance, in fact, to Ban of the Reich (or total anathema and cutting off from fire and water): but in none of these, in Ban as little as any, did it come to practical result at all, or acquire the least title to be remembered at this day. Finis of Ban, some eight months hence, has something of attractive as futility, the curious Death of a Futility. Finis of Ban (October 14th, already indicated) we may for one moment look in upon, if there be one moment to spare;

the rest — readers shall fancy it; and read only of the actuality and fighting part, which will itself be enough for them on such a matter.

Friedrich suddenly marches on Prag.

Four Invasions, from their respective points of the compass, north-east, north-west, south-east and southwest: here is a formidable outlook for the one man against whom they are all advancing open-mouthed. The one man, — with nothing but a Duke of Cumberland and his Observation Army for backing in such duel, — had need to look to himself! Which, we well know, he does; wrapt in profoundly silent vigilance, with his plans all laid. Of the Four Invasions, three, the Russian, French, Austrian, are very large; and the two latter, especially the last, are abundantly formidable. The Swedish, of which there is rumouring, he hopes may come to little, or not come at all. Nor is Russia, though talking big, and actually getting ready above 100,000 men, so immediately alarming. Friedrich always hopes the English, with their guineas and their managements, will do something for him in that quarter; and he knows, at worst, that the Russian Hundred-Thousand will be a very slow-moving entity. The Swedish Invasion Friedrich, for the present, leaves to chance: and against Russia, he has sent old Marshal Lehwald into those Baltic parts; far eastward, towards the utmost Memel Frontier, to put the Country upon its own defence, and make what he can of it with 30,000 men, — West-Prussian militias a good few of them. This is all he can spare on the Swedish-Russian side: Austria and France are the perilous pair of entities; not to be managed except by intense concentration of stroke; and by going on them in succession, if one have luck! —

Friedrich's motions and procedures in canton-quarters, through Winter and in late months, have led to the belief that he means to stand on the defensive; that the scene of the Campaign will probably be Saxony; and that Austria, for recovering injured Saxony, for recovering dear Silesia, will have to take an invasive attitude. And Austria is busy everywhere preparing with that view. Has Tolpatcheries, and advanced Brigades, still harassing about in the Lausitz. A great Army assembling at Prag, — Browne forward towards the Metal Mountains securing posts, gathering magazines, for the crossing into Saxony there. There, it is thought, the tug of war will probably be. Furious, and strenuous, it is not doubted, on this Friedrich's part: but against such odds, what can he do? With Austrians in front, with Russians to left, with French to right and a-rear, not to mention Swedes and appendages: surely here, if ever, is a lost King! —

It is by no means Friedrich's intention that Saxony itself shall need to be invaded. Friedrich's habit is, as his enemies might by this time be beginning to learn, not that of standing on the defensive, but that of *going* on it, as the preferable method wherever possible. March 24th, Friedrich had quitted Dresden City; and for a month after (headquarters Lockwitz, edge of the Pirna Country), he had been shifting, redistributing, his cantoned Army, — privately into the due Divisions, due readiness for march. Which done, on fixed days, about the end of April, the whole Army, he himself from Lockwitz, April 20th, — to the surprise of Austria and the world, Friedrich in three grand Columns, Bevern out of the Lausitz, King himself over the Metal Mountains, Schwerin out of Schlesien, is marching with extraordinary rapidity direct for Prag; in the notion that a right plunge into the heart of Bohemia will be the best defence for Saxony and the other places under menace.

This is a most unexpected movement; which greatly astonishes the world-theatre, pit, boxes and gallery alike (as Friedrich's sudden movements often do); and which is, above all, interesting on the stage itself, where the actors had been counting on a quite opposite set of entries and activities! Feldmarschall Browne, and General Königseck (not our old friend Königseck, who used to drynurse in the Netherlands, but his nephew and heir) may cease gathering Magazines, in those Lausitz and Metal-Mountain parts: happy could they give wings to those already gathered! Magazines, for Austrian service, are clearly not the things wanted there. One does not burn one's Magazines till the last extremity; but wings they have none; and such is the enigmatic velocity of those Prussian movements, one seldom has time even to burn them, in the last crisis of catastrophe! Considerable portions of that provender fell into the Prussian throat; as much as "three-months provision for the whole Army," count they, — adding to those Frontier sundries, the really important Magazine which they seized at Jung-Bunzlau farther in.* It is one among their many greater advantages from this surprisal of the enemy, and sudden topsy-turvying of his plans. Browne and Königseck have to retire on Prag at their swiftest; looking to more important results than Magazines.

* *Helden-Geschichte*, iv. 6-13; &c.

It is Friedrich's old plan. Long since, in 1744, we saw a march of this kind, Three Columns rushing with simultaneous rapidity on Prag; and need not repeat the particulars on this occasion. Here are some Notes on the subject, which will sufficiently bring it home to readers:

"The Three Columns were, for a part of the way, Four; "the King's being, at first, in two branches, till they united "again, on the other side of the Hills. For the King," what is to be noted, "had shot out, three weeks before, a small pre- "liminary branch, under Moritz of Dessau; who marched, "well westward, by Eger (starting from Chemnitz in Saxony); "and had some tusseling with our poor old friend Duke "d'Ahremberg, Browne's subordinate in those parts. "D'Ahremberg, having 20,000 under him, would not quit "Eger for Moritz; but pushed out Croats upon him, and sat "still. This, it was afterwards surmised, had been a feint on "Friedrich's part; to give the Austrians pleasant thoughts: "'Invading us, is he? Would fain invade us, but cannot!' "Moritz fell back from Eger; and was ready to join the "King's march, 'at Linay, April 23d' (third day from Lock- "witz, on the King's part). Onwards from which point the "Columns are specifically Three; in strength, and on routes, "somewhat as follows:

1º. "The *First* Column or King's, — which is 60,000 after "this junction, 45,000 foot, 15,000 horse, — quitted Lockwitz "(headquarter for a month past), *Wednesday, April 20th.* "They go by the Pascopol and other roads; through Pirna, "for one place: through Karbitz, Aussig, are at Linay on "the 23d; where Moritz joins: 24th, in the united state, for- "ward again (leave Lobositz two miles to left); to Trebnitz, "25th, and rest there one day.

"At Aussig an unfortunate thing befel. Zastrow, respect- "able old General Zastrow, was to drive the Austrians out of "Aussig: Zastrow does it, April 22d-23d, drives them well "over the heights; April 25th, however, marching forward "towards Lobositz, Zastrow is shot through both temples "(Pandour hid among the bushes and cliffs, *other* side of Elbe), "and falls dead on the spot. Buried in *Gottleube* Kirk, "1st May."

In these Aussig affairs, especially in recapturing the Castle of Tetschen near by, Colonel Mayer, father of the new "Free-Corps," did shining service; — and was approved of, he and they. And, a day or two after, was detached with a Fifteen Hundred of that kind, on more important business: First to pick up one or two Bohemian Magazines lying handy; after which, — to pay a visit to the Reich and its bluster about Execution-Army, and teach certain persons, who it is they are thundering against in that awkwardly truculent manner! Errand shiningly done by Mayer, as perhaps we may hear, — and certainly as all the Newspapers loudly heard, — in the course of the next two months.

At crossing of the Eger, Friedrich's Column had some chasing of poor D'Ahremberg; attempting to cut him off from his Bridges, Bridge of Koschlitz, Bridge of Budin; but he made good despatch, Browne and he; and, except a few prisoners of Ziethen's gathering, and most of his Magazines unburnt, they did him no damage. The chase was close enough; more than once, the Austrian head-quarter of tonight was that of the Prussians tomorrow. Monday, May 2d, Friedrich's Column was on the Weissenberg of Prag; Browne, D'Ahremberg, and Prince Karl, who is now come up to take command, having hastily filed through the City, leaving a fit garrison, the day before. Except his Magazines, nothing the least essential went wrong with Browne; but Königseck, who had not a Friedrich on his heels, — Königseck, trying more, as his opportunities were more, — was not quite so lucky.

2º. "Column *Second*, to the King's left, comes from the "Lausitz under Brunswick-Bevern, — 18,000 foot, 5,000 "horse. This is the Bevern who so distinguished himself at

"Lobositz last year; and he is now to culminate into a still "brighter exploit, — the last of his very bright ones, as it "proved. Bevern set out from about Zittau (from Grottau, "few miles south of Zittau), the same day with Friedrich, that "is April 20th; — and had not well started till he came upon "formidable obstacles. Came upon General Königseck, "namely: a Königseck manœuvering ahead, in superior "force; a Macguire, Irish subordinate of Königseck's, com- "ing from the right to cut off our baggage (against whom "Bevern has to detach); a Lacy, coming from the left; — or "indeed, Königseck and Lacy in concert, intending to offer "battle. Battle of Reichenberg, which accordingly ensued, "April 21st," — of which, though it was very famous for so small a Battle, there can be no account given here.

The short truth is, Königseck falling back, Parthian-like, with a force of 30,000 or more, has in front of him nothing but Bevern; who, as he issues from the Lausitz, and till he can unite with Schwerin farther southward, is but some 20,000 odd: cannot Königseck call halt, and bid Bevern return, or do worse? Königseck, a diligent enough soldier, determines to try; chooses an excellent position, — at or round Reichenberg, which is the first Bohemian Town, one march from Zittau in the Lausitz, and then one from Liebenau, which latter would be Bevern's *second* Bohemian stage on the Prag road, if he continued prosperous. Reichenberg, standing nestled among hills in the Neisse Valley (one of those Four Neisses known to us, the Neisse where Prince Karl got exploded, in that signal manner, Winter 1745, by a certain King), offers fine capabili-ties; which Königseck has laid hold of. There is especially one excellent Hollow (on the left or western bank of Neisse River, that is, *across* from Reichenberg), backed by woody hills, nothing but hills, brooks, woods all round; Hollow scooped out as if for the purpose;

and altogether of inviting character to Königseck. There "Wednesday, April 20th," Königseck posts himself, plants batteries, fells abatis; plenty of cannon, of horse and foot, and, say all soldiers, one of the best positions possible.

So that Bevern, approaching Reichenberg at evening, evening of his first march, Wednesday, April 20th, finds his way barred; and that the difficulties may be considerable. "Nothing to be made of it tonight," thinks Bevern; "but we must try tomorrow!" and has to take camp, "with a marshy brook in front of him," some way on the hither side of Reichenberg; and study overnight what method of unbarring there may be. Thursday morning early, Bevern, having well reconnoitred and studied, was at work unbarring. Bevern crossed his own marshy brook; courageously assaulted Königseck's position, left wing of Königseck; stormed the abatis, the batteries, plunged in upon Königseck, man to man, horse to horse, and after some fierce enough but brief dispute, tumbled Königseck out of the ground. Königseck made some attempt to rally; attempted twice, but in vain; had fairly to roll away, and at length to run, leaving 1,000 dead upon the field, about 500 prisoners; one or two guns, and I forget how many standards, or whether any kettle-drums. This was thought to be a decidedly bright feat on Bevern's part (rather mismanaged latterly on Königseck's);[*] — much approved by Friedrich, as he

---

[*] Tempelhof, i. 100; *Helden-Geschichte*, iii. 1077 (Friedrich's own Account, "Linay in Böhmen, 24th April 1757"); &c. &. There is, in Büsching's *Magazin* (xvi. 189 et seq.), an intelligible sketch of this Action of Reichenberg, with satirical criticisms, which have some basis, on Lacy, Macguire and others, by an Anonymous Military Cynic,— who gives many

hears of it, at Linay, on his own prosperous march Prag-ward. A comfortable omen, were there nothing more.

Königseck and Company, torn out of Reichenberg, and set running, could not fairly halt again and face about till at Liebenau, twenty miles off, where they found some defile or difficult bit of ground fit for them; and this too proved capable of yielding pause for a few hours only. For Schwerin, with his Silesian Column, was coming up from the north-east, threatening Königseck on flank and rear: Königseck could only tighten his straps a little at this Liebenau, and again get under way; and making vain attempts to hinder the junction of Schwerin and Bevern, to defend the Jung-Buntzlau Magazine, or do any good in those parts, except to detain the Schwerin-Bevern people certain hours (I think, one day in all), had nothing for it but to gird himself together, and retreat on Prag and the Ziscaberg, where his friends now were.

The Austrian force at Reichenberg was 20,000; would have been 30 and odd thousands, had Macguire come up (as he might have done, had not the appearances alarmed him too much); Bevern, minus the Detachment sent against Macguire, was but 15,000 in fight; and he has quite burst the Austrians away, who had plugged his road for him in such force: is it not a comfortable little victory, glorious in its sort; and a good omen for the bigger things that are coming? Bevern marched composedly on, after this inspiriting tussle, through Liebenau and what defiles there were;

---

such in *Büsching* (that of Fontenoy, for example), not without force of judgment, and signs of wide study and experience in his trade.

April 24th, at Turnau, he falls into the Schwerin Column; incorporates himself therewith, and, as subordinate constituent part, accompanies Schwerin thenceforth.

3º. "Column *Third* was Schwerin's, out of Schlesien; "counted to be 32,000 foot, 12,000 horse. Schwerin, gathering "himself, from Glatz and the northerly country, at Landshut, "— very careless, he, of the pleasant Hills, and fine scattered "peaks of the Giant Mountains thereabouts, — was com- "pletely gathered foremost of all the Columns, having "farthest to go. And on Monday, 18th April, started from "Landshut, Winterfeld leading one Division. In our days, "it is the finest of roads; high level Pass, of good width, "across the Giant Range; pleasant painted hamlets sprinkling "it, fine mountain ridges and distant peaks looking on; "Schneekoppe (*Snowfell*, its head bright white till July come) "attends you, far to the right, all the way: — probably Sprite "Rübezahl inhabits there; and no doubt River Elbe begins "his long journey there, trickling down in little threads over "yonder, intending to float navies by and by: considerations "infinitely indifferent to Schwerin. 'The road,' says my "Tourist, 'is not Alpine; it reminds you of Derbyshire-Peak "'country; more like the road from Castletown to Sheffield "'than any I could name;' — we have been in it before, my "reader and I, about Schatzlar and other places. Trautenau, "well down the Hills, with swift streams, more like torrents, "bound Elbe-wards, watering it, is a considerable Austrian "Town, and the Bohemian end of the Pass, — Sohr only a "few miles from it: heartily indifferent to Schwerin at this "'moment; who was home from the Army, in a kind of dis- "favour, or mutual pet, at the time Sohr was done. Schwerin's "March we shall not give; his junction with Bevern (at "Turnau, on the Iser, April 24th), then their capture of Jung- "Buntzlau Magazine, and crossing of the Elbe at Melnick, "these were the important points; and, in spite of Königs- "eck's tusselings, these all went well, and nothing was lost "except one day of time."

The Austrians, some days ago, as we observed,

filed *through* Prag, — Sunday, May 1st, not a pleasant holiday spectacle to the populations; — and are all encamped on the Ziscaberg high ground, on the other side of the City. Had they been alert, now was their time to attack Friedrich, who is weaker than they, while nobody has yet joined him. They did not think of it, under Prince Karl; and Browne and the Prince are said to be in bad agreement.

CHAPTER II.

BATTLE OF PRAG.

MONDAY morning, 2d May 1757, the Vanguard, or advanced troops of Friedrich's Column, had appeared upon the Weissenberg, north-west corner of Prag (ground known to them in 1744, and to the poor Winter-King in 1620): Vanguard in the morning; followed shortly by Friedrich himself; and, hour after hour, by all the others, marching in. So that, before sunset, the whole force lay posted there; and had the romantic City of Prag full in view at their feet. A most romantic, high-piled, many-towered, most unlevel old City; its skylights and gilt steeplecocks glittering in the western sun, — Austrian Camp very visible close beyond it, spread out miles in extent on the Ziscaberg Heights, or eastern side; — Prag, no doubt, and the Austrian Garrison of Prag, taking intense survey of this Prussian phenomenon, with commentaries, with emotions, hidden now in eternal silence, as is fit enough. One thing we know, "Headquarter was in Welleslawin:" there, in that small Hamlet, nearly to north, lodged Friedrich, the then busiest man of Europe; whom Posterity is still striving for a view of, as something memorable.

Prince Karl, our old friend, is now in chief command yonder; Browne also is there, who was in chief command; their scheme of Campaign gone all awry. And to Friedrich, last night, at his quarters "in the

Monastery of Tuchomirsitz," where these two Gentlemen had lodged the night before, it was reported that they had been heard in violent altercation;* — both of them, naturally, in ill-humour at the surprising turn things had taken; and Feldmarschall Browne firing up, belike, at some platitude past or coming, at some advice of his rejected, some imputation cast on him, or we know not what. Prince Karl is now chief; and indignant Browne, as may well be the case, dissents a good deal, — as he has often had to do. Patience, my friend, it is near ending now! Prince Karl means to lie quiet on the Ziscaberg, and hold Prag; does not think of molesting Friedrich in his solitary state; and will undertake nothing, "till Königseck, from Jung-Buntzlau, come in," victorious or not; or till perhaps even Daun arrive (who is, rather slowly, gathering reinforcement in Mähren): "What can the enemy attempt on us, in a Post of this strength?" thinks Prince Karl. And Browne, whatever his insight or convictions be, has to keep silence.

"Weissenberg," let readers be reminded, "is on the hither "or western side of Prag: the Hradschin" (pronounce Rad-*sheen*, with accent on the last syllable, as in "Schwerín" and other such cases), "the Hradschin, which is the topmost summit "of the City and of the Fashionable Quarter, — old Bohemian "Palace, still occasionally habitable as such, and in constant "use as a *Downing-Street*, — lies on the slope or shoulder of "the Weissenberg, a good way from the top; and has a web "of streets rushing down from it, steepest streets in the world; "till they reach the Bridge, and broad-flowing Moldau "(broad as Thames at half-flood, but nothing like so deep); "after which the streets become level, and spread out in in- "tricate plenty to right and to left, and ahead eastward, "across the River, till the Ziscaberg, with frowning pre-

* *Helden-Geschichte*, iv. 11. (exact 'Diary of the march' given there).

"cipitous brow, suddenly puts a stop to them, in that particu-
"lar direction. From Ziscaberg top to Weissenberg top may
"be about five English miles; from the Hradschin to the foot
"of Ziscaberg, north-west to south-east, will be half that
"distance, the greatest length of Prag City. Which is rather
"rhomboidal in shape, its longer diagonal this that we men-
"tion. The shorter diagonal, from northmost base of Zisca-
"berg to southmost of Hradschin, is perhaps a couple of
"miles. Prag stands nestled in the lap of mountains; and is
"not in itself a strong place in war: but the country round it,
"Moldau ploughing his rugged chasm of a passage through
"the piled table-land, is difficult to manœuvre in.
"Moldau Valley comes straight from the south, crosses
"Prag; and, — making, on its outgate at the northern end of
"Prag (end of "shortest diagonal" just spoken of), one big
"loop, or bend and counter-bend, of horse-shoe shape," which
will be notable to us anon, — "again proceeds straight north-
"ward and Elbe-ward. It is narrow everywhere, especially
"when once got fairly north of Prag; and runs along like a
"Quasi-Highland Strath, amid rocks and Hills. Big Hill-
"ranges, not to be called barren, yet with rock enough on
"each hand, and fine side valleys opening here and there: the
"bottom of your Strath, which is green and fertile, with
"pleasant busy Villages (much intent on water-power and
"cotton-spinning in our time), is generally of few furlongs in
"breadth. And so it lasts, this pleasant Moldau-Valley, mile
"after mile, on the northern or Lower Moldau, generally
"straight north, though with one big bend eastward just
"before ending; and not till near Melnick, or the mouth of
"Moldau, do we emerge on that grand Elbe Valley, —
"glanced at once already, from Pascopol or other Height, in
"the Lobositz times."

Friedrich's first problem is the junction with
Schwerin: junction not to be accomplished south of the
Ziscaberg in the present circumstances; and which
Friedrich knows to be a ticklish operation, with those
Austrians looking on from the high grounds there.
Tuesday 3d May, in the way of reconnoitring, and

decisively on Wednesday 4th, Friedrich is off northward, along the western heights of Lower Moldau, proper force following him, to seek a fit place for the pontoons, and get across in that northern quarter. "How dangerous that Schwerin is a day too late!" murmurs he; but hopes the Austrians will undertake nothing. Keith, with 30,000, he has left on the Weissenberg, to straiten Prag and the Austrian Garrison on that side: our wagon-trains arrive from Leitmeritz on that side, Elbe-boats bring them up to Leitmeritz; very indispensable to guard that side of Prag. Friedrich's fixed purpose also is to beat the Austrians, on the other side of it, and send them packing; but for that, there are steps needful!

Up so far as Lissoley, the first day, Friedrich has found no fit place; but on the morrow, Thursday 5th, farther up, at a place called Seltz, Friedrich finds his side of the Strath to be "a little higher than the other," — proper, therefore, for cannonading the other, if need be; — and orders his pontoons to be built together there. He knows accurately of the Schwerin Column, of the comfortable Bevern Victory at Reichenberg, and how they have got the Jung-Buntzlau Magazine, and are across the Elbe, their bridges all secured, though with delay of one day; and do now wait only for the word, — for the three cannon-shot, in fact, which are to signify that Friedrich is actually crossing to their side of Lower Moldau.

Friedrich's Bridge is speedily built (trained human hands can be no speedier), his batteries planted, his precautions taken: the three cannon-shot go off, audible to Schwerin; and Friedrich's troops stream speedily across, hardly a Pandour to meddle with them. Nay, before the passage was complete — what light-horse squadrons are these? Hussars, seen to be Seidlitz's (missioned by Schwerin), appear on the outskirts: a meeting worthy of three-cheers, surely, after such a march on both sides! Friedrich lies on the eastern Hilltops that night (Hamlet of Czimitz his Headquarter, discoverable if you wish it, scarcely three miles north of Prag); and accurate appointment is made with Schwerin as to the meeting-place tomorrow morning. Meeting-place is to be the environs of Prossik Village, south-eastward over yonder, short way north of the Prag-Königgrätz Highway; and rather nearer Prag than we now are, in Czimitz here: time at Prossik to be 6 A.M. by the clock; and Winterfeld and Schwerin to come in person and speak with his Majesty. This is the program for Friday, May 6th, which proves to be so memorable a day.

Schwerin is on foot by the stroke of midnight; comes along "over the heights of Chaber," by half-a-dozen, or I know not how many roads; visible in due time to Friedrich's people, who are likewise punctually on the advance: in a word, the junction is accomplished with all correctness. And, while the Columns are marching up, Schwerin and Winterfeld ride about in personal conference with his Majesty; taking survey, through spyglasses, of those Austrians encamped yonder on the broad back of their Zisca Hill, a couple of miles to southward. "What a set of Austrians," exclaim military critics; "to permit such junction, without effort to devour the one half or the other, in good time!" Friedrich himself, it is probable, might partly be of the same opinion; but he knew his Austrians, and had made bold to venture. Friedrich, we can observe, always got to know his man, after fighting him a month or two; and took liberties with him, or did not take, accordingly. And, for most part,— not quite always, as one signal exception will show, — he does it with perfect accuracy; and often with vital profit to his measures. "If the Austrian cooking-tents are a-smoke "before eight in the morning," note she, "you may cal- "culate, n such case, the Austrians will march that "day."* With a surprising vividness of eye and mind (beautiful to rival, if one could), he watches the signs of the times, of the hours and the days and the places; and prophesies from them; — reads men and their procedures, as if they were mere handwriting, not too cramp for him. — The Austrians have, by this time, got their Königseck home, very unvictorious, but still on foot, all but a thousand or two: they are already stronger than the Prussians by count of heads; and till even Daun come up, what hurry in a Post like this? The Austrians are viewing Friedrich, too, this morning; but in the blankest manner: their outposts fire a cannon-shot or two on his group of adjutants and him, without effect; and the Head people send their cavalry out to forage, so little prophecy have they from signs seen.

Zisca Hill, where the Austrians now are, rises sheer up, of well-nigh precipitous steepness, though there are trees and grass on it, from the eastern side of Prag, say five or six hundred feet. A steep, picturesque, massive green Hill; Moldau River, turning suddenly to right, strikes the north-west corner of it (has flowed well to west of it, till then), and winds eastward round its northern base. As will be noticed

* *Military Instructions.*

presently. The ascent of Ziscaberg, by roads, is steep and tedious: but once at the top, you find that it is precipitous on two sides only, the City, or westward side, and the Moldau or northward. Atop it spreads out, far and wide, into a waving upland level; bare of hedges; ploughable all of it, studded with littery hamlets and farmsteadings: far and wide, a kind of Plain, sloping with extreme gentleness, five or six miles to eastward, and as far to southward, before the level perceptibly rise again.

Another feature of the Ziscaberg, already hinted at, is very notable: that of the Moldau skirting its northern base, and scarping the Hill, on that side too, into a precipitous, or very steep condition. Moldau having arrived from southward, fairly past the end of Ziscaberg, had, so to speak, made up his mind to go right eastward, quarrying his way through the lower uplands there. And he proceeds, accordingly, hugging the northern base of Ziscaberg, and making it steep enough; but finds, in the course of a mile or so, that he can no more; upland being still rock-built, not underminable farther; and so is obliged to wind round again, to northward, and finally straight westward, the way he came, or parallel to the way he came; and has effected that great Horse-shoe Hollow we heard of lately. An extremely pretty Hollow, and curious to look upon; pretty villas, gardens, and a "Belvedere Park," laid out in the bottom part; with green mountain-walls rising all round it, and a silver ring of river at the base of them: length of Horse-shoe, from heel to toe, or from west to east, is perhaps a mile; breadth, from heel to heel, perhaps half as much. Having arrived at his old distance to west, Moldau, like a repentant prodigal, and as if ashamed of his frolic, just over against the old point he swerved from, takes straight to northward again. Straight northward; and quarries out that fine narrow valley, or Quasi-Highland Strath, with its pleasant busy villages, where he turns the overshot machinery, and where Friedrich and his men had their pontoons swimming yesterday.

It is here, on this broad back of the Ziscaberg, that the Austrians now lie; looking northward over to the King, and trying cannon-shots upon him. There they have been encamping, and diligently entrenching themselves for four days past; diligent especially since yesterday, when they heard of Friedrich's crossing the River. Their groups of tents, and batteries at all the good points, stretch from near the crown of Ziscaberg eastward to the Villages of Hlaupetin, Kyge, and their Lakes, near four miles; and rearward into the interior one knows not how far; — Prince Karl, hardly awake yet, lies at Nussel, near the Moldau, near the Wischerad or south-eastmost point of Prag; six good miles west-by-south of Kyge, at the other end of the diagonal line. About the same distance, right east from Nussel, and a mile or more to south of Kyge over yonder, is a littery Farmstead named Sterbohol, which is not yet occupied by the Austrians, but will become very famous in their War-Annals, this day! —

Where the Austrian Camp or various Tent-groups were, at the time Friedrich first cast eye on them, is no great concern of his or ours; inasmuch as, in two or three hours hence, the Austrians were obliged, rather suddenly, to take Order of Battle; and that, and not their camping, is the thing we are curious upon. Let us step across, and take some survey of that Austrian

CHAP. II.]   BATTLE OF PRAG.   33
6th May 1757.

ground, which Friedrich is now surveying from the distance, fully intending that it shall be a battle-ground in few hours; and try to explain how the Austrians drew up on it, when they noticed the Prussian symptoms to become serious more and more. By nine in the morning, — some two hours after Friedrich began his scanning, and the Austrian outposts their firing of stray cannon-shots on him, — it is Battle-lines, not empty Tents (which there was not time to strike), that salute the eye over yonder.

From behind that verdant Horse-shoe Chasm we spoke of, buttressed by the inaccessible steeps, and the Moldau, double-folded in the form of Horse-shoe, all along the brow of that sloping expanse, stands (by 9 A.M. "foragers all suddenly called in") the Austrian front; the second line and the reserve, parallel to it, at good distances behind. Ranked there; say, 65,000 regulars (Prussian force little short of the same), on the brow of Ziscaberg slope, some four miles long. Their right wing ends, in strong batteries, in intricate marshes, knolls, lakelets, between Hlaupetin and Kyge: the extreme of their left wing looks over on that Horse-shoe Hollow, where Moldau tried to dig his way, but could not, and had to turn back. They have numerous redoubts, in front and in all the good places; and are busy with more, some of them just now getting finished, treble-quick, while the Prussians are seen under way. As many as sixty heavy cannon in battery up and down: of field-pieces they have a hundred and fifty. Excellent always with their Artillery, these Austrians; plenty of it, well placed, and well served: thanks to Prince Lichtenstein's fine labours, within these ten

Carlyle, Frederick the Great. X.   3

years past.* The villages, the farmsteads, are occupied; every rising ground especially has its battery, — Homoly Berg, Tabor Berg, "Mount of Tabor;" say *Knoll of Tabor* (nothing like so high as Battersea Rise, hardly even as Constitution Hill), though scriptural Zisca would make a Mount of it; — these, and other *Bergs* of the like type.

That is the Austrian Battle Order (as it stood about nine, though it had still to change a little, as we shall see): their first line, straight or nearly so, looking northward, stands on the brow of the Zisca Slope; their second and their third, singularly like it, at the due distances behind; — in the intervals, their tents, which stand scattered, in groups wide apart, in the ample interior to southward. The cavalry is on both wings; left wing, behind that Moldau Chasm, cannot attack nor be attacked, — except it were on hippogriffs, and its enemy on the like, capable of fighting in the air, overhead of these Belvedere Pleasure-grounds: perhaps Prince Karl will remedy this oversight; fruit of close following of the orthodox practice? Prince Karl, supreme Chief, commands on the left wing; Browne on the right, where he can attack or be attacked, *not* on hippogriffs. As we shall see, and others will! Light horse, in any quantity, hang scattered on all outskirts. With foot, with cannon batteries, with horse, light or heavy, they cover in long broad flood the whole of that Zisca Slope, to near where it ceases, and the ground to eastward begins perceptibly to rise again.

In this latter quarter, Zisca Slope, now nearly ended, begins to get very swampy in parts; on the eastern border of the Austrian Camp, at Kyge, Hostn-

---

* *Œuvres de Frédéric* (in several places); see Hormayr, § Lichtenstein.

witz, and beyond it southward, about Sterboho! and Michelup, there are many little lakelets; artificial fish-ponds, several of them, with their sluices, dams and apparatus: a ragged broadish lacing of ponds and lakelets (all well dried in our day) straggles and zigzags along there, connected by the miserablest Brook in nature, which takes to oozing and serpentising forward thereabouts, and does finally get emptied, now in a rather livelier condition, into the Moldau, about the *toe*-part of that Horse-shoe or Belvedere region. It runs in sight of the King, I think, where he now is; this lower livelier part of it: little does the King know how important the upper oozing portion of it will be to him this day. Near Michelup are lakelets worth noticing; a little under Sterbohol, in the course of this miserable Brook, is a string of fish-ponds, with their sluices open at this time, the water out, and the mud bottom sown with herb-provender for the intended carps, which is coming on beautifully, green as leeks, and nearly ready for the fish getting to it again.

Friedrich surveys diligently what he can of all this, from the northern verge. We will now return to Friedrich: and will stay on his side, through the terrible Action that is coming. Battle of Prag, one of the furious Battles of the World; loud as Doomsday; — the very Emblem of which, done on the Piano by females of energy, scatters mankind to flight who love their ears! Of this great Action the Narratives old and modern are innumerable; false some of them, unintelligible well nigh all. There are three in Lloyd, known probably to some of my readers. Tempelhof, with criticisms of these three, gives a fourth, — perhaps the one Narrative which human nature, after much study, can in some sort understand. Human readers, especially military, I refer to that as their finale.* Other interest than military-scientific the Action now has not much. The stormy fire of soul that blazed that day (higher in no ancient or modern Fight of men) is extinct, hopeless of resuscitation for English readers. Approximately what the thing to human eyes might be like; what Friedrich's procedure, humour and physiognomy of soul was in it: this, especially the latter head, is what we search for, — had lazy Dryasdust given us almost anything on this latter head! What little can be gleaned from him on both heads let us faithfully give, and finish our sad part of the combat.

Friedrich, with his Schwerin and Winterfeld, surveying these things from the northern edge, admits that the Austrian position is extremely strong; but he has no doubt that it must be, by some good method, attacked straightway, and the Austrians got beaten. Indisputably the enterprise is difficult. Unattackable clearly, the Austrians, on that left wing of theirs; not in the centre well attackable, nor in the front at all, with that stiff ground, and such redoubts and points of strength: but round on their right yonder; take them

---

* In Lloyd, i. 38 et seq. (the Three); in Tempelhof, i. 133 (the Fourth) ib. i. 144 (strength of each Army), 105-149 (*remarks* of Tempelhof). The "*History,*" or Series of Lectures on the Battles, &c. of this War, "*by the Royal Staff-Officers,*" — which, for the last thirty or forty years, is used as Text-Book, or Military *Euclid*, in the Prussian Cadet-Schools, — appears to possess the fit professorial lucidity and amplitude; and, in regard to all Official details, enumerations and the like, is received as of *canonical* authority: it is not accessible to the general Public, — though liberally enough conceded in special cases; whereby, in effect, the main results of it are now become current in modern Prussian Books. By favour in high quarters, I had once possession of a copy, for some months; but not, at that time, the possibility of thoroughly reading any part of it.

in flank, — cannot we? On as far as Kyge, the Three have ridden reconnoitring; and found no possibility upon the front; nor at Kyge, where the front ends in batteries, pools and quagmires, is there any. "Difficult, not undoable," persists the King: "and it must be straightway set about, and got done." Winterfeld, always for action, is of that opinion, too; and, examining farther down along their right flank, reports that there the thing is feasible.

Feasible perhaps: "but straightway?" objects Schwerin. His men have been on foot since midnight, and on forced marches for days past: were it not better to rest for this one day? "Rest: — and Daun, coming on with 30,000 of reinforcement to them, might arrive this night? Never, my good Feldmarschall;" — and as the Feldmarschall was a man of stiff notions, and had a tongue of some emphasis, the Dialogue went on, probably with increasing emphasis on Friedrich's side too, till old Schwerin, with a quite emphatic flash of countenance, crushing the hat firm over his brow, exclaims: "Well, your Majesty: the fresher fish the better fish (*frische Fische, gute Fische*): straightway, then!" and springs off on the gallop southward, he too, seeking some likely point of attack. He too, — conjointly or not with Winterfeld, I do not know: Winterfeld himself does not say; whose own modest words, on the subject, readers shall see before we finish. But both are mentioned in the Books as searching, at hand-gallop, in this way: and both, once well round to south, by the Podschernitz quarter,* with the Austrian right flank full in view, were agreed that here the thing was

---

* "Podschernitz," is pronounced *Potsheralts* (should we happen to mention it again); "Kyge," *Krega*.

possible. "Infantry to push from this quarter towards Sterbohol yonder, and then plunge into their redoubts and them! Cavalry may sweep still farther southward, if found convenient, and even take them in rear." Both agree that it will do in this way: ground tolerably good, slightly downwards for us, then slightly upwards again; tolerable for horse even: — the intermediate lacing of dirty lakelets, the fishponds with their sluices drawn, Schwerin and Winterfeld either did not notice at all, or thought them insignificant, interspersed with such beautiful "pasture-ground," — of unusual verdure at this early season of the year.

The deployment, or "marching up (*Aufmarschiren*)" of the Prussians was wonderful; in their squadrons, in their battalions, horse, foot, artillery, wheeling, closing, opening; strangely chequering a country-side, — in movements intricate, chaotic to all but the scientific eye. Conceive them, flowing along, from the Heights of Chaber, behind Prossik Hamlet (right wing of infantry plants itself at Prossik, horse westward of them); and ever onwards in broad many-chequered tide-stream, eastward, eastward, then southward ("our artillery "went through Podschernitz, the foot and horse a little "on this westward side of it"): intricate, many-glancing tide of coming battle; which, swift, correct as clockwork, becomes two lines, from Prossik to near Chwala ("baggage well behind at Gbell"); thence round by Podschernitz quarter; and descends, steady, swift, tornado-storm so beautifully hidden in it, towards Sterbohol, there to grip-to. Gradually, in stirring up those old dead pedantic record-books, the fact rises on us: silent whirlwinds of old Platt-Deutsch fire, beautifully held down, dwell in those mute masses; better human stuff there is not than that old Teutsch (Dutch, English, Platt-Deutsch, and other varieties); and so disciplined as here it never was before or since. "In an hour and half," what military men may count almost incredible, they are fairly on their ground, motionless the most of them by 9 A.M.; the rest wheeling rightward, as they successively arrive in the Chwala-Podschernitz localities; and, descending diligently, Sterbohol way; and will be at their harvest-work anon.

Meanwhile the Austrians, seeing, to their astonishment, these phenomena to the north, and that it is a quite serious thing, do also rapidly bestir themselves; swarming like bees; — bringing in their foraging Cavalry, "No time to change your jacket for a coat:" rank, double-quick! Browne is on that right wing of theirs: "Bring the left wing over hither," suggests Browne; "cavalry is useless yonder, unless they had hippogriffs!" — and (again Browne suggesting) the Austrians make a change in the position of their right wing, both horse and foot: change which is of vital importance, though unnoted in many Narratives of this Battle. Seeing, namely, what the Prussians intend, they wheel their right wing (say the last furlong or two of their long Line of Battle) half round to right; so that the last furlong or two stands at right angles ("*en potence*," gallows-wise, or joiner's-square-wise to the rest); and, in this way, make front to the Prussian onslaught, — front now, not flank, as the Prussians are anticipating. This is an important wheel to right, and formation in joiner's-square manner; and involves no end of interior wheeling, marching and deploying; which Austrians cannot manage with Prussian velocity.

"Swift with it, here about Sterbohol at least, my men! For here *are* the Prussians within wind of us!" urges Browne. And here straightway the hurricane does break loose.

Winterfeld, the van of Schwerin's infantry (Schwerin's own regiment, and some others, with him), is striding rapidly on Sterbohol; Winterfeld catches it before Browne can. But near by, behind that important post, on the Homoly Hill (*Berg* or "Mountain," nothing like so high as Constitution Mountain), are cannon-batteries of devouring quality; which awaken on Winterfeld, as he rushes out double-quick on the advancing Austrians; and are fatal to Winterfeld's attempt, and nearly to Winterfeld himself. Winterfeld, heavily wounded, sank in swoon from his horse; and awakening again in a pool of blood, found his men all off, rushing back upon the main Schwerin body; "Austrian grenadiers "gazing on the thing, about eighty paces off, not "venturing to follow." Winterfeld, half-dead, scrambled across to Schwerin, who is now come up with the main body, his front line fronting the Austrians here. And there ensued, about Sterbohol and neighbourhood, led on by Schwerin, such a death-wrestle as was seldom seen in the Annals of War. Winterfeld's miss of Sterbohol was the beginning of it; the exact course of sequel none can describe, though the end is well known.

The Austrians now hold Sterbohol with firm grip, backed by those batteries from Homoly Hill. Redoubts, cannon-batteries, as we said, stud all the field; the Austrian stock of artillery is very great; arrangement of it cunning, practice excellent; does honour to Prince Lichtenstein, and indeed is the real force of the Austrians on this occasion. Schwerin must have Sterbohol, in spite of batteries and ranked Austrians, and Winterfeld's recoil tumbling round him: — and rarely had the oldest veteran such a problem. Old Schwerin (fiery as ever, at the age of 73) has been in many battles, from Blenheim onwards; and now has got to his hottest and his last. "Vanguard could not do it; main body, we hope, kindling all the hotter, perhaps may!" A most willing mind is in these Prussians of Schwerin's: fatigue of over-marching has tired the muscles of them; but their hearts, — all witnesses say, these (and through these, their very muscles, 'always fresh again, after a few minutes of breathing time') were beyond comparison, this day!

Schwerin's Prussians, as they 'march up' (that is, as they front and advance upon the Austrians), are everywhere saluted by case-shot, from Homoly Hill and the batteries northward of Homoly; but march on, this main line of them, finely regardless of it or of Winterfeld's disaster by it. The general Prussian Order this day is: "By push of bayonet; no firing, none, at any rate, till you see the whites of their eyes!" Swift, steady as on the parade-ground, swiftly making up their gaps again, the Prussians advance, on these terms, and are now near those "fine sleek pasture-grounds, unusually green for the season." Figure the actual stepping upon these "fine pasture-grounds:" — mud-tanks, verdant with mere "bearding oat-crop" sown there as carp-provender! Figure the sinking of whole regiments to the knee; to the middle, some of them; the steady march become a wild sprawl through viscous mud, mere case-shot singing round you, tearing you away at its ease! Even on those terrible terms, the Prussians, by dams, by footpaths, sometimes one man abreast, sprawl steadily forward, trailing their cannon with them; only a few regiments, in the footpath parts, cannot bring their cannon. Forward; rank again, when the ground will carry; ever forward, the case-shot getting ever more murderous! No human pen can describe the deadly chaos which ensued in that quarter. Which lasted, in desperate fury, issue dubious, for above three hours; and was the crisis, or essential agony, of the Battle. Foot-chargings (once the mud-transit was accomplished), under storms of grape-shot from Homoly Hill; by and by, Horse-chargings, Prussian against Austrian, southward of Homoly and Sterbohol, still farther to the Prussian left; huge whirlpool of tumultuous death-wrestle, every species of spasmodic effort, on the one side and the other; — King himself present there, as I dimly discover; Feldmarschall Browne eminent, in the last of his fields; and, as the old *Niebelungen* has it, "a murder grim and great" going on.

Schwerin's Prussians, in that preliminary struggle through the mud-tanks (which Winterfeld, I think, had happened to skirt, and avoid), were hard bested. This, so far as I can learn, was the worst of the chaos, this preliminary part. Intolerable to human nature, this, or nearly so; even to human nature of the Platt-Teutsch type, improved by Prussian drill. Winterfeld's repulse we saw; Schwerin's own Regiment in it. Various repulses, I perceive, there were, — "fresh regiments from our Second Line" storming in thereupon; till the poor repulsed people "took breath," repented, "and themselves stormed in again," say the Books. Fearful tugging, swagging and swaying is conceivable, in this Sterbohol problem! And after long scanning, I rather judge it was in the wake of that first repulse, and not of some other farther on, that the veteran Schwerin himself got his death. No one times it for us; but the fact is unforgettable; and in the dim whirl of sequences, dimly places itself there. Very certain it is, "at sight of his own regiment in retreat," Feldmarschall Schwerin seized the colours, — as did other Generals, who are not named, that day. Seizes the colours, fiery old man: "*Heran, meine Kinder* (This way, my sons)!" and rides ahead, along the straight dam again; his 'sons' all turning, and with hot repentance following. "On, my children, *Heran!*" Five bits of grape-shot, deadly each of them, at once hit the old man; dead he sinks there on his flag; and will never fight more. "*Heran!*" storm the others with hot tears; Adjutant von Platen takes the flag; Platen, too, is instantly shot; but another takes it. "*Heran*, On!" in wild storm of rage and grief: — in a word, they managed to do the work at Sterbohol, they and the rest. First line, Second line, Infantry, Cavalry (and even the very Horses, I suppose), fighting inexpressibly; conquering one of the worst problems ever seen in War. For the Austrians too, especially their grenadiers there, stood to it toughly, and fought like men; — and "every "grenadier that survived of them," as I read afterwards, "got double pay for life."

Done, that Sterbohol work; — those Foot-chargings, Horse-chargings; that battery of Homoly Hill; and, hanging upon that, all manner of redoubts and batteries to the rightward and rearward: — but how it was done no pen can describe, nor any intellect in clear sequence understand. An enormous *mêlée* there: new Prussian battalions charging, and ever new, irrepressible by case-shot, as they successively get up:

Marshal Browne too sending for new battalions at double-quick from his left, disputing stiffly every inch of his ground. Till at length (hour not given), a cannon-shot tore away his foot; and he had to be carried into Prag, mortally wounded. Which probably was a most important circumstance, or the most important of all.

Important too, I gradually see, was that of the Prussian Horse of the Left Wing. Prussian Horse of extreme left, as already noticed, had, in the mean while, fallen in, well southward, round by certain lakelets about Michelup, on Browne's extreme right; furiously charging the Austrian Horse, which stood ranked there in many lines; breaking it, then again half broken by it; but again rallying, charging it a second time, then a third time, "both to front and "flank, amid whirlwinds of dust" (Ziethen busy there, not to mention indignant Warnery and others); — and at length, driving it wholly to the winds: "beyond "Nussel, towards the Sazawa Country;" never seen again that day. Prince Karl (after Browne's death-wound, or before, I never know) came galloping to rally that important Right Wing of horse. Prince Karl did his very utmost there; obtesting, praying, raging; threatening: — but to no purpose; the Zietheners and others so heavy on the rear of them: — and at last there came a cramp, or intolerable twinge of spasm, through Prince Karl's own person (breast or heart), like to take the life of him: so that he too had to be carried into Prag to the doctors. And his Cavalry fled at discretion; chased by Ziethen, on Friedrich's express order, and sent quite over the horizon. Enough, "by about "half-past one," Sterbohol work is thoroughly done;

and the Austrian Battle, both its Commanders gone, has heeled fairly downwards, and is in an ominous way.

The whole of this Austrian Right Wing, horse and foot, batteries and redoubts, which was put *en potence*, or square-wise, to the main battle, is become a ruin; gone to confusion; hovers in distracted clouds, seeking roads to run away by, which it ultimately found. Done all this surely was; and poor Browne, mortally wounded, is being carried off the ground; but in what sequence done, under what exact vicissitudes of aspect, special steps of cause and effect, no man can say; and only imagination, guided by these few data, can paint to itself. Such a chaotic whirlwind of blood, dust, mud, artillery-thunder, sulphurous rage, and human death and victory, — who shall pretend to describe it, or draw, except in the gross, the scientific plan of it?

For, in the mean time, — I think while the dispute at Sterbohol, on the extreme of the Austrian right wing "in joiner's-square form," was past the hottest (but nobody will give the hour), — there has occurred another thing, much calculated to settle that. And, indeed, to settle everything; — as it did. This was a volunteer exploit, upon the very elbow or angle of said "joiner's square;" in the wet grounds between Hlaupetin and Kyge, a good way north of Sterbohol. Volunteer exploit; on the part of General Mannstein, our old Russian friend; which Friedrich, a long way off from it, blames as a rash fault of Mannstein's, made good by Prince Henri and Ferdinand of Brunswick running up to mend it; but which Winterfeld, and subsequent good judges, admit to have been highly salutary, and to have finished everything. It went, if I read right, somewhat as follows.

In the Kyge-Illaupetin quarter, at the corner of that Austrian right wing *en potence*, there had, much contrary to Browne's intention, a perceptible gap occurred; the corner is open there; nothing in it but batterries and swamps. The Austrian right wing, wheeling southward, there to form *potence;* and scrambling and marching, then and subsequently, through such ground at double-quick, had gone too far (had thinned and lengthened itself, as is common, in such scrambling, and double-quick movement, thinks Tempelhof), and left a little gap at elbow; which always rather widened as the stress at Sterbohol went on. Certain enough, a gap there is, covered only by some half-moon battery in advance: into this, General Mannstein has been looking wistfully a long time: "Austrian Line fallen out at elbow yonder; clouted by some battery in advance?" — and at length cannot help dashing loose on it with his Division. A man liable to be rash, and always too impetuous in battle-time.

He would have fared ill, thinks Friedrich, had not Henri and Ferdinand, in pain for Mannstein (some think, privately in preconcert with him), hastened in to help; and done it altogether in a shining way; surmounting perilous difficulties not a few. Hard fighting in that corner, partly on the Sterbohol terms; batteries, mud-tanks; chargings, rechargings: "Comrades, you have got honour enough, *Kameraden, ihr habt Ehre genug*" (the second man of you lying dead); "let us now try!" said a certain Regiment to a certain other, in this business. * Prince Henri shone especially, the gallant little gentleman: coming upon one of those mud-tanks with battery beyond, his men were spreading file-wise, to cross

* Archenholtz, i. 75; Tempelhof, &c.

it on the dams; "*Bursche*, this way!" cried the Prince, and plunged in middle-deep, right upon the battery, and over it, and victoriously took possession of it. In a word, they all plunge forward, in a shining manner; rush on those halfmoon batteries, regardless of results; rush over them, seize and secure them. Rush, in a word, fairly into that Austrian hole-at-elbow, torrents more following them, — and irretrievably ruin both fore-arm and shoulder-arm of the Austrians thereby.

Fore-arm (Austrian right wing, if still struggling and wriggling about Sterbohol) is taken in flank; shoulder-arm, or main line, the like; we have them both in flank; with their own batteries to scour them to destruction here: — the Austrian Line, throughout, is become a ruin. Has to hurl itself rapidly to rightwards, to rearwards, says Tempelhof, behind what redoubts and strong points it may have in those parts; and then, by sure stages (Tempelhof guesses three, or perhaps four), as one redoubt after another is torn from the loose grasp of it, and the stand made becomes ever weaker, and the confusion worse, — to roll pell-mell into Prag, and hastily close the door behind it. The Prussians, Sterbohol people, Mannstein-Henri people, left wing and right, are quite across the Zisca Back, on by Nussel (Prince Karl's head-quarter that was), and at the Moldau Brink again, when the thing ends. Ziethen's Hussars have been at Nussel, very busy plundering there, ever since that final charge and chase from Sterbohol. Plundering; and, I am ashamed to say, mostly drunk; "Your Majesty, I cannot rank a hundred sober," answered Ziethen (doubtless with a kind of blush); when the King applied for them. The King himself has got to Branik, farther up stream.

Part of the Austrian foot fled, leftwards, southwards, as their right wing of horse had all done, up the Moldau. About 16,000 Austrians are distractedly on flight that way. Towards the Sazawa Country; to unite with Daun, as the now advisable thing. Near 40,000 of them are getting crammed into Prag; in spite of Prince Karl, now recovered of his cramp, and risen to the frantic pitch; who vainly struggles at the Gate against such inrush, and had even got through the Gate, conjuring and commanding, but was himself swum in again by those panic torrents of ebb-tide.

Rallying within, he again attempted, twice over, at two different points, to get out, and up the Moldau, with his broken people; but the Prussians, Nussel-Branik way, were awake to him: "No retreat up the Moldau for you, Austrian gentlemen!" They tried by another Gate, on the other side of the River; but Keith was awake too: "In again, ye Austrian gentlemen! Closed gates here too. What else?" Browne, from his bed of pain (deathbed, as it proved), was for a much more determined outrush: "In the dead of night, rank, deliberately adjust yourselves; storm out, one and all, and cut your way, night favouring!" That was Browne's last counsel; but that also was not taken. A really noble Browne, say all judges; died here in about six weeks, — and got away from Kriegs-Hofraths and Prince Karls, and the stupidity of neighbours, and the other ills that flesh is heir to, altogether.

At Branik the victorious King had one great disappointment: Prince Moritz of Dessau, who should have been here long hours ago, with Keith's right wing, a fresh 15,000, to fall upon the enemy's rear; — no Moritz visible; not even now, when the business is to chase! "How is this!" "Ill luck, your Majesty!" Moritz's Pontoon Bridge would not reach across, when he tried it. That is certain: "just three poor pontoons wanting," Rumour says: — three or more; spoiled, I am told, in some narrow road, some short cut which Moritz had commanded for them: and now they are not; and it is as if three hundred had been spoiled. Moritz, would he die for it, cannot get his Bridge to reach: his fresh 15,000 stand futile there; not even Seidlitz with his light horse could really swim across, though he tried hard, and is fabled to have done so. Beware of short cuts, my Prince: your Father that is gone, what would he say of you here! It was the worst mistake Prince Moritz ever made. The Austrian Army might have been annihilated, say judges (of a sanguine temper), had Moritz been ready, at his hour, to fall on from rear-ward; — and where had their retreat been? As it is, the Austrian Army is not annihilated; only bottled into Prag, and will need sieging. The brightest triumph has a bar of black in it, and might always have been brighter. Here is a flying Note, which I will subjoin:

"Friedrich's dispositions for the Battle, this day, are "allowed to have been masterly; but there was one signal "fault, thinks Retzow: That he did not, as Schwerin coun- "selled, wait till the morrow. Fault which brought many in "the train of it; that of his 'tired soldiers,' says Retzow, being "only a first item, and small in comparison. 'Had he waited "till the morrow, those fish-ponds of Sterbohol, examined in "the interim, need not have been mistaken for green meadows; "Prince Moritz, with his 15,000, would have been a fact, "instead of a false hope; the King might have done his "marching down upon Sterbohol in the night-time, and been "ready for the Austrians, flank, or even rear, at daybreak: "the King might' — In reality, this fault seems to have been

"considerable; to have made the victory far more costly to
"him, and far less complete. No doubt he had his reasons for
"making haste: Daun, advancing Prag-ward, with 30,000,
"was within three marches of him; General Beck, Daun's
"vanguard, with a 10,000 of irregulars, did a kind of feat at
"Brandeis, on the Prussian post there (our Saxons deserting
"to him, in the heat of action), this very day, May 6th; and
"might, if lucky, have taken part at Ziscaberg next day. And
"besides these solid reasons, there was perhaps another. Ret-
"zow, who is secretly of the Opposition-party, and well worth
"hearing, knows personally a curious thing. He says:
"'Being then' (in March or April, weeks before we left
"'Saxony) employed to translate the *Plan of Operations* into
"'French, for Marshal Keith's use, who did not understand
"'German, I well know that it contained the following three
"'main objects: 1º. "'All Regiments cantoning in Silesia as
"'well as Saxony march for Bohemia on one and the same day.
"'2º. Whole Army arrives at Prag, May 4th'"" (Schwerin was
a day later, and got scolded in consequence); "'"'if the Enemy
"'stand, he is attacked, May 6th, and beaten. 3º. So soon as
"'Prag is got, Schwerin, with the gross of the Army, pushes
"'into Mähren,'" and the heart of Austria itself; "'"King ha-
"'stens with 40,000 to help of the Allied Army"'"'—Royal Highness of Cumberland's; who will much need it by that time!*

"Here is a very curious fact and consideration. That the
"King had so prophesied and preordained: 'May 4th, Four
"Columns arrive at Prag; May 6th, attack the Austrians, beat
"them,'—and now wished to keep his word! This is an aerial
"reason, which I can suspect to have had its weight among
"others. There were twirls of that kind in Friedrich; intricate
"weak places; *knots* in the sound straight-fibred mind he had
"(as in whose mind are they not?),—which now and then
"cost him dear! The Anecdote-Books say he was very ill of
"body, that day, May 6th; and called for something of drug
"nature, and swallowed it (drug not named), after getting on
"horseback. The Evening Anecdote is prettier: How, in the
"rushing about, Austrians now flying, he got eye on Brother
"Henri" (clayey to a degree); "and sat down with him, in the
"blessed sunset, for a minute or two, and bewailed his sad
"losses of Schwerin and others.

* Retsow, i. 84 n.

"Certain it is, the victory was bought by hard fighting; "and but for the quality of his troops, had not been there. "But the bravery of the Prussians was exemplary, and covered "all mistakes that were made. Nobler fire, when did it burn "in any Army? More perfect soldiers I have not read of. "Platt-Teutsch fire, — which I liken to anthracite, in con- "tradistinction to Gaelic blaze of kindled straw, — is thrice "noble, when, by strict stern discipline, you are above it "withal; and wield your fire-element, as Jove his thunder, by "rule! Otherwise it is but half-admirable: Turk Janissaries "have it otherwise; and it comes to comparatively little."

This is the famed Battle of Prag; fought, May 6th, 1757; which sounded through all the world, — and used to deafen us in drawing-rooms within man's memory. Results of it were: On the Prussian side, killed, wounded and missing 12,500 men; on the Austrian, 13,300 (prisoners included), with many flags, cannon, tents, much war-gear gone the wrong road; — and a very great humiliation and dispiritment; though they had fought well: "No longer the old Austrians, by any means," as Friedrich sees; but have iron ramrods, all manner of Prussian improvements, and are "learning to march," as he once says, with surprise not quite pleasant!

Friedrich gives the cipher of loss, on both sides, much higher: "This Battle," says he, "which began "towards nine in the morning, and lasted, chase in- "cluded, till eight at night, was one of the bloodiest "of the age. The Enemy lost 24,000 men, of whom "were 6,000 prisoners; the Prussian loss amounted to "18,000 fighting men, — without counting Marshal "Schwerin, who alone was worth above 10,000." "This day saw the pillars of the Prussian Infantry "cut down," says he mournfully, seeming almost to "think the "laurels of victory" were purchased too dear. His account of the Battle, as if it had been a painful object, rather avoided in his after thoughts, is unusually indistinct; — and helps us little in the extreme confusion that reigns otherwise, both in the thing itself and in the reporters of the thing. Here is a word from Winterfeld, some private Letter, two days after; which is well worth reading for those who would understand this Battle.

"The Enemy had his Left Wing leaning on the City, close "by the Moldau," at Nussel; "and stretched with his Right "Wing across the high Hill" (of Zisca) "to the village of "Lieben" (so he *had* stood, looking into Prag; but faced about, on hearing that Friedrich was across the River); "having "before him those terrible Defiles" (*die terriblen Defilées*, 'Horse-shoe of the Moldau,' as we call it), "and the Village of "Prossik, which was crammed with Pandours. It was about "half-past six in the morning, when our Schwerin Army" (myself part of it, at this time) "joined with the twenty battalions "and twenty squadrons, which the King had brought across "to unite with us, and which formed our right wing of battle "that day" (our left wing were Schweriners, Sterbohol and the fighting done by Schweriners after their long march). "The King was at once determined to attack the Enemy; as "also were Schwerin" (say nothing of the arguing) "and your "humble servant (*meine Wenigkeit*): but the first thing was, to "find a hole whereby to get at him.

"This too was selected, and decided on, my proposal "being found good; and took effect in manner following: "We" (Schweriners) "had marched off left-wise, foremost; "and we now, without halt, continued marching so with the "Left Wing" of horse, "which had the van (*tête*); and moved "on, keeping the road for Hlaupetin, and ever thence onwards "along for Kyge, round the Ponds of Unter-Podschernitz, "without needing to pass these, and so as to get them in "our rear.

"'The Enemy, who at first had expected nothing bad, and "never supposed that we would attack him at once, *flagrante* "*delicto*, and least of all in this point; and did not believe it "possible, as we should have to wade, breast-deep in part, "through the ditches, and drag our cannon, — was at first "quite tranquil. But as he began to perceive our real design "(in which, they say, Prince Karl was the first to open "Marshal Browne's eyes), he drew his whole Cavalry over "towards us, as fast as it could be done, and stretched them "out as Right Wing; to complete which, his Grenadiers and "Hungarian Regulars of Foot ranked themselves as they got "up" (makes his *potence*, *Haken*, or joiner's-square, outmost "end of it Horse).

"The Enemy's intention was to hold with the Right Wing "of his infantry on the Farmstead which they call Sterbaholy" (Sterbohol, a very dirty Farmstead at this day); "I, however, "had the good luck, plunging on, head foremost, with six "battalions of our Left Wing and two of the Flank, to get to "it before him. Although our Second Line was not yet come "forward, yet, as the battalions of the First were tolerably "well together, I decided, with General Fouquet, who had "charge of the Flank, to begin at once; and, that the Enemy "might not have time to post himself still better, I pushed "forward, quick step, out of the Farmstead" of Sterbohol "to "meet him, — so fast, that even our cannon had not time to "follow. He did, accordingly, begin to waver; and I could "observe that his people here, on this Wing, were making "right-about.

"Meanwhile, his fire of case-shot opened" (from Homoly Hill, on our left), "and we were still pushing on, — might now "be about two hundred steps from the Enemy's Line, when I "had the misfortune, at the head of Regiment Schwerin, to "get wounded, and, swooning away (*vor Tod*), fell from my "horse to the ground. Awakening after some minutes, and "raising my head to look about, I found nobody of our people "now here beside or round me; but all were already behind, "in full flood of retreat (*hoch Anschlagen*). The Enemy's "Grenadiers were perhaps eighty paces from me; but had "halted, and had not the confidence to follow us. I struggled "to my feet, as fast as, for weakness, I possibly could; and "got up to our confused mass" (*confusen Klumpen*, — exact place, where?): "but could not, by entreaties or by threats, "persuade a single man of them to turn his face on the Enemy, "much less to halt and try again.

"In this embarrassment the deceased Foldmarschall found "me, and noticed that the blood was flowing stream-wise "from my neck. As I was on foot, and none of my people now "near, he bade give me his led horse which he still had"— (and sent me home for surgery? Winterfeld, handsomely effacing himself when no longer good for anything, hurries on to the Catastrophe, leaving us to guess that he was *not* an eye-witness farther)—"bade give me the led horse which he still "had; *and*" (as if that had happened directly after, which surely it did not? "*and*) snatched the Flag from Captain Rohr, "who had taken it up to make the Bursche turn, and rode "forward with it himself. But before he could succeed in the "attempt, this excellent man, almost in a minute, was hit with "five case-shot balls, and fell dead on the ground; as also his "brave Adjutant von Platen was so wounded that he died "next day.

"During this confusion and repulse, by which, as already "mentioned, the Enemy had not the heart to profit, not only "was our Second Line come on, but those of the First, who "had not suffered, went vigorously (*frisch*) at the Enemy,"— and in course of time (perhaps two hours yet), and by dint of effort, we did manage Sterbohol and its batteries:—"Like "as" (still in one sentence, and without the least punctuation; Winterfeld being little of a grammarian, and in haste for the close), "Like as Prince Henri's Royal Highness with our "Right Wing," Mannstein and he, "without waiting for order, "attacked so *prompt* and with such *fermeté*," in that elbow-hole far north of *us*, "that everywhere the Enemy's Line began "to give way; and instead of continuing as Line, sought "corps-wise to gain the Heights, and there post itself. And "as, without winning said Heights, we could not win the "Battle, we had to storm them all, one after the other; and "this it was that cost us the best, most, and bravest people.

"The late Colonel von Goltz" (if we glance back to Ster-bohol itself), "who, with the regiment Fouquet, was advancing, "right-hand of Schwerin regiment" and your servant, "had "likewise got quite close to the Enemy; and had he not, at the "very instant when he was levelling bayonets, been shot "down, I think that he, with myself and the Schwerin regi-

"ment, would have got in," — and perhaps have there done the job, special and general, with much less expense, and sooner!*

This is what we get from Winterfeld; a rugged, not much grammatical man, but (as I can perceive) with excellent eyes in his head, and interior talent for twenty grammatical people, had that been his line. These, faithfully rendered here, without change but of pointing, are the only words I ever saw of his: to my regret, — which surely the Prussian Dryasdust might still amend a little? — in respect of so distinguished a person, and chosen Peer of Friedrich's. This his brief theory of Prag Battle, if intensely read, I find to be of a piece with his practice there.

Schwerin was much lamented in the Army; and has been duly honoured ever since. His body lies in Schwerinsburg, at home, far away; his Monument, finale of a series of Monuments, stands, now under special guardianship, near Sterbohol on the spot where he fell. A late Tourist says:

"At first there was a monument of wood" (*tree* planted, I will hope), "which is now all gone; round this Kaiser Joseph II. "once, in the year 1776, holding some review there, made his "grenadier battalions and artilleries form circle, fronting the "sky all round, and give three volleys of great arms and "small, Kaiser in the centre doffing hat at each volley, in "honour of the hero. Which was thought a very pretty thing "on the Kaiser's part. In 1824, the tree, I suppose, being gone "to a stump, certain subscribing Prussian Officers had it "rooted out, and a modest Pyramid of red veined marble built "in its room. Which latter the then King of Prussia, Friedrich

---

* Preuss, ii. 45-47 (in Winterfeld's hand; dated, "Camp at Prag, 8th May 1757;" addressed to one knows not whom; first printed by Preuss).

"Wilhelm III., determined to improve upon; and so, in 1839, "built a second Pyramid close by, bigger, finer, and of "Prussian iron, this one; — purchasing also, from the Austrian "Government, a rood or two of ground for site; and appoint- "ing some perpetual Peculium, or increase of Pension to an "Austrian Veteran of merit for taking charge there. All "which, perfectly in order, is in its place at this day. The "actual Austrian Pensioner of merit is a loud-voiced, hard- "faced, very limited, but honest little fellow; who has worked "a little polygon ditch and miniature hedge round the two "Monuments; keeps his own cottage, little garden, and self, "respectably clean; and leads stoically a lone life, — no com- "pany, I should think, but the Sterbohol hinds, who probably "are Czechs and cannot speak to him. He was once 'of the "regiment Hohenlohe;' suffers somewhat from cold, in the "winter time, in those upland parts (the 'cords of wood' "allowed him being limited); but complains of nothing else. "Two English names were in his Album, a military two, and "no more. '*Ehret den Held* (Honour the Hero)!' we said to "him, at parting. 'Don't I?' answered he; glancing at his "muddy bare legs and little spade, with which he had been "working in the Polygon Ditch when we arrived. I could wish "him an additional '*Klafter Holz*' (cord more of firewood), now "and then, in the cold months! —

"Sterbohol Farmstead has been new-built, in man's me- "mory, but is dirty as ever. Agriculture, all over this table- "land of the Ziscaberg, I should judge to be bad. Not so the "prospect; which is cheerfully extensive, picturesque in parts, "and to the student of Friedrich offers good commentary. "Roads, mansions, villages: Prossik, Kyge, Podschernitz, "from the Heights of Chaber round to Nussel and beyond: "from any knoll, all Friedrich's Villages, and many more, lie "round you as on a map, — their dirt all hidden, nothing "wanting to the landscape, were it better carpeted with green "(green instead of russet), and shaded here and there with "wood. A small wild pink, bright-red, and of the size of a "star, grows extensively about; of which you are tempted "to pluck specimens, as memorial of a Field so famous in "War."*

* Tourist's Note (September 1858).

CHAPTER III.

PRAG CANNOT BE GOT AT ONCE.

WHAT Friedrich's emotions after the Battle of Prag were, we do not much know. They are not inconceivable, if we read his situation well; but in the way of speech, there is, as usual, next to nothing. Here are two stray utterances, worth gathering from a man so uncommunicative in that form.

Friedrich a Month before Prag (From Lockwitz, 25th March, to Princess Amelia, at Berlin). — "My dearest Sister, I give "you a thousand thanks for the hints you have got me from "Dr. Eller on the illness of our dear Mother. Thrice welcome "this; and reassures me" (alas, not on good basis!) "against "a misfortune which I should have considered very great "for me.

"As to us and our posture of affairs, political and military, "— place yourself, I conjure you, *above* every event. Think "of our Country; and remember that one's first duty is to "defend it. If you learn that a misfortune happens to one of "us, ask, 'Did he die fighting?' and if Yes, give thanks to "God. Victory or else death, there is nothing else for us; "one or the other we must have. All the world here is of that "temper. What! you would have everybody sacrifice his life "for the State, and you would not have your Brothers give the "example? Ah, my dear Sister, at this crisis, there is no room "for bargaining. Either at the summit of glorious success, or "else abolished altogether. This Campaign now coming is "like that of Pharsalia for Rome, or that of Leuctra for the "Greeks" — a Campaign we verily shall have to win, or go to wreck upon!"*

* Œuvres de Frédéric, XXVII. i. 291.

Friedrich shortly after Prag (To his Mother, Letter still extant in Autograph, without date). — "My Brothers and I "are still well. The whole Campaign runs risk of being lost "to the Austrians; and I find myself free, with 150,000 men. "Add to this, that we are masters of a Kingdom" (Bohemia here), "which is obliged to furnish us with troops and money. "The Austrians are dispersed like straw before the wind. I "will send a part of my troops to compliment Messieurs the "French; and am going" (if I once had Prag!) "to pursue the "Austrians with the rest of my Army."*

Friedrich, who keeps his emotions generally to himself, does not, as will be seen, remain quite silent to us throughout this great Year; but, by accident, has left us some rather impressive gleanings in that kind; — and certainly in no year could such accident have been luckier to us; this of 1757 being, in several respects, the greatest of his Life. From nearly the topmost heights down to the lowest deeps, his fortunes oscillated this year; and probably, of all the sons of Adam, nobody's outlooks and reflexions had in them, successive and simultaneous, more gigantic forms of fear and of hope. He is on a very high peak at this moment; suddenly emerging from his thick cloud, into thunderous victory of that kind; and warning all Pythons what they get by meddling with the Sungod! Loud enough, far-clanging, is the sound of the silver bow; gazetteers and men all on pause at such new Phœbus Apollo risen in his wrath; — the Victory at Prag considered to be much more annihilative than it really was. At London, Lord Holderness had his Tower-guns in readiness, waiting for something of the kind; and "the joy of the people was frantic."**

---

* *Œuvres de Frédéric,* xxvi. 76.
** *Mitchell Papers and Memoirs* (i. e. the Printed Selection, 2 voll.,

CHAP. III.] PRAG CANNOT BE GOT AT ONCE. 59
9th May — 13th June 1757.

Very dominant, our "Protestant Champion" yonder, on his Ziscaberg; bidding the enormous Pompadour-Theresa combinations, the French, Austrian, Swedish, Russian populations and dread sovereigns, check their proud waves, and hold at mid-flood. It is thought, had he in effect "annihilated" the Austrian force at Prag, that day (Friday, 6th May, as he might have done by waiting till Saturday 7th), he could then, with the due rapidity, rapidity being indispensable in the affair, have become master of Prag, which meant of Bohemia altogether; and have stormed forward, as his program bore, into the heart of an Austria still terror-stricken, unrallied; — in which case, it is calculated, the French, the Russians, Swedes, much more the Reich and such like, would all have drawn bridle; and Austria itself have condescended to make Peace with a Neighbour of such quality, and consent to his really modest desire of being let alone! Possible, all this, — think Retzow and others.* But the King had not waited till to-morrow; no persuasion could make him wait: and it is idle speculating on the small turns which here, as everywhere, can produce such deflections of course.

Beyond question, Prag is not captured, and may, as now garrisoned, require a great deal of capturing: — and perhaps it is but a *peak*, this high dominancy of Friedrich's, not a solid table-land, till much more have been done! Friedrich has nothing of the Gascon: but there may well be conceivable at this time a certain

---

London, 1850; — which will be the oftenest cited by us, "Papers and Memoirs"), L. 249 : " Holderness to Mitchell, 20th May 1757." Mitchell is now attending Friedrich; his Letter from Keith's Camp, during the thunder of "Friday, May 6th," is given, ib. i. 248.

* See Retzow, i. 100-108; &c.

glow of internal pride, like that of Phœbus amid the piled tempests,—like that of the One Man prevailing, if but for a short season, against the Devil and All Men: "I have made good my bit of resolution so far: here are the Austrians beaten at the set day, and Prag summoned to surrender, as per program!" —

Intrinsically, Prag is not a strong City: we have seen it taken in few days; in one night; — and again, as in Belleisle's time, we have seen it making tough defence for a series of weeks. It depends on the garrison, what extent of garrison (the circuit of it being so immense), and what height of humour. There are now 46,000 men caged in it, known to have considerable magazines; and Friedrich, aware that it will cost trouble, bends all his strength upon it, and from his two camps, Ziscaberg, Weissenberg, due Bridges uniting, Keith and he batter it violently, aiming chiefly at the Magazines (which are not all bomb-proof); and hope they may succeed before it is too late.

The Vienna people are in the depths of amazement and discouragement; almost of terror, had it not been for a few, or especially for one high heart among them. Feldmarschall Daun, on the news of May 6th, hastily fell back, joined by the wrecks of the right wing, which fled Sazawa way. Brunswick-Bevern, with a 20,000, is detached to look after Daun; finds Daun still on the retreat; greedily collecting reinforcements from the homeward quarter; and hanging back, though now double or so of Bevern's strength. Amazement and discouragement are the general feeling among Friedrich's enemies. Notable to see how the whole hostile world marching in upon him, — French, Russians, much more the Reich, poor faltering entity, — pauses, as with its breath taken away, at news of Prag; and, arrested on the sudden, with lifted foot, ceases to stride forward; and merely tramp-tramps on the same place (nay in part, in the Reich part, visibly tramps backward), for above a month ensuing! Who knows whether, practically, any of them will come on;* and not leave Austria by itself to do the duel with Friedrich? If Prag were but got, and the 46,000 well locked away, it would be very salutary for Friedrich's affairs! — Week after week, the City holds out; and there seems no hope of it, except by hunger, and burning their Magazines by red-hot balls.

Colonel Mayer with his "Free-Corps" Party makes a Visit, of didactic Nature, to the Reich.

Friedrich, as we saw, on entering Böhmen, had shot off a Light Detachment under Colonel Mayer, southward, to seize any Austrian Magazines there were, especially one big Magazine at Pilsen:—which Mayer has handsomely done, May 2d (Pilsen "a bigger Magazine than Jung-Buntzlau, even"); after which Mayer is now off westward, into the Ober-Pfalz, into the Nürnberg Countries; to teach the Reich a small lesson, since they will not listen to Plotho. Prag Battle, as happens, had already much chilled the ardour of the Reich! Mayer has two Free-Corps, his own and another; about 1,300 of foot; to which are added a 200 of hussars. They have 5 cannon, carry otherwise a minimum of baggage; are swift wild fellows, sharp of stroke; and

* See *Correspondance du Comte de Saint-Germain*, an Eye-witness, t. 109 cited in Preuss, ii. 50); &c. &c.

do, for the time, prove didactic to the Reich; bringing home to its very bosom the late great lesson of the Ziscaberg, in an applied form. Mayer made a pretty course of it, into the Ober-Pfalz Countries; scattering the poor Execution Drill-Sergeants and incipiencies of preparation, the deliberative County Meetings, *Kreis-Convents*: ransoming Cities, Nürnberg for one city, whose cries went to Friedrich on the Ziscaberg, and wide over the world.* Nürnberg would have been but too happy to "refuse its contingent to the Reich's Army," as many others would have been (poor Kur-Baiern hurrying off a kind of Embassy to Friedrich, great terror reigning among the wigs of Regensburg, and everybody drawing back that could), — had not Imperial menaces, and an Event that fell out by and by in Prag Country, forced compliance.

Mayer's Expedition made a loud noise in the Newspapers; and was truly of a shining nature in its kind; very perfectly managed on Mayer's part, and has traits in it which are amusing to read, had one time. Take one small glance from Pauli:

"At Fürth in Anspach, 1st June" (after six-days screwing of Nürnberg from without, which we had no cannon to take), "a Gratuity for the Prussian troops" (amount not stated) "was demanded and given: at Schwabach, farther up the "Regnitz River, they took quarters; no exemption made, "clergy and laity alike getting soldiers billeted. Meat and "drink had to be given them; as also 100 carolines" (guineas and better), "and twenty new uniforms. Upon which, next "day, they marched to Zirndorf, and the Reichsgraf Pückler's "Mansion, the Schloss of Farrenbach there. Mayer took

---

* In *Helden-Geschichte*, iv. 360-367, the Nürnberg Letter and Response (31st May-5th June 1757): in Pauli, *Leben grosser Helden* (iii. 159 et seq.), Account of the Mayer Expedition; also in *Militair-Lexikon*, iii. 89 (quoting from Pauli).

"quarter in the Schloss itself. Here the noble owners got up
"a ball for Mayer's entertainment; and did all they could
"contrive to induce a light treatment from him." Figure it,
the neighbouring nobility and gentry in gala; Mayer too in
his best uniform, and smiling politely, with those "bright
"little black eyes" of his! For he was a brilliant airy kind of
fellow, and had much of the chevalier, as well as of the partisan, when requisite!

"Out of Farrenbach, the Mayer people circulated upon all
"the neighbouring Lordships; at Wilhermsdorf, the Reichs-
"Fürst von Hohenlohe" (a too busy Anti-Prussian) "had the
"worst brunt to bear. The adjacent Baireuth lands" (dear
Wilhelmina, fancy her too in such neighbourhood!) "were to
"the utmost spared all billeting, and even all transit," —
though wandering sergeants of the Reich's Force, "one
"sergeant with the Würzburg Herr Commissarius and eight
"common men, did get picked up on Bayreuth ground: and
"this or the other Anspach Official (Anspach being dis-
"affected), too busy on the wrong side, found himself sud-
"denly Prisoner of War; but was given up, at Wilhelmina's
"gracious request. On Bamberg he was sharp as flint; and
"had to be; the Bambergers, reinforced at last by 'Circle-
"Militias *(Kreis-truppen)*' in quantity, being called out in
"mass against him; and at Vach, an actual Passage of Fight
"had occurred."

Of the "Affair at Vach," pretty little Drawn-Battle
(mostly an affair of art), Mayer *versus* "Kreis-troops ot
"the amount of 6,000, with twelve cannon, or some
"say twenty-four" (which they couldn't handle); and
how Mayer cunningly took a position unassailable,
"burnt Bridges of the Regnitz River," and, plying his
five cannon against these ardent awkward people, stood
cheerful on the other side; and then at last, in good
time, whisked himself off to the Hill of Culmbach,
with all his baggage, inexpugnable there for three days:
— of all this, though it is set down at full length, we

can say nothing.* And will add only that, having girt himself and made his packages, Mayer left the Hill of Culmbach; and deliberately wended home, by Coburg and other Countries where he had business, eating his way; and early in July was safe in the Metal Mountains again; having fluttered the Volscians in their Frankenland Corioli to an unexpected extent. It is one of five or six such sallies Friedrich made upon the Reich, sometimes upon the Austrians and Reich together, to tumble up their magazines and preparations. Rapid unexpected inroads, year after year; done chiefly by the Free-Corps; and famous enough to the then Gazetteers. Of which, or of their doers, as we can in time coming afford little or no notice, let us add this small Note on the Free-Corps topic, which is a large one in the Books, but must not interrupt us again:

"Before this War was done" say my Authorities, "there "came gradually to be twenty-one Prussian Free-Corps," — foot almost all; there being already Hussars in quantity, ever since the first Silesian experiences. "Notable Aggregates "they were of loose wandering fellows, broken Saxons, "Prussians, French; 'Hungarian-Protestant' some of them, "'Deserters from all the Armies' not a few; attracted by the "fame of Friedrich, — as the Colonels enlisting them had "been; Mayer himself, for instance, was by birth a Vienna "man; and had been in many services and wars, from his "fifteenth year and onwards. Most miscellaneous, these "Prussian Free-Corps; a swift faculty the indispensable "thing, by no means a particular character: but well-dis- "ciplined, well-captained; who generally managed their "work well.

"They were, by origin, of Anti-Tolpatch nature, got up "on the diamond-cut-diamond principle; they stole a good

* Pauli, III. 159, &c. (who gives Mayer's own *Letter*, and others, upon Yach).

"deal, with order sometimes, and oftener without; but there
"was nothing of the old Mentzel-Trenck atrocity permitted
"them, or ever imputed to them; and they did, usually with
"good military talent, sometimes conspicuously good, what
"was required of them. Regular Generals, of a high merit,
"one or two of their Captains came to be: Wunsch, for ex-
"ample; Werner, in some sort; and, but for his sudden
"death, this Mayer himself. Others of them, as Von Hordt
"(Hård is his Swedish name); and 'Quintus Icilius' (by
"nature, *Guichard*, of whom we shall hear a great deal in the
"Friedrich circle by and by), are distinguished as honourably
"intellectual and cultivated persons.*

"Poor Mayer died within two years hence (5th January
"1759); of fever, caught by unheard-of exertions and over-
"fatigues; after many exploits, and with the highest pro-
"spects opening on him. A man of many adventures, of many
"qualities; a wild dash of chivalry in him all along, and much
"military and other talent crossed in the growing. In the
"dull old Books, I read one other fact which is vivid to me,
"That Wilhelmina, as sequel of those first Franconian
"exploits and procedures, 'had given him her Order of
"Knighthood, *Order of Sincerity and Fidelity*.'" — poor dear
Princess, what an interest to Wilhelmina, this flash of her
Brother's thunder thrown into those Franconian parts, and
across her own pungent anxieties and sorrowfully affectionate
thoughts, in those weeks! —

Shortly after Mayer, about the time when Mayer
was wending homeward, General von Oldenburg, a very
valiant punctual old General, was pushed out westward
upon Erfurt, a City of Kur-Mainz's, to give Kur-Mainz
a similar monition. And did it handsomely, impressively
upon the Gazetteer world at least and the Erfurt populations, — though we can afford it no room in this

---

* Count de Hordt's *Memoirs* (autobiographical, or in the first-person; English Translation, London, 1806; *two* French Originals, a worse in 1789, and a better now at last), Preface, I.-XII. In *Helden-Geschichte*, v. 102-104, 93, a detailed "List of the Free-Corps in 1758" (twelve of foot, two of horse, at that time): see Preuss, II. 373 n.; Paull (ubi suprà), *Life of Mayer.*

place. Oldenburg's force was but some 2,000; Pirna Saxons most of them: — such a winter Oldenburg has had with these Saxons; bursting out into actual musketry upon him once; Oldenburg, volcanically steady, summoning the Prussian part, "To me, true Prussian Bursche!" — and hanging nine of the mutinous Saxons. And has coerced and compesced them (all that did not contrive to desert) into soldierly obedience; and, 20th June, appears at the Gate of Erfurt with them, to do his delicate errand there. Sharply conclusive, though polite and punctual. "Send to Kur-Mainz, say you? Well, as to your Citadel, and those 1,400 soldiers all moving peaceably off thither, — Yes. As to your City: within one hour, Gate open to us, or we open it!" * And Oldenburg marches in, as vice-sovereign for the time: — but, indeed, has soon to leave again; owing to what Event in the distance, will be seen!

If Prag Siege go well, these Mayer-Oldenburg expeditions will have an effect on the Reich: but if it go ill, what are they, against Austria with its force of steady pressure? All turns on the issue of Prag Siege: — a fact extremely evident to Friedrich too! But these are what in the interim can be done. One neglects no opportunity, tries by every method.

Of the singular quasi-bewitched Condition of England; and what is to be hoped from it, for the Common Cause, if Prag go amiss.

On the Britannic side too, the outlooks are not good; — much need Friedrich were through his Prag

---

* In *Helden-Geschichte* (v. 371-384), copious Account, with the Missives to and from, the Reichs-Pleadings that followed, the &c. &c. *Militair-Lexikon*, § Oldenburg.

affair, and "hastening with forty thousand to help his Allies," — that is, Royal Highness of Cumberland and Britannic Purse, his only allies at this moment. Royal Highness and Army of Observation (should have been 67,000, are 50 to 60,000, hired Germans; troops good enough, were they tolerably led) finds the Hanover Program as bad as Schmettau and Friedrich ever represented it; and, already, — unless Prag go well, — wears, to the understanding eye, a very contingent aspect. D'Estrées outnumbers him; D'Estrées, too, is something of a soldier, — a very considerable advantage in affairs of war.

D'Estrées, since April, is in Wesel; gathering in the revenues, changing the Officialities: much out of discipline, they say; — "hanging" gradually "1,000 marauders;" in round numbers 1,000 this year.* D'Estrées does not yet push forward, owing to Prag. If he do — It is well known how Royal Highness fared when he did, and what a Campaign Royal Highness made of it this Year 1757! How the Weser did prove wadeable, as Schmettau had said to no purpose; wadeable, bridgeable; and Royal Highness had to wriggle back, ever back; no stand to be made, or far worse than none: back, ever back, till he got into the Sea, for that matter, and to the *end* of more than one thing! Poor man, friends say he has an incurable Hanover Ministry, a Program that is inexecutable. As yet he has not lost head, any head he ever had: but he is wonderful, he; — and his England is! We shall have to look at him once again; and happily once only. Here, from my Constitutional Historian, are some Passages which we may as well read in the

* Stenzel, v. 65; Retzow, i. 173.

present interim of expectation. I label, and try to arrange:

1. *England in Crisis.* "England is indignant with its Hero "of Culloden and his Campaign 1757; but really has no "business to complain. Royal Highness of Cumberland, "wriggling helplessly in that manner, is a fair representative "of the England that now is. For years back, there has been, "in regard to all things Foreign or Domestic, in that Country, "by way of National action, the miserablest haggling as to "which of various little-competent persons shall act for the "Nation. A melancholy condition indeed!—

"But the fact is, his Grace of Newcastle, ever since his "poor Brother Pelham died (who was always a solid, loyal kind "of man, though a dull; and had always, with patient affection, "furnished his Grace, much *unsupplied* otherwise, with Com-"mon-Sense hitherto), is quite insecure in Parliament, and "knows not what hand to turn to. Fox is contemptuous of "him; Pitt entirely impatient of him; Duke of Cumberland "(great in the glory of Culloden) is aiming to oust him, and "bear rule with his Young Nephew, the new Rising Sun, as "the poor Papa and Grandfather gets old. Even Carteret "(Earl Granville, as they now call him, a Carteret much "changed since those high-soaring Worms-Hanau times!) "was applied to. But the answer was — what could the an-"swer be? High-soaring Carteret, scandalously overset and "hurled out in that Hanau time, had already tried once (long "ago, and with such result!) to spring in again, and 'deliver "'his Majesty from factions;' and actually had made a "'Granville Ministry;' Ministry which fell again in one day.*
"To the complete disgust of Carteret-Granville;—who, ever "since, sits ponderously dormant (kind of Fixture in the "Privy Council, this long while back); and is resigned, in a "big contemptuous way, to have had his really considerable "career closed upon him by the smallest of mankind; and, "except occasional blurts of strong rugged speech which "come from him, and a good deal of wine taken into him, dis-"dains making further debate with the world and its elect "Newcastles. Carteret, at this crisis, was again applied to,

* "11th February 1746" (Thackeray, *Life of Chatham*, 1. 166).

"'Cannot you? In behalf of an afflicted old King?' But Carteret answered, No.*

"In short, it is admitted and bewailed by everybody, seldom was there seen such a Government of England (and England has seen some strange Governments), as in these last Three Years. Chaotic Imbecility reigning pretty supreme. Ruler's Work, — policy, administration, governance, guidance, performance in any kind, — where is it to be found? For if even a Walpole, when his Talking-Apparatus gets out of gear upon him, is reduced to extremities, though the stoutest of men, — fancy what it will be, in like case, and how the Acting-Apparatuses and Affairs generally will go, with a poor hysterical Newcastle, now when his Common-Sense is fatally withdrawn! The poor man has no resource but to shuffle about in aimless perpetual fidget; endeavouring vainly to say Yes *and* No to all questions, Foreign and Domestic, that may rise. Whereby, in the Affairs of England, there has, as it were, universal St. Vitus'-dance supervened, at an important crisis: and the Preparations for America, and for a down-right Life-and-Death Wrestle with France on the *Jenkins's-Ear Question*, are quite in a bad way. In an ominously bad. Why cannot we draw a veil over these things!" —

2. *Pitt, and the Hour of Tide.* "The fidgetings and shufflings, the subtleties, inane trickeries, and futile hitherings and thitherings of Newcastle may be imagined: a man not incapable of trick; but anxious to be well with everybody; and to answer Yes *and* No to almost everything, — and not a little puzzled, poor soul, to get through, in that impossible way! Such a paralysis of wriggling imbecility fallen over England, in this great crisis of its fortunes, as is still painful to contemplate: and indeed it has been mostly shaken out of mind by the modern Englishman; who tries to laugh at it, instead of weeping and considering, which would better beseem. Pitt speaks with a tragical vivacity, in all ingenious dialects, lively though serious; and with a depth of sad conviction, which is apt to be slurred over and missed altogether by a modern reader. Speaks as if this brave English Nation were about ended; little or no hope left for it; here a gleam of possibility, and there a gleam, which

* Thackeray, *Life of Chatham*, t. 264.

"soon vanishes again in the fatal murk of impotencies, do-
"nothingisms. Very sad to the heart of Pitt. A once brave
"Nation arrived at its critical point, and doomed to higgle
"and puddle there till it drown in the gutters: considerably
"tragical to Pitt; who is lively, ingenious, and, though not
"quitting the Parliamentary tone for the Hebrew-Prophetic,
"far more serious than the modern reader thinks.

"In Walpole's Book * there is the liveliest Picture of this
"dismal Parliamentary Hellbroth, — such a Mother of Dead
"Dogs as one has seldom looked into! For the Hour is great;
"and the Honourable Gentlemen, I must say, are small. The
"Hour, little as you dream of it, my Honourable Friends, is
"pregnant with questions that are immense. Wide Con-
"tinents, long Epochs and Æons hang on this poor jargoning
"of yours; the Eternal Destinies are asking their much-
"favoured Nation, "Will you, can you?" — much-favoured
"Nation is answering in that manner. Astonished at its own
"stupidity, and taking refuge in laughter. The Eternal
"Destinies are very patient with some Nations; and can dis-
"regard their follies, for a long while; and have their Crom-
"well, have their Pitt, or what else is essential, ready for the
"poor Nation, in a grandly silent way!

"Certain it is, — though how could poor Newcastle know
"it at all! — here is again the hour of tide for England. Tide
"is full again; has been flowing long hundreds of years, and
"is full: certain, too, that time and tide wait on no man or
"nation. In a dialect different from Cromwell's or Pitt's, but
"with a sense true to theirs, I call it the Eternal Destinies
"knocking at England's door again: 'Are you ready for the
"'crisis, birth-point of long Ages to you, which is now come?'
"Greater question had not been, for centuries past. None to
"be named with it since that high Spiritual Question (truly a
"much higher, and which was in fact the *parent* of this, and of
"all of high and great that lay ahead), which England and
"Oliver Cromwell were there to answer: 'Will you hold by
"Consecrated Formulas, then, you English, and expect salva-
"tion from traditions of the elders; or are you for Divine
"Realities, as the one sacred and indispensable thing?'
"Which they did answer, in what way we know. Truly the
"Highest Question; which, if a Nation can answer *well*, it

* *Memoirs of the Last Ten Years of George II.*

"will grow in this world, and may come to be considerable,
"and to have many high Questions to answer, — this of Pitt's,
"for example. And the Answers given do always extend
"through coming ages; and do always bear harvests, ac-
"cursed or else blessed, according as the Answers were. A
"thing awfully true, if you have eye for it; — a thing to make
"Honourable Gentlemen serious, even in the age of percus-
"sion-caps! No, my friend, Newcastleisms, impious Pol-
"trooneries, in a Nation, do not die: — neither (thank God)
"do Cromwellisms and pious Heroisms; but are alive for the
"poor Nation, even in its somnambulencies, in its stupidest
"dreams. For Nations have their somnambulencies; and, at
"any rate, the questions put to Nations, in different ages, vary
"much. Not in any age, or turning-point in History, had
"England answered the Destinies in such a dialect as now,
"under its Newcastle and National Palaver."

3. *Of Walpole, as Recording Angel.* "Walpole's *George
"the Second* is a Book of far more worth than is commonly
"ascribed to it; almost the one original English Book yet
"written on those times, — which, by the accident of Pitt, are
"still memorable to us. But for Walpole, — burning like a
"small steady light there, shining faithfully, if stingily, on the
"evil and the good, — that sordid muddle of the Pelham
"Parliaments, which chanced to be the element of things now
"recognisable enough as great, would be forever unintel-
"ligible. He is unusually accurate, punctual, lucid; an
"irrefragable authority on English points. And if, in regard
"to Foreign, he cannot be called an understanding witness,
"he has read the best Documents accessible, has conversed
"with select Ambassadors (Mitchell and the like, as we can
"guess); and has informed himself to a degree far beyond
"most of his contemporaries. In regard to Pitt's Speeches,
"in particular, his brief jottings, done rapidly while the
"matter was still shining to him, are the only Reports that
"have the least human resemblance. We may thank Walpole
"that Pitt is not dumb to us, as well as dark. Very curious
"little scratchings and etchings, those of Walpole; frugal,
"swift, but punctual and exact; hasty pen-and-ink outlines;
"at first view, all barren; bald as an invoice, seemingly; but
"which yield you, after long study there and elsewhere, a
"conceivable notion of what and how excellent these Pitt

"Speeches may have been. Airy, winged, like arrow-flights
"of Phœbus Apollo; very superlative Speeches indeed.
"Walpole's Book is carefully printed, — few errors in it like
"that 'Chapeau' for *Chasot*," which readers remember: —
"but, in respect to editing, may be characterised as still want-
"ing an Editor. A Book *unedited*; little but lazy ignorance
"of a very hopeless type, thick contented darkness, traceable
"throughout in the marginal part. No attempt at an Index,
"or at any of the natural helps to a reader now at such
"distance from it. Nay, till you have at least marked, on
"the top of each page, what Month and Year it actually is,
"the Book cannot be read at all, — except by an idle crea-
"ture, doing worse than nothing under the name of reading!"

4. *Pitt's Speeches, foreshadowing What.* "It is a kind of
"epoch in your studies of modern English History when you
"get to understand of Pitt's Speeches, that they are not Par-
"liamentary Eloquences, but things which with his whole soul
"he means, and is intent to *do*. This surprising circumstance,
"when at last become undeniable, makes, on the sudden, an
"immense difference for the Speeches and you! Speeches are
"not a thing of high moment to this Editor; it is the Thing
"spoken, and how far the speaker means to do it, that this
"Editor inquires for. Too many Speeches there are, which
"he hears admired all round, and has privately to entertain a
"very horrid notion of! Speeches, the finest in quality (were
"quality really 'fine' conceivable in such case), which *want* a
"corresponding fineness of source and intention, correspond-
"ing nobleness of purport, conviction, tendency; these, if we
"will reflect, are frightful instead of beautiful. Yes; — and
"always the frightfuller, the 'finer' they are; the faster and
"and farther they go, sowing themselves in the dim vacancy
"of men's minds. For Speeches, like all human things,
"though the act is now little remembered, do always rank
"themselves as forever blessed or as forever unblessed.
"Sheep or goats; on the right hand of the Final Judge, or
"else on the left. There are Speeches which can be called
"true; and, again, Speeches which are not true: — Heavens,
"only think what these latter are! Sacked wind, which you
"are intended to *sow*, — that you may reap the whirlwind!
"After long reading, I find Chatham's Speeches to be what he
"pretends they are: true, and worth speaking then and there.

"Noble indeed, I can call them with you: the highly noble
"Foreshadow, necessary preface and accompaniment of
"Actions which are still nobler. A very singular phenomenon
"within those walls, or without!

"Pitt, though nobly eloquent, is a Man of Action, not of
"Speech; an authentically Royal kind of Man. And if there
"were a Plutarch in these times, with a good deal of leisure
"on his hands, he might run a Parallel between Friedrich and
"Chatham. Two radiant Kings; very shining Men of Action
"both; both of them hard bested, as the case often is. For
"your born King will generally have, if not 'all Europe
"against him,' at least pretty much all the Universe. Chat-
"ham's course to Kingship was not straight or smooth, — as
"Friedrich, too, had his well-nigh fatal difficulties on the
"road. Again says the Plutarch, they are very brave men
"both; and of a clearness and veracity peculiar among their
"contemporaries. In Chatham, too, there is something of the
"flash of steel; a very sharp-cutting, penetrative, rapid in-
"dividual, he too; and shaped for action, first of all, though
"he has to talk so much in the world. Fastidious, proud, no
"King could be prouder, though his element is that of Free-
"Senate and Democracy. And he has a beautiful poetic
"delicacy, withal; great tenderness in him, playfulness,
"grace; in all ways, an airy as well as a solid loftiness of
"mind. Not born a King, — alas, no, not officially so; only
"naturally so; has his kingdom to seek. The Conquering of
"Silesia, the Conquering of the Pelham Parliaments — But
"we will shut up the Plutarch with time on his hands.

"Pitt's Speeches, as I spell them from Walpole and the
"other faint tracings left, are full of genius in the vocal kind,
"far beyond any Speeches delivered in Parliament: serious
"always, and the very truth, such as he has it; but going in
"many dialects and modes; full of airy flashings, twinkles
"and coruscations. Sport, as of sheet-lightning glancing
"about, the bolt lying under the horizon; bolt *hidden*, as is fit,
"under such a horizon as he had. A singularly radiant man.
"Could have been a Poet, too, in some small measure, had
"he gone on that line. There are many touches of genius,
"comic, tragic, lyric, something of humour even, to be read
"in those Shadows of Speeches taken down for us by Wal-
"pole. * *

"In one word, Pitt, shining like a gleam of sharp steel in
"that murk of contemptibilities, is carefully steering his way
"towards Kingship over it. Tragical it is (especially in Pitt's
"case, first and last) to see a Royal Man, or Born King,
"wading towards his throne in such an element. But, alas,
"the Born King (even when he tries, which I take to be the
"rarer case) so seldom can arrive there at all;—sinful Epochs
"there are, when Heaven's curse has been spoken, and it is
"that awful Being, the Born Sham-King, that arrives! Pitt,
"however, does it. Yes; and the more we study Pitt, the more
"we shall find he does it in a peculiarly high, manful, and
"honourable as well as dextrous manner; and that English
"History has a right to call him 'the acme and highest man
"of Constitutional Parliaments; the like of whom was not in
"any Parliament called Constitutional, nor will again be.'"

Well, probably enough; too probably! But what it more concerns us to remember here, is the fact, That in these dismal shufflings which have been, Pitt, — in spite of Royal dislikes and Newcastle peddlings and chicaneries, — has been actually in Office, in the due topmost place, the poor English Nation ardently demanding him, in what ways it could. Been in Office; — and is actually out again, in spite of the Nation. Was without real power in the Royal Councils; though of noble promise, and planting himself down, hero-like, evidently bent on work, and on ending that unutterable "St. Vitus'-dance" that had gone so high all round him. Without real power, we say; and has had no permanency. Came in, 11th-19th November 1756; thrown out, 5th April 1757. After six months trial, the St. Vitus finds that it cannot do with him; and will prefer going on again. The last act his Royal Highness of Cumberland did in England was to displace Pitt: "Down you, I am the man!" said Royal Highness; and went to the Weser Countries on those terms.

Would the reader wish to see, in summary, what Pitt's Offices have been, since he entered on this career about thirty years ago? Here, from our Historian, is the List of them in order of time; *Stages of Pitt's Course,* he calls it:

1º. "*December* 1734, Comes into Parliament, age now "twenty-six; Cornet in the Blues as well; being poor, and in "absolute need of some career that will suit. *April* 1736, "makes his First Speech: — Prince Frederick the subject, — "who was much used as battering-ram by the Opposition; "whom perhaps Pitt admired for his madrigals, for his Liter-"ary patronisings, and favour to the West-Wickham set. "Speech, full of airy lightning, was much admired. Followed "by many, with the lightning getting denser and denser; "always on the Opposition side" (once on the *Jenkins's-Ear Question*, as we saw, when the Gazetteer Editor spelt him Mr. Pitts): "so that Majesty was very angry, sulky Public much "applausive; and Walpole was heard to say, 'We must "muzzle, in some way, that terrible Cornet of Horse!' — but "could not, on trial; this man's 'price,' as would seem, being "awfully high! *August-October* 1744, Sarah Duchess of Marl-"borough bequeathed him 10,000*l.*, as Commissariat equip-"ment in this his Campaign against the Mudgods,* — glory "to the old Heroine for so doing! Which lifted Pitt out of the "Cornetcy or Horseguards element, I fancy; and was as the "nailing of his Parliamentary colours to the mast.

2º. "*February 14th,* 1746, Vice-Treasurer for Ireland: on "occasion of that Pelham-Granville 'As-you-were!' (Carteret "Ministry, which lasted One Day), and the slight shufflings "that were necessary. Now first in Office, — after such Ten "Years of colliding and conflicting, and fine steering in diffi-"cult waters. Vice-Treasurer for Ireland: and 'soon after, on "Lord Wilmington's death,' *Paymaster of the Forces.* Continued "Paymaster about nine years. Rejects, quietly and totally, "the big income derivable from Interest of Government "Moneys lying delayed in the Paymaster's hand ('Dishonest, "I tell you!') — and will none of it, though poor. Not yet

* Thackeray, i. 138.

"high, still low over the horizon, but shining brighter and
"brighter. Greatly contemptuous of Newcastle and the Pla-
"titudes and Poltrooneries; and still a good deal in the Op-
"position strain, — and *not* always tempering the wind to the
"shorn lamb. For example, Pitt (still Paymaster) to New-
"castle on King of the Romans Question (1752 or so): 'You
"engage for Subsidies, not knowing their extent; for Treaties,
"not knowing the terms!' — 'What a bashaw!' moan New-
"castle and the top Officials. 'Best way is, don't mind it,'
"said Mr. Stone" (one of their terriers, — a hard-headed
fellow, whose brother became Primate of Ireland by and by).

3°. "*November 20th*, 1755, Thrown out: — on Pelham's
"death, and the general hurlyburly in Official regions, and
"change of partners with no little difficulty, which had then
"ensued! Sir Thomas Robinson," our old friend, "made
"Secretary, — not found to answer. Pitt sulkily looking on
"America, on Minorca; on things German, on things in
"general; warily set on returning, as is thought; but How?
"*Fox* to Pitt: 'Will you join *me?*' — *Pitt:* 'No,' — with such
"politeness, but in an unmistakable way! Ten months of con-
"summate steering on the part of Pitt; Chancellor Hardwicke
"coming as messenger, he among others; Pitt's answer to him
"dextrous, modestly royal. Pitt's bearing, in this grand
"juncture and crisis, is royal, his speakings and also his
"silences notably fine. *October 20th*, 1756: to Newcastle face
"to face, 'I will accept no situation under your Grace!' —
"and, about that day month, comes *in*, on his own footing.
"That is to say,

"*November 19th*, 1756, to England's great comfort, Sees
"himself Secretary of State (age now just forty-eight.) Has
"pretty much all England at his back; but has, in face of him,
"Fox, Newcastle and Company, offering mere impediment
"and discouragement; Royal Highness of Cumberland looking
"deadly sour. Till finally,

"*April 5th*, 1757, King bids him resign; Royal Highness
"setting off for Germany the second day after. Pitt had been
"*in* rather more than Four months. England, at that time a
"silent Country in comparison, knew not well what to do;
"took to offering him Freedoms of Corporations in very great
"quantity. Town after Town, from all the four winds, sym-
"pathetically firing off, upon a misguided Sacred Majesty,

"its little Box, in this oblique way, with extraordinary
"diligence. Whereby, after six-months bombardment by
"Boxes, and also by Events, *June 29th*, 1757"— We will expect
June 29th.*

In these sad circumstances, Preparations, so-called,
have been making for Hanover, for America; — such
preparations as were never seen before. Take only
one instance; let one be enough:

"By the London Gazette, well on in February 1756, we
"learn that Lord Loudon, a military gentleman of small
"faculty, but of good connexions, has been nominated to
"command the Forces in America; and then, more obscurely,
"some days after, that another has been nominated: — one of
"them ought certainly to make haste out, if he could; the
"French, by account, have 25,000 men in those countries,
"with real officers to lead them! Haste out, however, is not
"what this Lord Loudon or his rival can make. In March, we
"learn that Lord Loudon has been again nominated; in an
"improved manner, this time; — and still does not look like
"going. 'Again nominated, why again?' Alas, reader, there
"have been hysterical fidgettings in a high quarter; internal
"shiftings and shufflings, contradictions, new proposals, one
"knows not what.** One asks only: How is the business ever
"to be done, if you cannot even settle what imbecile is to go
"and try it?

"Seldom had Country more need of a Commander than
"America now. America itself is of willing mind; and surely
"has resources, in such a Cause; but is full of anarchies as
"well: the different States and sections of it, with their dis-
"crepant Legislatures, their half-drilled Militias, pulling each
"a different way, there is, as in the poor Mother Country, little
"result except of the St. Vitus kind. In some Legislatures are
"anarchic Quakers, who think it unpermissible to fight with
"those hectoring French, and their tail of scalping Indians;

* Thackeray, 1. 231, 264. Almon, *Anecdotes of Pitt* (London, 1810),
1. 151, 188, 218.
** *Gentleman's Magazine* for 1756, pp. 92, 150, 359, 450.

"and that the 'method of love' ought to be tried with them.
"What is to become of those poor people, if not even a Lord
"Loudon can get out?"

The result was, Lord Loudon had not in his own poor person come to hand in America till August 1756, Season now done; and could only write home, "All is St. Vitus out here! Must have reinforcement of 10,000 men!" "Yes," answers Pitt, who is now in Office: "you shall have them; and we will take Cape Breton, please Heaven!"— but was thrown out; and by the wrigglings that ensued, nothing of the 10,000 reached Lord Loudon till Season 1757 too was done. Nor did they then stead his Lordship much, then or afterwards; who never took Cape Breton, nor was like doing it; — but wriggled too and fro a good deal, and revolved on his axis, according to pattern given. And set (what chiefly induces us to name him here) his not reverent enough Subordinate, Lord Charles Hay, our old Fontenoy friend, into angry impatient quizzing of him; — and by and by into Court Martial for such quizzing.* Court Martial, which was much puzzled by the case; and could decide nothing, but only adjourn and adjourn; — as we will now do, not mentioning Lord Loudon farther, or the numerous other instances at all.

Pitt, we just saw, far from being confirmed and furthered, has been thrown out by Royal Highness of Cumberland; the last thing before crossing to that exquisite Weser Problem. "Nothing now left at home to hinder *us* and our Hanover and Weser Problem!" thinks Royal Highness. No, indeed: a comfortable pacific No-government, or Battle of the Four Elements, left yonder; the Anarch Old waggling his addle head

* Peerage Books, § Tweeddale.

over it; ready to help everybody, and bring fire and
water, and Yes and No, into holy matrimony, if he
could! — Let us return to Prag. Only one remark
more; upon "April 5th." That was the Day of Pitt's
Dismissal at St. James's: and I find, at Schönbrunn it
is likewise the day when *Reichs-Hofrath* (Kaiser in
Privy Council) decides, in respect to Friedrich, that
Ban of the Reich must be proceeded with, and recom-
mends Reich's Diet to get through with the same.*
Official England ordering its Pitt into private life, and
Official Teutschland its Friedrich into outlawry ("Be
quiet henceforth, both of *you!*") — are, by chance,
synchronous phenomena.

Phenomena of Prag Siege: — Prag Siege is interrupted.

Friedrich's Siege of Prag proved tedious beyond expectation. In four days he had done that exploit in
1744; but now, to the world's disappointment, in as
many weeks he cannot. Nothing was omitted on his
part: he seized all egresses from Prag, rapidly enough;
had beset them with batteries, on the very night or
morrow of the Battle; every egress beset, cannon and
ruin forbidding any issue there. On the 9th of May,
cannonading began; proper siege-cannon and ammunition, coming up from Dresden, were completely come
May 19th; after which the place is industriously battered, bombarded with redhot balls; but except by
hunger, it will not do. Prag, as a fortress, is weak,
but as a breastwork for 50,000 men it is strong. The
Austrians tried sallies; but these availed nothing, —
very ill-conducted, say some. The Prussians, more

* *Helden-Geschichte* (Reichs-Procedures, *ubi supra*).

than once, had nearly got into the place by surprisal; but, owing to mere luck of the Austrians, never could, — say the same parties.*

A *Diarium* of Prag Siege is still extant, Two *Diariums;* punctual diurnal account, both Austrian and Prussian:** which it is far from our intention to inflict on readers, in this haste. Siege lasted six weeks; four weeks extremely hot, — from May 19th, when the proper artilleries, in complete state, got up from Dresden. Line of siege-works, or intermittent series of batteries, is some twelve miles long; from Branik southward, to beyond the Belvedere northward, on both sides of the Moldau. King's Camp is on the Ziscaberg; Keith's on the Lorenz Berg, embracing and commanding the Weissenberg; there are two Bridges of communication, Branik and Podoli: King lodges in the Parsonage of Michel, — the busiest of all the sons of Adam; what a set of meditations in that Parsonage! The Besieged, 46,000 by count, offer to surrender Prag on condition of "Free withdrawal:" "No; you shall engage, such of you as won't enlist with us, not to serve against me for six years." Here are some select Specimens; Prussian chiefly, in an abridged state:

"*May 19th,* No sooner was our artillery come (all the "grounds and beds for it had been ready beforehand), than as "evening fell, it began to play in terrific fashion."

"*Night of the 23d-24th May,* There broke out a furious sally; "their first, and much their hottest, say the Prussians: a very "serious affair; — which fell upon Keith's quarter, west side "of the Moldau. Sally, say something like 10,000 strong; "picked men all, and strengthened with half a pound of horse-

* Archenholtz, i. 85, 87.
** In *Helden-Geschichte,* iv. 42-56, Prussian *Diarium;* ib. 73-86, Austrian.

"flesh each"(unluckily without salt): judge what the common diet must have been, when that was generous! "No salt to it; "but a fair supplement of brandy. Browne, from his bed of "pain (died, 26th June), had been strongly urgent. Aim is, "To force the Prussian lines, by determination, and the help "of darkness, in some weak point: the whole Army, standing "ranked on the walls, shall follow, if things go well; and storm "itself through, — away Daun-wards, across the River by "Podoli Bridge.

"Sally broke out between 1 and 2 A.M.; but we had wind of "it, and were on the alert. Sally tried on this place and on "that; very furious in places, but could not anywhere prevail. "The tusseling lasted for near six hours (Prince Ferdinand "of Preussen, King's youngest Brother, "and others of us, "getting hurts and doing exploits), — till, about 7 A.M., it was "wholly swept in, with loss of 1,000 dead. Upon which, their "whole Army retired to its quarters, in a hopeless condition. "Escape impossible. Near 50,000 of them; but in such a "posture. Provision of bread, the spies say, is not scarce, "unless the Prussians can burn it, which they are indus- "triously trying (diligent to learn where the Magazines are, "and to fire incessantly upon the same): plenty of meal "hitherto; but for butcher's meat, only what we saw. Forage "nearly done, and 12,000 horses standing in the squares and "market-places, — not even stabling for them, not to speak of "food or work, — slaughtering and salting" (if one but had salt!) "the one method. Horse-flesh two kreutzers a pound; "rises gradually to double that value.

"*May 29th*, About sunset there came a furious burst of "weather: rain-torrents mixed with battering hail; — some "flaw of water-spout among the Hills; for it lasted hour on "hour, and Moldau came down roaring double-deep, above a "hundred yards too wide each way; with cargoes of ruin, torn- "up trees, drowned horses; which sorely tried our Bridge at "Branik. Bridge, half of it, did break away (Friedrich's half, "forty-four pontoons; Keith's people got their end of the "Bridge doubled-in and saved): the Austrians, in Prag, fished "out twenty-four of Friedrich's pontoons; the other twenty "we caught at our Bridge of Podoli farther down. A most "wild night for the Prussian Army in tents; and indeed for "Prag itself, the low parts of which were all under water;

"unfortunate individuals getting drowned in the cellars; and,
"still more important, a great deal of Austrian meal, which
"had been carried thither, to be safe from the red-hot balls.
"It was thought the Austrians, our Bridge being down,
"might try a sally again. To prevent which, hardly was the
"rain done, when, on our part, a rocket flew aloft; and there
"began on the City, from all sides, a deluge of bombs and
"red-hot balls. So that the still-dripping City was set fire to,
"in various parts; and we could hear" (what this Editor never
can forget) "the *Weh-Klagen* (wail) of the Townsfolk as they
"tried to quench it, and it always burst out again. The fire-
"deluge lasted for six hours."—Human *Weh-Klagen*, through
the hollow of Night, audible to the Prussians and us: 'Woe's
me! water-deluges, then fire-deluges; death on every hand!'
According to the Austrian accounts, there perished, by
bursting of bomb-shells, falling of walls, by hunger and other
misery and hurts, "above 9,000 Townsfolk in this Siege." Yes,
my Imperial friends; War is not a thing of streamering and
ornamental trumpeting alone; War is an inexorable, dangerously incalculable thing. Is it not a terrible question, at whose
door lies the beginning of a War!

"*June 5th*, 12,000 poor people of Prag were pushed out:
"'Useless mouths, will you contrive to disappear some way:'
"But, after haggling about all day, they had to be admitted
"in again, under penalty of being shot.

"*June 8th*, City looking black and ruinous, whole of the
"Neustadt in ashes; few houses left in the Jew Town; in the
"Altstadt the fire raged on, *wüthete fort*. Nothing but ruin and
"confusion over there; population hiding in cellars, getting
"killed by falling buildings. Bürgermeister and Townsfolk
"besiege Prince Karl, 'For the Virgin's sake, have pity on us,
'Your Serenity!" Poor Prince Karl has to be deaf, whatever
"his feelings.

"He was diligent in attending mass, they say: he alone of
"the Princes, of whom there were several; two Saxon Princes
"among others, Prince Xavier the elder of them, who will be
"heard of again. A profane set, these, lodging in the *Clemen-*
"*tinum*" (vast Jesuit Edifice, which had been cleared out for
them, and "the windows filled with dung outside," against
balls): "there, with wines of fine vintage, and cookeries
"plentiful and exquisite, that know nothing of famine outside,

"they led an idle disorderly life, — ran races in the long cor-
"ridors"(not so bad a course), "dressed themselves in Priests'
"vestures" (which are abundant in such locality), "and made
"travesties and mummeries of Holy Religion; the wretched
"creatures, defying despair, as buccaneers might when their
"ship is sinking. To surrender, everything forbids; of escape,
"there is no possibility.*

"*June 9th*, The bombardment abates; a *Laboratorium* of
"our own flew aloft by some spark or accident; and killed
"thirteen men.

"*June 15th*, From the King's Camp a few bombs" (King
himself now gone) "kindled the City in three places:" — but
there is, by this time, new game afield; Prag Siege awaiting
its decision not at Prag, but some way off.

Friedrich has being doing his utmost; diligent, by
all methods, to learn where the Austrian Magazines
were, that is, on what special edifices and localities
shot might be expended with advantage; and has fired
into these "about 12,000 bombs.' Here is a small
thing still remembered:

"Spies being, above all, essential in this business, Friedrich
"had bethought him of one Käsebier, a supreme of House-
"breakers, whom he has, safe with a ball at his ancle, doing
"forced labour at Spandau"(in Stettin, if it mattered). "Käse-
"bier was actually sent for, pardon promised him if he could
"do the State a service. Käsebier smuggled himself twice,
"perhaps three times, into Prag; but the fourth time he did
"not come back."** Another Note says: "Käsebier was a
"Tailor, and Son of a Tailor, in Halle; and the expertest of
"Thieves. Had been doing forced labour, in Stettin, since
"1748; twice did get into Prag; third time, vanished. A highly
"celebrated Prussian thief; still a myth among the People,
"like Dick Turpin or Cartouche, except that his was always
"theft without violence." ***

* Archenholtz, i. 86; *Helden-Geschichte*, iv. 73-84.
** Retzow, i. 108 n.
*** Preuss, ii. 57 n.

We learn vaguely that the price of horse-flesh in Prag has risen to double; famine very sore: but still one hears nothing of surrender. And again there is vague rumour that the City may be as it will; but that the Garrison has meal, after all we have ruined, which will last till October. Such a Problem has this King: soluble within the time; or not soluble? Such a question for the whole world, and for himself more than any.

CHAPTER IV.

BATTLE OF KOLIN.

On and after June 9th, the bombardment at Prag abated, and never rose to briskness again; the place of trial for decision of that Siege having flitted elsewhither, as we said. About that time, rumours came in, not so favourable, from the Duke of Bevern; which Friedrich, strong in hope, strove visibly to disbelieve, but at last could not. Bevern reports that Daun is actually coming on, far too strong for his resisting; — in other terms, that the Siege of Prag will not decide itself by bombardment, but otherwise and elsewhere. Of which we must now give some account; brief as may be, especially in regard to the preliminary or marching part.

Daun, whose light troops plundered Brandeis (almost within wind of the Prussian Rear) on the day while Prag Battle was fighting, had, on that fatal event, gradually drawn back to Czaslau, a place we used to know fifteen years ago; and there, or in those neighbourhoods, defensively manœuvering, and hanging upon Kuttenberg, Kolin, especially upon his Magazine of Suchdol, Daun, always rather drawing back, with Brunswick Bevern vigilantly waiting on him, has continued ever since; diligently recruiting himself; ranking the remains of the right wing defeated at Prag; drawing regiments out of Mähren, or whencesoever to be had. Till, by these methods, he is grown 60,000 strong; nearly thrice superior to Bevern; though being a 'Fabius Cunctator' (so called by and by), he as yet attempts nothing. Forty thousand in Prag, with Sixty here in the Czaslau Quarter,* that

---

* Tempelhof, i. 196; Retzow (i. 107, 109) counts 46,000 + 66,000.

makes 100,000; say his Prussian Majesty has two-thirds of the number: can the Fabius Cunctator attempt nothing, before Prag utterly famish?

Order comes to him from Vienna: "Rescue Prag; straightway go upon it, cost what it like!" Daun does go upon it; advances visibly towards Prag, Bevern obliged to fall back in front of him. Sunday, 12th June, Daun despatches several Officers to Prince Karl at Prag, with notice that, "On the 20th, Monday come a week, he will be in the neighbourhood of Prag with this view: — they, of course, to sally out, and help from rearward." "Several Officers, under various disguises," go with that message, June 12th; but none of them could get into the City; and some of them, I judge, must have fallen into the Prussian Hussar Parties: — at any rate, the news they carried did get into the Prussian circuit, and produced an instant resolution there. Early next morning, Monday 13th, King Friedrich, with what disposable force is on the spot, — 10,000 capable of being spared from siegework, and 4,000 more that will be capable of following, under Prince Moritz, in two days, — sets forth in all speed. Joins Bevern, that same night; at Kaurzim, thirty-five miles off, which is about midway from Prag to Czaslau, and only three miles or so from Daun's quarters that night, — had the King known it, which he did not.

Daun must be instantly gone into; and shall, — if he is there at all, and not fallen back at the first rumour of us, as Friedrich rather supposes. In any case, there are preliminaries indispensable: the 4,000 of Prince Moritz still to come up; secondly, bread to be had for us, which is baking at Nimburg, across the Elbe, twenty miles off; lastly (or rather firstly, and most indispensable of all), Daun to be reconnoitred. Friedrich reconnoitres Daun with all diligence; pushes on everything according to his wont; much obstructed in the reconnoitring by Pandour clouds; under which Daun has veiled himself, which far outnumber our small Hussar force. Daun, as usual, — showing always great skill in regard to camps and positions, — has planted himself in difficult country: a little river with its boggy pools in front; behind and around, an intricate broken country of knolls and swamps, one ridge in it which they even call a *Berg* or Hill, Kamhayek Berg; not much of a Hill after all,

BATTLE OF KOLIN.

but forming a long backbone to the locality, west end of it straight behind Daun's centre, at present. Friedrich's position is from north to south; like Daun's, taking advantage of what heights and brooks there are; and edging northward to be near his bread-ovens: right wing still holds by Kaurzim, left wing looking down on Planian, a little Town on the High Road (*Kaiser-Strasse*) from Prag to Vienna. Little Town destined to get up its name in a day or two, — next little Town to which, twelve miles farther on, is Kolin, secretly destined to become and continue still more famous among mankind. Kolin is close to the Elbe, left or south bank; Elbe hereabouts strikes into his long north-eastern course (to Wittenberg all the way; Pirna, say 150 miles off, is his halfway house in that direction); — strikes off northward hereabouts, making for Nimburg, among other places: Planian, right south of Nimburg, is already fifteen good miles from Elbe.

This is Friedrich's position, Wednesday June 15th and the day following; somewhat nearer his ovens than yesterday. Daun is yet parallel to him, has his centre behind Swoyschitz, an insignificant Village, at the foot of those Kamhayek Heights, which is, ever since, to be found in Maps. Friday 17th, Friedrich's bread-wagons and 4,000 having come in, as doubtless the Pandours report in the proper place, Daun does not quite like his strong position any more, but would prefer a stronger. Friday about sunset, "great clouds of dust" rise from Daun: changing his position, the Prussians see, if for Pandours and gathering darkness they can at present see little else. Daun, truly, observing the King to have in that manner edged up, towards Planian, is afraid of his right wing from such a neighbour. So that the reader must take his Map again. Or if he care not for such things, let him skip, and leave me solitary to my sad function; till we can meet on easier ground, and report the Battle which ensued. Daun hustles his right wing back out of that dangerous proximity; wheels his whole right wing and centre ninety degrees round, so as to reach out now towards Kolin, and lie on the north slope of the Kamhayek ridge; places his left wing *en potence* (gibbet-wise), hanging round the western *end* of said Kamhayek, its southern extremity at Swoyschitz, its northern at Hradenin, where (not a mile from Planian) his right wing had formerly been; — with other intricate movements not worth following, under my questionable guidance, on a Map with unpronounceable names. Enough to say that Daun's right wing is now far east at Kreczhorz, well beyond Chotzemitz, whereabouts his centre now comes to stand (and most of his horse *there*, both the wings being hilly and rough, unfit for horse); — and that this being nearly the last of Daun's shiftings and hustlings for the present, or indeed in essential respects the very last, readers may as well note the above main points in it.

Hustled into this still stronger place, with wheeling and shoving, which lasted to a late hour, Daun composes himself for the night. He lies now, with centre and right looking northward, pretty much parallel to the Planian-Kolin or Prag Vienna Highway, and about a mile south of the same; extreme posts extending almost to Kolin on that side; left wing well planted *en potence*; Kamhayck ridge, north face and west end of it, completely his on both the exposed or Anti-Prussian faces. Friedrich feels uncertain whether he has not gone his ways altogether; but proposes to ascertain by break of day.

By break of day Friedrich starts, having cleared off certain Pandour swarms visible in places of difficulty, who go on first notice, and without shot fired.[*] Marches through Planian in two columns, along the Kolin Highway and to north of it; marches on, four or five miles farther, nothing visible but the skirts of retiring Pandours, — "Daun's rearguard probably?" — Friedrich

[*] Lloyd, i. 61 et seq. (or Tempelhof's Translation, i. 151-164); Tempelhof's own Account is, i. 179-196; Retzow's, i. 120-149 (fewer errors of detail than usual); Kutzen, *Der Tag von Kolin* (Breslau, 1857), a useful little compilation from many sources. Very incorrect most of the common accounts are: Kausler's *Schlachten*, Jomini, and the like.

himself is with Ziethen, who has the vanguard, as Friedrich's wont is, eagerly enough looking out; reaches a certain Inn on the wayside (*Wirthshaus* "of Slatislunz or *Golden-Sun*," say the Modern Books,—though I am driven to think it Novomiesto, nearer Planian; but will not quarrel on the subject); Inn of good height for one thing; and there, mounting to the top-story or perhaps the leads, descries Daun, stretching far and wide, leant against the Kamhayek, in the summer morning. What a sight for Friedrich: "Big game *shall* be played, then; death sure, this day, to thousands of men: and to me—? — Well!"

Friedrich calls halt: rest here a little; to consider, examine, settle how. A hot close morning; rest for an hour or two, till our rear from Kaurzim come up: horses and men will be the better for it, — horses can have a mouthful of grass, mouthful of water; some of them "had no drink last night, so late in getting home." Poor quadrupeds, they also have to get into a blaze of battle-rage this day, and be blown to pieces a great many of them, — in a quarrel not of their seeking! Horse and rider are alike satisfied on that latter point; silently ready for the task *they* have; and deaf on questions that are bottomless.

At this Hostelry of Novomiesto (not of Slatislunz or "*Golden-Sun*" at all, which is a "Sun" fallen dismally eclipsed in other ways*), Friedrich halted for

---

* "The Inn of Slati-Slunz was burnt, about twenty years ago; nothing "of it but the stone walls now dates from Friedrich's time. It is a biggish "solid-looking House of two stories (whether ever of three, I could not "learn); stands pleasantly, at the crown of a long rise from Kolin; — and "inwardly, alas, in our day, offers little but bad smells and negative "quantities! Only the ground-floor is now inhabited. From the front, "your view, northward, Nimburg way, across the Elbe Valley, is fertile, "wide-waving, pretty; but rearward, upstairs, — having with difficulty

three hours and more; saw Daun developing himself into new Order of Battle, "every part of his position visible;" considered with his whole might what was to be tried upon him; — and about noon, having made up his mind, called his Generals, in sight of the phenomenon itself there, to give them their various orders and injunctions in regard to the same. The Plan of Fight, which was thought then, and is still thought by everybody, an excellent one, — resting on the "oblique order of attack," Friedrich's favourite mode, — was, if the reader will take his Map, conceivable as follows.

Daun has by this time deployed himself; in three lines, or two lines and a reserve; on the high-lying Champaign south of the Planian-Kolin Great Road; south, say a mile, and over the crests of the rising ground, or Kamhayek ridge, so that from the Great Road you can see nothing of him. His line, swaying here and there a little, to take advantage of its ground, extends nearly five miles, from east to west; pointing towards Planian side, the left wing of it; from Planian, eastward, the way Friedrich has marched, Daun's left wing may be four miles distant. On the other side, Daun's right wing, — main line always pretty parallel to the Highway, and pointing rather southward of Kolin, — reaches to the small Hamlet of Krzeczhorz, which is two miles off Kolin. In front of his centre is a Vil-

---

"got permission, — you find bare balks, tattered feathers, several hundred-weight of pigeon's dung, and no outlook at all, except into walls of office-houses and the overhanging brow of Heights, — fatal, clearly, to any view of Daun, even from a third story!" (*Tourist's Note*, 1858.) — Tempelhof (*ubi suprá*) seems to have known the right place; not Retzow, or almost anybody since: and indeed the question, except for expressly Military people, is of no moment.

lage called Chotzemitz (from which for a while, in those months, the Battle gets its name, "Battle of Chotzemitz," by Daun's christening): in front of him, to right or to left of Chotzemitz, are some four or even six other Villages (dim rustic Hamlets, invisible from the High Road), every Village of which Daun has well beset with batteries, with good infantry, not to speak of Croat parties hovering about, or dismounted Pandours squatted in the corn. That easternmost Village of his is spelt "Krzeczhorz" (unpronounceable to mankind); a dirty little place; in and round which the Battle had its hinge or cardinal point: the others, as abstruse of spelling, all but equally impossible to the human organs, we will forbear to name, except in case of necessity. Half a mile behind Krzeczhorz (let us write it Kreczor, for the future: what can we do?), is a thin little Oakwood, bushes mainly, but with sparse trees too, which is now quite stubbed out, though it was then important enough, and played a great part in the result of this day's work. Radowesnitz, a pronounceable little Village, half a mile farther or southward of the Oak-bush, is beyond the extremity of Daun's position; low down on a marshy little Brook, which oozes through lakes and swamps towards Kolin, in the northerly direction.

Most or all of these Villages are on little Brooks (natural thirst so leading them): always some little runlet of water, not so swampy when there is any fall for it; in general lively when it gets over the ridge, and becomes visible from this Highway. And it is curious to see what a considerable dell, or green ascending chasm, this little thread of water, working at all moments for thousands of years, has hollowed out for itself in the sloping ground; making a great military obstacle, if you are mounting to attack there. Poor Czech Hamlets all of them, dirty, dark, malodorous, ignorant, abhorrent of German speech; — in what nook those inarticulate inhabitants, diving underground at a great rate this morning, have hidden themselves today, I know not. The country consists of knolls and slopes, with swamps intermediate; rises higher on the Planian side; but except the top of that Kamhayek ridge on the Planian side, and "Friedrich's-Berg" on the Kolin side, there is nothing that you could think of calling a Hill, though many Books (and even Friedrich's Book) rashly say otherwise. Friedrich's-Berg now so called, is on the north side of the Highway: half a mile northeastward of Slatislunz, the malodorous Inn. A conical height of perhaps a hundred and fifty feet; rises rather suddenly from the still-sloping ground, checking the slope there; on which the Austrian populations have built some memorial lately, notable to Tourists. Here Friedrich "stood during the Battle," say they; and the Prussians "had a battery there." Which remains uncertain to me, at least the battery part of it: that Friedrich himself was there, now and then, can be believed; but not that he kept "standing there" for long together. Friedrich's-Berg does command some view of the Kreczor scene, which at times was cardinal, at others not: but Friedrich did not stand anywhere: "oftenest in the thick of the fire," say those who saw.

Friedrich, from his Inn near Planian, seeing how Daun deploys himself, considers him impregnable on the left wing; impregnable, too, in front: not so on the Kreczor side, right flank and rear; but capable of being rolled together, if well struck at there. Thither, therefore; that is his vulnerable point. March along his front; quietly parallel in due Order of Battle, till we can bend round, and plunge in upon that. The Van, which consists of Ziethen's Horse and Hülsen's Infantry; Van, having faced to right at the proper moment and so become Left Wing, will attack Kreczor; probably carry it; each Division following will in like manner face to right when it arrives there, and fall on in regular succession in support of Hülsen (at Hülsen's right flank, if Hülsen be found prospering): our Right Wing is to refuse itself, and be as a Reserve, — no fighting on the road, you others, but steady towards Hülsen, in continual succession, all you; no facing round, no fighting anywhere, till we get thither: — "March!"

The word is given about 2 P. M.; and all, on the instant, is in motion; rolls steadily eastward, in two columns, which will become First Line and Second. One along the Highway, the second at due distance leftward on the green ground, no hedge or other obstacle obstructing in that part of the world. Daun's batteries, on the right, spit at them in passing, to no purpose; sputters of Pandour musketry, from coverts, there may be: Prussians finely disregarding, pass along; flowing tide-like towards *their* goal and place of choice. An impressive phenomenon in the sunny afternoon; with Daun expectant of them, and the Czech populations well hidden underground! —

Ziethen, vanmost of all, finds Nadasti and his Austrian squadrons drawn across the Highway, hitherward of the Kreczor latitude: Ziethen dashes on Nadasti; tumbles his squadrons and him away; clears the Road, and Kreczor neighbourhood, of Nadasti: drives him quite into the hollow of Radowesnitz, where he stood inactive for the rest of the day. Hülsen now at the level of Kreczor (in the latitude of Kreczor, as we phrased it), halts, faces to right; stiffly presses up, opens his cannon-thunders, his bayonet-charges and platoon-fires upon Kreczor. Stiffly pressing up, in spite of the violent counter-thunders, Hülsen does manage Kreczor without very much delay, completely enough, and like a workman; takes the battery, two batteries; overturns the Infantry; — in a word, has seized Kreczor, and, as new tenant, swept the old, and their litter, quite out. Of all which Ziethen has now the chase, and by no means will neglect that duty. Ziethen, driving the rout before him, has driven it in some minutes past the little Oak-wood above mentioned; and, or rather *but*, — what is much to be noted, — is there taken in flank with cannon-shot and musketry, Daun having put batteries and Croat parties in the Oak-wood; and is forced to draw bridle, and get out of range again.

Hülsen, advancing towards this little Oak-wood, is surprised to discover, not the wood alone, but a strong Austrian force, foot and horse, to rear of it; — such had been Daun's and Nadasti's precaution, on view of those Friedrich phenomena, flowing on from Planian, guessed to be hitherward. At sight of which Wood and foot-party, Hülsen, no new Battalion having yet arrived to second him, pauses, merely cannonading from the distance, till new Battalions shall arrive. Unhappily they did not arrive, or not in due quantity at the set time, — for what reason, by what strange mistake? men still ask themselves. Probably by more mistakes than one. Enough, Hülsen, struggling here all day, with reinforcements never adequate, did take the Wood, and then lose it; did take and lose this and that; — but was unable to make more of it than keep his ground thereabouts. A resolute man, says Retzow, but without invention of his own, or head to mend the mistakes of others. In and about Kreczor, Hülsen did maintain himself with more and more tenacity, till the general avalanche, fruit of said mistakes, swept *him*, quite spasmodically struggling at that period, off to the edge of it, and all the others clean away! Mistakes have been to rightwards, one or even two, the fruit of which, small at first, suffices to turn the balance, and ends in an avalanche, or precipitous descent of ruin on the Prussian side.

One mistake there was, miles westward on the right wing; due to Mannstein, our too impetuous Russian friend. Mannstein well to right, while marching forward according to order, has Croat musketry spitting upon him from amid the high corn, to an inconvenient extent: such was the common lot, which others had borne and disregarded: perhaps it was beyond the average on Mannstein, or Mannstein's patience was less infinite; anyway it provoked Mannstein to boil over; and in evil moment he said, "Extinguish me that Croat canaille, then!" Regiment Bornstedt faced to right, accordingly; took to extinguishing the Croat canaille, which of course fled at once, or squatted closer, but came back with reinforcements; drew Mannstein deeper in, fatally delayed Bornstedt, and proved widely ruinous. For now he stopped the way to those following him: regiments marching on to rear of Mannstein see Mannstein halted, volleying with the Austrians; ask themselves, "How? Is there new order come? Attack to be in this point?" And successively fall on to support

Mannstein, as the one clear point in such dubiety. So that the whole right wing from Regiment Bornstedt westward is storming up the difficult steeps, in hot conflict with the Austrians there, where success against them had been judged impracticable; — and there is now no reserve force anywhere to be applied to in emergency, for Hülsen's behoof or another's; and the Plan of Battle from Mannstein westward has been fatally overturned. Poor Mannstein, there is no doubt, committed this error, being too fiery a man. Surely to him it was no luxury, and he paid the smart for it in skin and soul: "badly wounded in this business;" nay, in direct sequel, not many weeks after, killed by it, as we shall see! —

To Mannstein's mistake, Friedrich himself, in his account of Kolin mainly imputes the disaster that followed; and such, then and afterwards, was the universal judgment in military circles; loading the memory of too impetuous Mannstein with the whole.* Much talk there was in Prussian military circles; but there must also have been an admirable silence on the part of some. To Three Persons it was known that another strange incident had happened far ahead, far eastward, of Mannstein's position: incident, which did not by any means tend to alleviate, which could only strengthen and widen, the evil results of Mannstein; and which might have lifted part of the load from Mannstein's memory! Not till the present Century, after the lapse of almost fifty years, was this secret slowly dug out of silence, and submitted to modern curiosity.

The incident is this; — never whispered of for

* See Retzow, i. 135; Tempelhof, i. 214, 220.

near fifty years (so silent were the three); and endlessly tossed about since that; the sense of it not understood till almost now.* The three parties were: King Friedrich; Moritz of Dessau, leading on the centre here; Moritz's young Nephew Franz, Heir of Dessau, a brisk lad of seventeen, learning War here as Aide-de-camp to Moritz: the exact spot is not known to me, — probably the ground near that Inn of Slatislunz, or Golden Sun; between the foot of Friedrich's-Berg and that: — fact indubitable, though kept dark so long. Moritz is marching with the centre, or main battle, that way, intending to wheel and turn hillwards, Kreczor-wise, as per order, certain furlongs ahead; when Friedrich (having, so I can conceive it, seen from his Hill-top, how Hülsen had done Kreczor, altogether prosperous there; and what endless capability there was of prospering to all lengths and speeding the general winning, were Hülsen but supported soon enough, were there any safe short cut to Hülsen) dashed from his Hill-top in hot haste toward Prince Moritz, General of the centre, intending to direct him upon such short cut; and hastily said, with Olympian brevity and fire, "Face to right *here!*" With Jove-like brevity, and in such blaze of Olympian fire as we may imagine. Moritz himself is of brief, crabbed, fiery mind, brief in temper; and answers to the effect, "Impossible to attack the enemy here, your Majesty; postured as they are; and we with such orders gone abroad!" — "Face to right, I tell you!" said the King, still more Olympian, and too emphatic for explaining. Moritz, I hope, paused, but rather think he did not, before remon-

---

* See Retzow, i. 126; Berenhorst; &c. &c.; — then *finally*, Kutzen, pp. 99, 217.

strating the second time; neither perhaps was his voice so low as it should have been: it is certain Friedrich dashed quite up to Moritz at this second remonstrance, flashed out his sword (the only time he ever drew his sword in battle); and now, gone all to mere Olympian lightning and thunder-tone, asks in *this* attitude, "*Will Er* (will He) obey orders, then?" — Moritz, fallen silent of remonstrance, with gloomy rapidity obeys.

Prince Franz, the young Nephew of Moritz, alone witnessed this scene; scene to be locked in threefold silence. In his old age, Franz had whispered it to Berenhorst, his bastard Half-Uncle, a famed military Critic, — who is still in the highest repute that way (Berenhorst's *Kriegskunst*, and other deep Books), and is recognisable, to *lay* readers, for an abstruse strong judgment; with equal strength of abstruse temper hidden behind it, and very privately a deep grudge towards Friedrich, scarcely repressible on opportunity. From Berenhorst it irrepressibly oozed out;[*] much more to Friedrich's disadvantage than it now looks when wholly seen into. Not change of plan, not ruinous caprice on Friedrich's part, as Berenhorst, Retzow, and others would have it; only excess of brevity towards Moritz, and accident of the Olympian fire breaking out. Friedrich is chargeable with nothing, except perhaps (what Moritz knows the evil of) trying for a short cut! Such is now the received interpretation. Prince Franz, to his last day, refused to speak again on the subject; judiciously repentant, we can fancy, of having spoken at all, and brought such a

---

[*] "Heinrich von Berenhorst" (a natural son of the Old Dessauer's), "in his *Betrachtungen über die Kriegskunst*, is the first that alludes to it in print (Leipzig, 1797, — page in second edition, 1798, is, i. 219)."

matter into the streets and their pie-powder adjudications.* For the present, he is Adjutant to Moritz, busy obeying to the letter.

Friedrich, withdrawing to his Height again, and looking back on Moritz, finds that he is making right in upon the Austrian line; which was by no means Friedrich's meaning, had not he been so brief. Friedrich, doubtless with pain, remembers now that he had said only, "Face to right!" and had then got into Olympian tempest, which left things dark to Moritz. "*Halb-links*, Half to left withal!" he despatches that new order to Moritz, with the utmost speed: "Face to right; *then*, forward half to left." Had Moritz, at the first, got that commentary to his order, there had probably been no remonstrance on Moritz's part, no Olympian scene to keep silent; and Moritz, taking that diagonal direction from the first, had hit in at or below Kreczor, at the very point where he was needed. Alas, for overhaste; short cuts, if they are to be good, ought at least to be made clear! Moritz, on the new order reaching him, does instantly steer half-left: but he arrives now above Kreczor, strikes the Austrian line on this side of Kreczor; disjoined from Hülsen, where he can do no good to Hülsen: in brief, Moritz, and now the whole line with him, have to do as Mannstein and sequel are doing, attack in face, not in flank; and try what, in the proportion of one to two, uphill, and against batteries, they can make of it in that fashion!

And so, from right wing to left, miles long, there is now universal storm of volleying, bayonet-charging, thunder of artillery, case-shot, cartridge-shot, and sul-

* In *Kutters*, pp. 217-257, a long dissertation on it.

phurous devouring whirlwind; the wrestle very tough and furious, especially on the assaulting side. Here, as at Prag, the Prussian troops were one and all in the fire; each doing strenuously his utmost, no complaint to be made of their performance. More perfect soldiers, I believe, were rarely or never seen on any field of war. But there is no reserve left: Mannstein and the rest, who should have been reserve, and at a General's disposal, we see what they are doing! In vain, or nearly so, is Friedrich's tactic or manœuvering talent; what now is there to manœuvre? All is gone up into one combustion. To fan the fire, to be here, there, fanning the fire where need shows: this is now Friedrich's function; "everywhere in the hottest of the fight," that is all we at present know of him, invisible to us otherwise. This death-wrestle lasted perhaps four hours; till seven or towards eight o'clock in the June evening; the sun verging downwards; issue still uncertain.

And, in fact, at last the issue turned upon a hair; — such the empire of Chance in War matters. Cautious Daun, it is well known, did not like the aspect of the thing; cautious Daun thinks to himself, "If we get pushed back into that Camp of yesternight, down the Kamhayek Heights, and right into the impassable swamps; the reverse way, Heights now *his*, not ours, and impassable swamps waiting to swallow us? Wreck complete, and surrender at discretion — !" — Daun writes in pencil: "The retreat is to Suchdol" (Kuttenberg way, southward, where we have heights again and magazines); Daun's Aide-de-camp is galloping everywhither with that important Document; and Generals are preparing for retreat accordingly, — one

General on the right wing has, visibly to Hülsen and us, his cannon out of battery, and under way rearwards; a welcome sight to Hülsen, who, with imperfect reinforcement, is toughly maintaining himself there all day.

And now the Daun Aide-de-camp, so Chance would have it, cannot find Nostitz the Saxon Commandant of Horse in that quarter; finds a "Saxon Lieutenant-Colonel B—" ("Benkendorf" all Books now write him plainly), who, by another little chance, had been still left there: "Can the Herr Lieutenant-Colonel tell me where General Nostitz is?" Benkendorf can tell; — will himself take the message: but Benkendorf looks into the important Pencil Document; thinks it premature, wasteful, and that the contrary is feasible; persuades Nostitz so to think; persuades this regiment and that (Saxon, Austrian, horse and foot); though the cannon in retreat go trundling past them: "Merely shifting their battery, don't you see: — Steady!" And, in fine, organises, of Saxon and Austrian horse and foot in promising quantity (Saxons in great fury on the Pirna score, not to say the Striegau, and other old grudges), a new unanimous assault on Hülsen.

The assault was furious, and became ever more so; at length irresistible to Hülsen. Hülsen's horse, pressing on as to victory, are at last hurled back; could not be rallied;* fairly fled (some of them); confusing Hülsen's foot, — foot is broken, instantly ranks itself, as the manner of Prussians is; ranks itself in impromptu squares, and stands fiercely defensive again, amid the

* That of "*Racker, wollt ihr ewig leben*, Rascals, would you live forever?" with the "Fritz, for eight groschen, this day there has been enough!" — is to be counted pure myth; not unsuccessful, in its withered kind.

slashing and careering: wrestle of extreme fury, say the witnesses. 'This for Striegau!' cried the Saxon dragoons, furiously sabring.* Yes; and is there nothing to account of Pirna, and the later scores? Scores unliquidated, very many still; but the end is, Hülsen is driven away; retreats, Parthian-like, down hill, some space; whose sad example has to spread rightwards like a powder-train, till all are in retreat, — northward, towards Nimburg, is the road;—and the Battle of Kolin is finished.

Friedrich made vehement effort to rally the Horse, to rally this and that; but to no purpose: one account says he did collect some small body, and marched forth at the head of it against a certain battery; but, in his rear, man after man fell away, till Lieutenant-Colonel Grant (not "Le Grand," as some call him, and indeed there is an *accent* of Scotch in him, still audible to us here) had to remark, "Your Majesty and I cannot take the battery ourselves!" Upon which Friedrich turned round; and, finding nobody, looked at the Enemy through his glass, and slowly rode away** — on a different errand.

Seeing the Battle irretrievably lost, he now called Bevern and Moritz to him; gave them charge of the retreat — "To Nimburg; cross Elbe there" (fifteen good miles away); "and in the defiles of Planian have especial care!" and himself rode off thitherward, his Garde-du-Corps escorting. Retzow says, "a swarm of fugitive "horse-soldiers, baggage-people, grooms and led horses "gathered in the train of him: these latter, at one point," Retzow has heard in Opposition circles, "rushed up, "galloping: 'Enemy's hussars upon us!' and set the

* Archenholtz, i. 100.   ** Retzow, i. 139.

"whole party to the gallop for some time, till they found the alarm was false."* Of Friedrich we see nothing, except as if by cloudy moonlight in an uncertain manner, through this and the other small Anecdote, perhaps semi-mythical, and true only in the essence of it.

Daun gave no chase anywhere; on his extreme left he had, perhaps as preparative for chasing, ordered out the cavalry; "General Stampach and cavalry from the centre," with cannon, with infantry and appliances, to clear away the wrecks of Mannstein, and what still stands, to right of him, on the Planian Highway yonder. But Stampach found "obstacles of ground," wet obstacles and also dry, — Prussian posts, smaller and greater, who would not stir a handbreadth: in fact, an altogether deadly storm of Negative, spontaneous on their part, from the indignant regiments thereabouts, King's First Battalion, and two others; who blazed out on Stampach in an extraordinary manner, tearing to shreds every attempt of his, themselves stiff as steel: "Die, all of us, rather than stir!" And, in fact, the second man of these poor fellows did die there.** So that Bevern, Commander in that part, who was absent speaking with the King, found on his return a new battle broken out; which he did not forbid but encourage; till Stampach had enough, and withdrew in rather torn condition. This, if this were some preparative for chasing, was what Daun did of it, in the cavalry way; and this was all. The infantry he strictly prohibited to stir from their position, — "No saying, if we come into the level ground, with such an enemy!" — and passed the

* Retzow, i. 140.
** Kaisen, p. 188 (from the canonical, or "*Staff-Officers*" enumeration: see *supra*, p. 83 n.).

night under arms. Far on our left, or what was once our left, Ziethen with all his squadrons, nay Hülsen with most of his battalions, continued steady on the ground; and marched away at their leisure, as rear-guard.

"It seemed," says Tempelhof, in splenetic tone, "as if Feldmarshall Daun, like a good Christian, would "not suffer the sun to go down on his wrath. This "day, nearly the longest in the year, he allowed the "Prussian cavalry, which had beaten Nadasti, to stand "quiet on the field till ten at night" (till nine); "he "did not send a single hussar in chase of the infantry. "He stood all night under arms; and next day, returned "to his old Camp, as if he had been afraid the King "would come back. Arriving there himself, he could "see, about ten in the morning, behind Kaurzim and "Planian, the whole Prussian Baggage fallen into such "a coil that the wagons were with difficulty got on "way again; nevertheless he let it, under cover of the "grenadier battalion Manteuffel, go in peace."* A man that for caution and slowness could make no use of his victory!

The Austrian force in the Field this day is counted to have been 60,000; their losses in killed, wounded, and missing, 8,114. The Prussians, who began 34,000 in strength, lost 13,773; of whom prisoners (including all the wounded), 5,380. Their baggage, we have seen, was not meddled with: they lost 45 cannon, 22 flags, — a loss not worth adding, in comparison to this sore havoc, for the second time, in the flower of the Prussian Infantry."

* Tempelhof, I. 195.
" Retzow, L 141 (whose numbers are apt to be inaccurate); Kutzen, p. 144 (who depends on the Canonical *Staff-Officer* Account).

The news reached Prag Camp at two in the morning (Sunday 19th): to the sorrowful amazement of the Generals there; who "stood all silent; only the Prince "of Prussia breaking out into loud lamentations and "accusations," which even Retzow thinks unseemly. Friedrich arrived that Sunday evening: and the Siege was raised, next day; with next to no hindrance or injury. With none at all on the part of Daun; who was still standing among the heights and swamps of Planian, — busy singing, or shooting, universal *Te Deum*, with very great rolling fire and other pomp, that day while Friedrich gathered his Siege-goods and got on march.

The Maria-Theresa Order, new Knighthood for Austria.

No tongue can express the joy of the Austrians over this victory, — vouchsafed them, in this manner, by Lieutenant-Colonel Benkendorf and the Powers Above. Miraculously, behold, they are not upon the retreat to Suchdol, at double-quick, and in ragged ever-lengthening line; but stand here, keeping rank all night, on the Planian-Kolin upland of the Kamhayek: — behold, they have actually beaten Friedrich; for the first time, not been beaten by him. Clearly beaten that Friedrich, by some means or other. With such a result, too; consider it, — drawn sword was at our throat; and marvellously now it is turned round upon his (if Daun be alert), and we — let us rejoice to all lengths, and sing *Te Drum* and *Te Daunum* with one throat, till the Heavens echo again.

There was quite a hurricane, or lengthened storm, of jubilation and tripudiation raised at Vienna on this victory: New *Order of Maria Theresa*, in suitable Olympian fashion, with no end of regulating and inaugurating, — with Daun the first Chief of it; and "Pensions to Merit" a conspicuous part of the plan, we are glad to see. It subsists to this day: the grandest Military Order the Austrians yet have. Which then deafened the world, with its infinite solemnities, patentings, discoursings, trumpetings, for a good while. As was natural, surely, to that high Imperial Lady with the magnanimous heart; to that loyal solid Austrian People with its pudding-heart. Daun is at the top of the Theresa Order, and of military renown in Vienna circles; — of Lieutenant-Colonel Benkendorf I never heard that he got the least pension or recognition; — continued quietly a military lion to discerning men, for the rest of his days.*

Nay once, on Daun's *Te-Deum* day, he had a kind of recognition; — and even, by good accident, can tell us of it in his own words.**

"I was sent for to headquarters by a trumpeter," — Benkendorf was, — "when all was ready for the *Te Deum*. "Feldmarschall Daun was pleased to say at sight of me, "'That as I had had so much to do with the victory, it was but "right I should thank our Herr Gott along with him.' Having "no change of clothes, — as the servant who was to have a "uniform and some linens ready for me, had galloped off "during the Fight, and our baggage was all gone to rearward, "— I tried to hustle out of sight among the crowd of Imperial "Officers all in gala: but the reigning Duke of Würtemberg" (Wilhelmina's Son-in-law, a perverse obstinate Herr, growing ever more perverse; one of Wilhelmina's sad afflictions in these days) "called me to him, and said, 'He would give his

---

* "Died at Dresden, General of Cavalry," 5th May 1801 (Rödenbeck, i. 338, 539).

** Katsch (citing some *Biography* of Benkendorf), p. 142.

"whole wardrobe, could he wear that dusty coat with such "honour as I!'" — yes; and tried hard, in his perverse way, for some such thing; but never could, as we shall see.

How lucky that Polish Majesty had some remains of Cavalry still at Warsaw in the Pirna time; that they were made into a Saxon Brigade, and taken into the Austrian service; Brigade of three Regiments, Nostitz for Chief, and this Benkendorf a Lieutenant-Colonel, among them; — and that Polish Majesty, though himself lost, has been the saving of Austria twice within one year!

CHAPTER V.

FRIEDRICH AT LEITMERITZ, HIS WORLD OF ENEMIES COMING ON.

Of Friedrich's night-thoughts at Nimburg; how he slept, and what his dreams were, we have no account. Seldom did a wearied heart sink down into oblivion on such terms. By narrow miss, the game gone; and with such results ahead. It was a right valiant plunge this that he made, with all his strength and all his skill, home upon the heart of his chief enemy. To quench his chief enemy before another came up: it was a valiant plan, and valiantly executed; and it has failed. To dictate peace from the walls of Vienna: that lay on the cards for him this morning; and at night —? Kolin is lost, the fruit of Prag Victory too is lost; and Schwerin and new tens of thousands, unreplaceable for worth in this world, are lost: much is lost! Courage, your Majesty, all is not lost, you not, and honour not.

To the young Graf von Anhalt, on the road to Nimburg, he is recorded to have said, "Don't you "know, then, that every man must have his reverses "(*Mais ne savez-vous donc pas que chaque homme doit* "*avoir ses revers*)? It appears I am to have mine."[*] And more vaguely, in the Anecdote-Books, is mention of some stanch ruggedly pious old Dragoon, who brought, in his steel cap, from some fine-flowing well

[*] Rödenbeck, i. 309.

he had discovered, a draught of pure water to the King; old Mother Earth's own gift, through her rugged Dragoon, exquisite refection to the thirsty wearied soul; and spoke, in his Dragoon dialect, — "Never mind, your Majesty! *Der Allmächtige* and we; it shall be mended yet. 'The Kaiserin may get a victory for once; 'but does that send us to the Devil (*davon holt uns der 'Teufel nicht*)!'" — words of rough comfort, which were well taken.

Next morning, several Books, and many Drawings and Sculptures of a dim unsuccessful nature, give us view of him, at Nimburg; sitting silent "on a *Brunnen-* "*Rohr*" (Fountain Apparatus, waste-pipe or feeding-pipe, too high for convenient sitting); he is stooping forward there, his eyes fixed on the ground, and is scratching figures in the sand with his stick, as the broken troops reassemble round him. Archenholtz says: "He surveyed "with speechless feeling the small remnant of his Life- "guard of Foot, favourite First Battalion; 1,000 strong "yesterday morning, hardly 400 now;" — gone the others, in that furious Anti-Stampach outburst which ended the day's work! "All soldiers of this chosen "Battalion were personally known to him; their names, "their age, native place, their history" (the pick of his Ruppin regiment was the basis of it): "in one day, "Death had mowed them down; they had fought like "heroes, and it was for him that they had died. His "eyes were visibly wet, down his face rolled silent "tears." *

In public I never saw other tears from this King, — though in private I do not warrant him; his sensibilities, little as you would think it, being very

* Archenholtz, L 104, 101; Kutzen, pp. 259, 158; Retzow, i. 142.

lively and intense. "To work however!" This King can shake away such things; and is not given overmuch to retrospection on the unalterable Past. "Like dewdrops from the lion's mane" (as is figuratively said); the lion swiftly rampant again! There was manifold swift ordering, considering and determining, at Nimburg, that day; and towards night Friedrich shot rapidly into Headquarters at Prag, where, by order, there is, as the first thing of all a very rapid business going on, well forward by the time he arrives.

To fold one's Siege-gear and Army neatly together from those Two Hill-tops, and march away with them safe, in sight of so many enemies: this has to be the first and rapidest thing; if this be found possible, as one calculates it may. After which, the world of enemies, held in the slip so long, will rush in from all the four winds, — unknown whitherward; one must wait to see whitherward and how.

Friedrich's History for the remaining six months of this Year falls, accordingly, into three Sections. Section *first:* Waiting how and towards what objects his enemies, the Austrians first of all, will advance; — this lasts for about a month, Friedrich waiting mainly at Leitmeritz, on guard there both of Saxony and of Silesia, till this slowly declare itself. Slowly, perhaps almost stupidly, but by no means satisfactorily to Friedrich, as will be seen! After which, Section *second* of his History lasts above two months; Friedrich's enemies being all got to the ground, and united in hope and resolution to overwhelm and abolish him; but their plans, positions, operations so extremely various that, for a long time (end of August to beginning of November), Friedrich cannot tell what to do with them; and has to scatter himself into thin threads, and roam about, chiefly in Thüringen and the West of Saxony, seeking something to fight with, and finding nothing; getting more and more impatient of such paltry misery; at times nigh desperate; and habitually drifting on desperation as on a lee shore in the night, despite all his efforts. Till, in Section *third*, which goes from November 5th, through December 5th, and into the New Year, he does find what to do; and does it, — in a forever memorable way.

Three Sections; of which the reader shall successively have some idea, if he exert himself; though it is only in snatches, suggestive to an active fancy, that we can promise to dwell on them, especially on the First Two, which lie pretty much *unsurveyable* in those chaotic records, like a world-wide coil of thrums. Let us be swift, in Friedrich's own manner; and try to disemprison the small portions of essential! Here, partly from Eyewitnesses, are some Notes in regard to Section First: *

"*Sunday, 19th June*, At 2 A. M., Major Grant arrives at "Prag" (must have started instantly after that of 'We two cannot take the battery, your Majesty!') — "goes to Prince "Ferdinand of Brunswick, interim Commander on the Zisca-"berg, with order To raise Siege. Consternation on the part "of some; worse, on the Prince of Prussia's part; the others "kept silence at least, — and set instantly to work. On both "Hills, the cannons are removed (across Moldau the Zisca-"Hill ones), batteries destroyed, Siege-gear neatly gathered "up, to go in wagons to Leitmeritz, thence by boat to "Dresden: all this lies ready done, the dangerous part of it "done, when Friedrich arrives.

* Westphalen, *Geschichte der Feldzüge des Herzogs Ferdinand* (and a Private Journal of W.'s there), n. 13-19; Retzow; &c.

"*Monday 20th*, before sunrise, Siege raised. At three in
"the morning, Friedrich marches from the Ziscaberg; to
"eastward he, to Alt-Buntzlau, thence to Alt-Lissa," —
Nimburg way, with what objects we shall see. "Marshal
"Keith's fine performance. Keith, from the Weissenberg,
"does not march, such packing and loading still; all the
"baggages and artilleries being with Keith. Not till four in
"the afternoon did Keith march; but beautifully then; and
"folded himself away, — rearguard under Schmettau 're-
"treating chequerwise,' nothing but Tolpatcheries attempt-
"ing on him, — westward, Budin-ward, without loss of a
"linstock, not to speak of guns. Very prettily done on the
"part of Keith. By Budin, to Leitmeritz, he; where the
"King will join him shortly."

Friedrich's errand in Alt-Lissa, eastward, while
Keith went westward, was, To be within due arm's-
length of the Moritz-Bevern, or beaten Kolin Army,
which is coming up that way; intending to take post,
and do its best, in those parts, with Zittau Magazine
and the Lausitz to rear of it. One of our Eyewitnesses,
a Herr Westphalen, Ferdinand of Brunswick's Secretary, — who, with his Chief, got into wider fields
before long, — yields these additional particulars face
to face:

"*Tuesday, 21st June 1757*. King's Headquarters in Lissa
"or neighbourhood till Friday next; which is central for both
"these movements, — Thursday, orders seven regiments of
"horse to reinforce Keith. No symptom yet of pursuit any-
"where.

"*Friday, 24th*. Prince Moritz with the Kolin Army made
"appearance, all safe, and is to command here; King in-
"tending for Keith. After dinner, and the due interchange
"of battalions to that end, King sets off, with Prince Henri,
"towards Keith; Headquarter in Alt-Buntzlau again. *Satur-
"day Night*, at Melnick; *Sunday*, Gastorf: *Monday Night*,
"*27th June*, Leitmeritz; King lodges in the Cathedral Close,
"in sight of Keith, wo is on the opposite side of Elbe, — but
"the town has a Bridge for tomorrow. 'Never was a quieter

"march; not the shadow of a Pandour visible. The Duke" (Ferdinand, my Chief, Chatham's jewel that is to be, and precious to England) "has suffered much from a" — in fact, from "a *cours de ventre*, temporary bowel-derangement, "which was very troublesome, owing to the excessive heats "by day, and coldness of the nights.

"*Tuesday, 28th.* Junction with Keith, — Bridge rightly "secured, due party of dragoons and foot left on the right "bank, to occupy a height which covers Leitmeritz. 'Clear-"ing of the Pascopol' (that is, sweeping the Pandours out of "it), is the first business; Colonel Loudon with his Pandours, "a most swift sharp-cutting man, being now here in those "parts; doing a deal of mischief. Three days ago, Satur-"day 25th, Keith had sent seven battalions, with the proper "steel-besoms, on that Pascopol affair; Tuesday, on junc-"tion, Majesty sends three more: job done on Wednesday; "reported 'done,' — though I should not be surprised," says Westphalen, "if some little highway robbery still went on "among the Mountains up there."

No; — and before quitting hold, what is this that Loudon (on the very day of the King's arrival, June 27th), on the old Field of Lobositz over yonder, has managed to do! General Mannstein, wounded at Kolin, happened, with others in like case, to be passing that way, towards Dresden and better surgery, — when Loudon's Croats set upon them, scattering their slight escort: "Quarter, on surrender! Prisoners?" "Never!" answered Mannstein; "Never!" that too impetuous man, starting out from his carriage, and snatching a musket: and was instantly cut down there. And so ends; — a man of strong head, and of heart only too strong. *

From Prag onwards, here has been a delicate set of operations; perfectly executed, — thanks to Friedrich's rapidity of shift, and also to the cautious slowly-

---

* Preuss, II. 58; *Militair-Lexikon*, III. 10.

puzzling mind of Daun. Had Daun used any diligence, had Daun and Prince Karl been broad awake, together or even singly! But Friedrich guessed they seldom or never were; that they would spend some days in puzzling; and that, with despatch, he would have time for everything. Daun, we could observe, stood singing *Te Deum*, greatly at leisure, in his old Camp, 20th June, while Friedrich, from the first gray of morning, and diligently all day long, was withdrawing from the trenches of Prag, — Friedrich's people, self, and goods getting folded out in the finest gradation, and with perfect success; no Daun to hinder him, — Daun leisurely doing *Te Deum*, forty miles off, helping on the *wrong* side by that exertion!* — "Poor Browne, he is dead "of his wounds, in Prag yonder," writes Westphalen in his Leitmeritz Journal, "news came to us, July 1st: "men said, 'Ah, that was why they lay asleep.'"

Till June 26th, Daun and Karl had not united; nor, except sending out Loudon and Croats, done anything, either of them. Sunday, June 26th, at Podschernitz on the old Field of Prag, a week and a day after Kolin, they did get together; still seemingly a little puzzled, "Shall we follow the King? Shall we follow Moritz and Bevern?" — nothing clear for some time, except to send out Pandour parties upon both. Moritz, since parting with the King in Alt-Buntzlau neighbourhood, has gone northward some marches, thirty miles or so, to *Jung*-Buntzlau, — meeting of Iser and Elbe, surely a good position: — Moritz, on receipt of these Pandour allowances of his, writes to the King, "Shall we retreat on Zittau, then, your Majesty? Straight upon Zittau?" Fancy Friedrich's astonishment; —

* Cogniazo, n. 867.

who well intends to eat the Country first, perhaps to fight if there be chance, and at least to lie *outside* the doors of Silesia and the Lausitz, as well as of Saxony here? — and answers, with his own hand, on the instant: "Your Dilection will not be so mad!"* And at once recals Moritz, and appoints the Prince of Prussia to go and take command. Who directly went; — a most important step for the King's interests and his own. Whose fortunes in that business we shall see before long! —

At Leitmeritz the King continues four weeks, with his Army parted in this way; waiting how the endless hostile element, which begirdles his horizon all round, will shape itself into combinations, that he may set upon the likeliest or the needfullest of these, when once it has disclosed itself. Horizon all round is black enough: Austrians, French, Swedes, Russians, Reichs Army; closer upon him or not so close, all are rolling in: Saxony, the Lausitz and Silesia, Brandenburg itself, it is uncertain which of these may soonest require his active presence.

The very day after his arrival in Leitmeritz, — Tuesday, 28th of June, while that junction with Keith was going on, and the troops were defiling along the Bridge for junction with Keith, — a heavy sorrow had befallen him, which he yet knew not of. An irreparable Domestic loss; sad complement to these Military and other Public disasters. Queen Sophie Dorothee, about whose health he had been anxious, but had again been set quiet, died at Berlin that day.** In her seventy-first year: of no definite violent disease; worn

* In Preuss, n. 58, the pungent little Autograph in full.
** Monbijou, 28th June 1757; born at Hanover, 27th March 1687.

down with chagrins and apprehensions, in this black whirlpool of Public troubles. So far as appears, the news came on Friedrich by surprise: — "bad cough," we hear of, and of his anxieties about it, in the Spring time; then again of "improvement, recovery, in the fine weather;" — no thought, just now, of such an event: and he took it with a depth of affliction, which my less informed readers are far from expecting of him.

July 2d, the news came: King withdrew into privacy; to weep and bewail under this new pungency of grief, superadded to so many others. Mitchell says: "For two days he had no levee; only the Princes dined "with him" (Princes Henri and Ferdinand; Prince of Prussia is gone to Jung-Buntzlau, would get the sad message there, among his other troubles): "yesterday, "July 3d, King sent for me in the afternoon, — the "first time he has seen anybody since the news came: "— I had the honour to remain with him some hours in "his closet. I must own to your Lordship I was most "sensibly afflicted to see him indulging his grief, and "giving way to the warmest filial affections; recalling "to mind the many obligations he had to her late Ma-"jesty; all she had suffered, and how nobly she bore it; "the good she did to everybody; the one comfort he "now had, to think of having tried to make her last "years more agreeable." * In the thick of public business, this kind of mood to Mitchell seems to have lasted all the time of Leitmeritz, which is about three weeks yet: Mitchell's Notebooks and Despatches, in that part, have

* *Papers and Memoirs,* i. 258; Despatch to Holdernesss, 4th July slightly abridged); — see ib. i. 357-359 (Private Journal). Westphalen, n. 14. See *Œuvres de Frédéric,* iv. 182.

a fine Biographic interest; the wholly human Friedrich wholly visible to us there as he seldom is. Going over his past Life to Mitchell; brief, candid, pious to both his Parents; — inexpressibly sad; like moonlight on the grave of one's Mother, silent that, while so much else is too noisy! —

This Friedrich, upon whom the whole world has risen like a mad Sorcerer's-Sabbath, how safe he once lay in his cradle, like the rest of us, mother's love wrapping him soft: — and now! These thoughts commingle in a very tragic way with the avalanche of public disasters which is thundering down on all sides. Warm tears the meed of this new sorrow; small in compass, but greater in poignancy than all the rest together. "My poor old Mother, oh, my Mother, that so loved me always, and would have given her own life to shelter mine!" — It was at Leitmeritz, as I guess, that Mitchell first made decisive acquaintance, that we may almost call intimacy, with the King: we already defined him as a sagacious, long-headed, loyal-hearted diplomatic gentleman, Scotch by birth and by turn of character; abundantly polite, vigilant, discreet, and with a fund of general sense and rugged veracity of mind; whom Friedrich at once recognised for what he was, and much took to, finding a hearty return withal; so that they were soon well with one another, and continued so. Mitchell, as orders were, "attended "the King's person" all through this War, sometimes in the blaze of battle itself and nothing but cannon-shot going, if it so chanced; and has preserved, in his multifarious Papers, a great many traits of Friedrich, not to be met with elsewhere.

Mitchell's occasional society, conversation with a

man of sense and manly character, which Friedrich always much loved, was, no doubt, a resource to Friedrich in his lonely roamings and vicissitudes in those dark years. No other British Ambassador ever had the luck to please him or be pleased by him, — most of them, as Ex-Exchequer Legge and the like Ex-Parliamentary people, he seems to have considered dull, obstinate, wooden fellows, of fantastic, abrupt, rather abstruse kind of character, not worth deciphering; — some of them, as Hanbury Williams, with the mischievous tic (more like galvanism or St. Vitus'-dance) which he called "wit," and the inconvenient turn for plotting and intriguing, Friedrich could not endure at all, but had them as soon as possible recalled, — of course, not without detestation on their part.

At Leitmeritz, it appears, he kept withdrawn to his closet, a good deal; gave himself up to his sorrows and his thoughts; would sit many hours drowned in tears, weeping bitterly like a child or a woman. This is strange to some readers; but it is true, — and ought to alter certain current notions. Friedrich, flashing like clear steel upon evil-doers and mendacious unjust persons and their works, is not by nature a cruel man, then, or an unfeeling, as Rumour reports? Reader, no, far the reverse; — and public Rumour, as you may have remarked, is apt to be an extreme blockhead, full of fury and stupidity on such points, and had much better hold its tongue till it know in some measure. Extreme sensibility is not sure to be a merit; though it is sure to be reckoned one, by the greedy dim fellows looking idly on: but, in any case, the degree of it that dwelt (privately, for most part) in Friedrich was great; and to himself it seemed a sad rather than joyful fact. Speaking of this matter, long afterwards, to Garve, a Silesian Philosopher, with whom he used to converse at Breslau, he says; — or let dull Garve himself report it, in the literal third-person:

"And herein, I," the Herr Garve (venturing to dispute, or qualify, on one of his Majesty's favourite topics) "believe, "lies the real ground of 'happiness:' it is the capacity and "opportunity to accomplish great things. This the King "would not allow; but said, That I did not sufficiently take "into account the natural feelings, different in different "people, which, when painful, embittered the life of the "highest as of the lowest. That, in his own life, he had ex- "perienced the deepest sufferings of this kind: 'And,' added "he, with a touching tone of kindness and familiarity which "never occurred again in his interviews with me, 'if you *(Er)* "knew, for instance, what I underwent on the death of my "Mother, you would see that I have been as unhappy as any "other, and unhappier than others, because of the greater "sensibility I had *(weil ich mehr Empfindlichkeit gehabt* "*habe*).'" *

There needed not this new calamity in Friedrich's lot just now! From all points of the compass, his enemies, held in check so long, are flooding on: the confluence of disasters and ill tidings, at this time, very great. From Jung-Buntzlau, close by, his Brother's accounts are bad; and grow ever worse, — as will be seen! On the extreme West, "July 3d," while Friedrich at Leitmeritz sat weeping for his Mother, the French take Embden from him; "July 5th," the Russians, Memel, on the utmost East. June 30th, six days

---

* *Fragmente zur Schilderung des Geistes, des Charakters und der Regierung Friedrichs des Zweiten*, von Christian Garve (Breslau, 1798), I. 314-316. An unexpectedly dull Book (Garve having talent and reputation); kind of monotonous Preachment upon Friedrich's character; almost nothing but the above fraction now derivable from it.

before, the Russians, after as many months of haggling, did cross the Border; 37,000 of them on this point; and set to bombarding Memel from land and sea. Poor Memel (garrison only 700) answered very fiercely, "sank two of their gunboats" and the like; but the end was as we see, — Feldmarschall Lehwald able to give no relief. For there were above 70,000 other Russians (Feldmarschall Apraxin with these latter, and Cossacks and Calmucks more than enough) crossing elsewhere, south in Tilsit Country, upon old Lehwald.* Lehwald, with 30,000, in such circumstances — what is to become of Preussen and him! Nearer hand, the Austrians, the French, the very Reichs Army, do now seem intent on business.

The Reichs Execution Army, we saw how Mayer and the Battle of Prag had checked it in the birth-pangs; and given rise to pangs of another sort; the poor Reichs Circles generally exclaiming, "What! Bring the war into our own borders? Bring the King of Prussia on our own throats!" — and stopping short in their enlistments and preparations; in vain for Austrian Officials to urge them. Watching there, with awe-struck eye, while the 12,000 bombs flew into Prag.

The Battle of Kolin has reversed all that; and the poor old Reich is again bent on business in the Execution way. Drumming, committeeing, projecting and endeavouring with all her might, in all quarters; and, from and after the event of Kolin, holding visible Encampment, in the Nürnberg Country; fractions of actual troops assembling there. "On the Plains of Fürth, "between Fürth and Farrenbach, east side the River

* *Helden-Geschichte,* iv. 407-413.

"Regnitz, there was the Camp pitched," says my Anonymous Friend; who gives me a cheerful Copperplate of the thing: red pennons, blue, and bright mixed colours; generals' tents; order-of-battle, and respective rallying points: with Bamberg Country in front, and the peaks of the Pine Mountains lying pleasantly behind: a sight for the curious.* It is the same ground where Mayer was careering lately; neighbouring nobility and gentry glad to come in gala, and dance with Mayer. Hither, all through July, come contingents straggling in, thicker and thicker; "August 8th," things now about complete, the Bishop of Bamberg came to take survey of the Reichs-Heer (Bishop's remarks not given); August 10th, came the young reigning Duke of Hildburghausen (Duke's granduncle is to be Commander), on like errand; August 11th, the Reichs-Heer got on march. Westward ho! — readers will see towards what.

A truly *elende*, or miserable, Reichs Execution Army (as the misprinter had made it); but giving loud voice in the Gazettes; and urged by every consideration to do something for itself. Prince of Hildburghausen, — a general of small merit, though he has risen in the Austrian service, and we have seen him with Seckendorf in old Turk times, — has, for his Kaiser's sake, taken the command; sensible perhaps that glory is not likely to be rife here; but willing to make himself useful. Kaiser and Austria urge, everywhere, with all their might: Prince of Hessen-Darmstadt, who lay on the Weissenberg lately, one of Keith's distinguished seconds there and a Prussian Officer of long standing,

* J. F. S. (whom I named *Anonymous of Hamburg* long since; who has boiled down, with great diligence, the old Newspapers, and gives a great many dates, notes &c., without Index), L. 211, 224 (the Copperplate).

has, on Kaiser's order, quitted all that, and become Hildburghausen's second here, in the Camp of Fürth; thinking the path of duty lay that way, — though his Wife, one of the noble women of her age, thought very differently.* A similar Kaiser's order, backed by what Law-thunder lay in the Reich, had gone out against Friedrich's own Brothers, and against every Reichs Prince who was in Friedrich's service; but, except him of Hessen-Darmstadt, none of them had much minded.** I did not hear that his strategic talent was momentous: but Prussia had taught him the routine of right soldiering, surely to small purpose; and Friedrich, no doubt, glanced indignantly at this small thing, among the many big ones.

From about the end of June, the Reichs Army kept dribbling in: the most inferior Army in the world; no part of it well drilled, most of it not drilled at all; and for variety in colour, condition, method, and military and pecuniary and other outfit, beggaring description. Hildburghausen does his utmost; Kaiser the like. The number should have far exceeded 50,000; but was not, on the field, of above half that number: 25,000; add at last 8,000 Austrian troops, two regiments of them cavalry; good these 8,000, the rest bad, — that was the Reichs Execution Army; most inferior among Armies; and considerable part of it, all the Protestant part, privately wishing well to Friedrich, they say. Drills itself multifariously in that Camp between Fürth and Farrenbach, on the east side of Regnitz River.

---

* Her Letter to Friedrich, "Berlin, 30th October 1757," (*Œuvres de Frédéric*, XXVII. II. 135.

** In Orlich, *Fürst Moritz von Anhalt-Dessau* (Berlin, 1842), pp. 74, 75, Prince Moritz's rather mournful Letter on the subject, with Friedrich's sharp Answer.

Fancy what a sight to Wilhelmina, if she ever drove
that way; which I think she hardly would. The Baireuth contingent itself is there; the Margraf would have
held out stiff on that point; but Friedrich himself advised compliance. Margraf of Anspach, — perverse
tippling creature, ill with his Wife, I doubt, — has
joyfully sent his legal hundreds; will vote for the Reichs
Ban against this worst of Germans, whom he has for
Brother-in-law. Dark days in the heart of Wilhelmina, those of the Camp at Fürth. Days which grow
ever darker, with strange flashings-out of empyrean
lightning from that shrill true heart; no peace more,
till the noble heroine die! —

This *elende* Reichs-Heer, miserable "Army of the
Circles," is mockingly called "the Hoopers, Coopers
(*Tonneliers*)," and gets quizzing enough, under that
and other titles, from an Opposition Public. Far other
from the French and Austrians; who are bent that it
should do feats in the world, and prove impressive on
a robber King. Thus too, "for Deliverance of Saxony,"
to cooperate with Reichs-Heer in that sacred object,
thanks to the zeal of Pompadour, Prince de Soubise
has got together, in Elsass, a supplementary 30,000
(40,330 said Theory, but Fact never quite so many);
and is passing them across the Rhine, in Frankfurt
Country, all through July, while the drilling at Fürth
goes on. With these, Soubise, simultaneously getting
under way, will steer north-eastward; join the Reichs-
Heer about Erfurt, before August end; and — and we
shall see what becomes of the combined Soubise and
Reichs Army after that!

It must be owned, the French, Pompadour and love
of glory urging, are diligent since the event of Kolin.

In select Parisian circles, the Soubise Army, or even that of D'Estrées altogether, — produced by the tears of a filial Dauphiness, — is regarded as a quasi-sacred, or uncommonly noble thing; and is called by her name, "*L'Armée de la Dauphine*," or for shortness, "*La Dauphine*" without adjunct. Thus, like a kind of chivalrous Bellona, vengeance in her right hand, tears and fire in her eyes, *The Dauphiness* advances; and will join Reichs-Heer at Erfurt before August end. Such the will of Pompadour; Richelieu encouraging, for reasons of his own. Soubise, I understand, is privately in pique against poor D'Estrées;* and intends to eclipse him by a higher style of diligence; though D'Estrées too is doing his best.

July 3d, we saw the D'Estrées people taking Embden; D'Estrées, quiet so long in his Camp at Bielefeld, had at once bestirred himself, Kolin being done; — shot out a detachment leftwards, and Embden had capitulated that day. Adieu to the Shipping Interests there, and to other pleasant things! "July 9th, after sunset," D'Estrées himself got on march from Bielefeld; set forth, in the cool of night, 60,000 strong, and 10,000 more to join him by the road (the rest are left as garrisons, reserves, — 1,000 marauders of them swing as monitory pendulums, on their various trees, for one item), — direct towards Hanover and Royal Highness of Cumberland; who retreats, and has retreated, behind the Ems, the Weser, back, ever back; and, to appearance, will make a bad finish yonder.

* "Reappeared unexpectedly in Paris" from D'Estrées's Army), "23d June" (four days after Kolin); got up this *Dauphiness Army*, by aid of Pompadour, with Richelieu, &c.: *Barbier*, iv. 227, 231. Richelieu "busy at Strasburg lately" (29th July: Collini's *Voltaire*, p. 191).

To Friedrich, waiting at Leitmeritz, all these things are gloomily known; but the most pressing of them is that of the Austrians and Jung-Buntzlau close by. Let us give some utterances of his to Wilhelmina, nearly all we have of direct from him in that time; and then hasten to the Prince of Prussia there:

Friedrich to Wilhelmina (at Baireuth).

Leitmeritz, 1st July 1757. * * "Sensible as heart can "be to the tender interest you deign to take in what concerns "me. Dear Sister, fear nothing on my score: men are "always in the hand of what we call Fate" ('Predestination, *Gnadenwahl,*' — Pardon us, Papa! — "*ce qu'on nomme le "destin*); accidents will befal people, walking on the streets, "sitting in their room, lying in their bed; and there are "many who escape the perils of war." * * "I think, through "Hessen will be the safest route for your Letters, till we see; "— and not to write just now except on occasions of im- "portance. Here is a piece in cipher; anonymous," — in- tended for the Newspapers, or some such road.

July 5th. "By a Courier of Plotho's, returning to Regens- "burg" (who passes near you), "I write to apprise my dear "Sister of the new misery which overwhelms us. We have "no longer a Mother. This loss puts the crown on my sorrows. "I am obliged to act; and have not time to give free course "to my tears. Judge, I pray you, of the situation of a "feeling heart put to so cruel a trial. All losses in the world "are capable of being remedied; but those which Death "causes are beyond the reach of hope."

July 7th. "You are too good; I am ashamed to abuse "your indulgence. But do, since you will, try to sound the "French, what conditions of Peace they would demand; one "might judge as to their intentions. Send that Mirabeau "(*ce M. de Mirabeau*) to France. Willingly will I pay the "expense. He may offer as much as five million thalers" (750,000*l.*) "to the Favourite" (yes, even to the Pompadour) "for Peace alone. Of course, his utmost discretion will be "needed;" — should the English get the least wind of it! But if they are gone to St. Vitus, and fail in every point, what can one do? *Ce M. de Mirabeau*, readers will be surprised to learn, is an Uncle of the great Mirabeau's; who has fallen into roving courses, gone abroad insolvent; and "directs the Opera at Baireuth," in these years! — One Letter we will give in full:

"Leitmeritz, 15th July 1757.

"MY DEAREST SISTER, — Your Letter has arrived: I see in "it your regrets for the irreparable loss we have had of the "best and worthiest Mother in this world. I am so struck "down with all those blows from within and without, that I "feel myself in a sort of stupefaction.

"The French have just laid hold of Friesland" (seized Embden, July 3d); "are about to pass the Weser: they have "instigated the Swedes to declare War against me; the "Swedes are sending 17,000 men" (rather more if anything; but they proved beautifully ineffectual) "into Pommern," — will be burdensome to Stralsund and the poor country people mainly; having no Captain over them but a hydra-headed National Palaver at home, and a Long-pole with Cocked-hat on it here at hand. "The Russians are besieging Memel" (have taken it, ten days ago): "Lehwald has them on his "front and in his rear. The Troops of the Reich," from your Plains of Fürth yonder, "are also about to march. All "this will force me to evacuate Bohemia, so soon as that "crowd of Enemies gets into motion.

"I am firmly resolved on the extremest efforts to save my "Country. We shall see *(quitte à voir)* if Fortune will take a "new thought, or if she will entirely turn her back upon me. "Happy the moment when I took to training myself in philo-"sophy! There is nothing else that can sustain the soul in a "situation like mine. I spread out to you, dear Sister, the "detail of my sorrows: if these things regarded only myself, "I could stand it with composure; but I am bound Guardian "of the safety and happiness of a People which has been put "under my charge. There lies the sting of it: and I shall "have to reproach myself with every fault, if, by delay or "by overhaste, I occasion the smallest accident; all the "more as, at present, any fault may be capital.

"What a business! Here is the liberty of Germany, and "that Protestant Cause for which so much blood has been "shed; here are those Two great Interests again at stake

"and the pinch of this huge game is such, that an unlucky
"quarter of an hour may establish over Germany the tyran-
"nous domination of the House of Austria forever! I am in
"the case of a traveller who sees himself surrounded and
"ready to be assassinated by a troop of cutthroats, who
"intend to share his spoils. Since the League of Cambrai"
(1508—1510, with a Pope in it and a Kaiser and Most
Christian King, iniquitously sworn against poor Venice;—
to no purpose, as happily appears), "there is no example of
"such a Conspiracy as that infamous Triumvirate" (Austria,
France, Russia) "now forms against me. Was it ever seen
"before that three great Princes laid plot in concert to
"destroy a Fourth, who had done nothing against them?
"I have not had the least quarrel either with France or with
"Russia, still less with Sweden. If, in common life, three
"citizens took it into their heads to fall upon their neighbour,
"and burn his house about him, they very certainly, by
"sentence of tribunal, would be broken on the wheel. What!
"and will Sovereigns, who maintain these tribunals and
"these laws in their States, give such example to their
"subjects?" — "Happy, my dear Sister, is the obscure man,
"whose good sense, from youth upwards, has renounced all
"sorts of glory; who, in his safe low place, has none to envy
"him, and whose fortune does not excite the cupidity of
"scoundrels!

"But these reflections are vain. We have to be what our
"birth, which decides, has made us in entering upon this
"world. I reckoned that, being King, it beseemed me to
"think as a Sovereign; and I took for principle, that the
"reputation of a Prince ought to be dearer to him than life.
"They have plotted against me; the Court of Vienna has
"given itself the liberty of trying to maltreat me; my honour
"commanded me not to suffer it. We have come to War; a
"gang of robbers falls on me, pistol in hand: that is the
"adventure which has happened to me. The remedy is diffi-
"cult: in desperate diseases there are no methods but
"desperate ones.

"I beg a thousand pardons, dear Sister: in these three
"long pages I talk to you of nothing but my troubles and
"affairs. A strange abuse it would be of any other person's
"friendship. But yours, my dear Sister, yours is known to

"me; and I am persuaded you are not impatient when I open "my heart to you:— a heart which is yours altogether; being "filled with sentiments of the tenderest esteem, with which "I am, my dearest Sister, your" (in truth, affectionate Brother at all times) "F." *

Prince August Wilhelm finds a bad Problem at Jung-Buntzlau; and does it badly: Friedrich thereupon has to rise from Leitmeritz, and take the Field elsewhere, in bitter Haste and Impatience, with Outlooks worse than ever.

The Prince of Prussia's Enterprise had its intricacies; but, by good management, was capable of being done. At least, so Friedrich thought;— though, in truth, it would have been better had Friedrich gone himself, since the chief pressure happened to fall there! The Prince has to retire, Parthian-like, as slowly as possible, with the late Kolin or Moritz-Bevern Army, towards the Lausitz, keeping his eye upon Silesia the while; of course securing the passes and strong places in his passage, for defence of his own rear at lowest; especially securing Zittau, a fine opulent Town, where his chief Magazine is, fed from Silesia now. The Army is in good strength (guess 30,000), with every equipment complete; in discipline, in health and in heart, such as beseems a Prussian Army,— probably longing rather, if it venture to long or wish for anything not yet commanded, to have a stroke at those Austrians again, and pay them something towards that late Kolin score.

The Prince arrived at Jung-Buntzlau, June 30th; Winterfeld with him, and, at his own request, Schmettau.

* *Œuvres de Frédéric,* xxvii. l. 294, 295, 296-8.

The Austrians have not yet stirred: if they do, it may be upon the King, it may be upon the Prince: in three or even in two marches, Prince and King can be together, — the King only too happy, in the present oppressive coil of doubts, to find the Austrians ready for a new passage of battle, and an immediate decision. The Austrians did, in fact, break out, — seemingly, at first, upon the King; but in reality upon the Prince, whom they judge safer game; and the matter became much more critical upon him than had been expected.

The Prince was thought to have a good judgment (too much talk in it, we sometimes feared), and fair knowledge in military matters. The King, not quite by the Prince's choice, has given him Winterfeld for Mentor; Winterfeld, who has an excellent military head in such matters, and a heart firm as steel, — almost like a second self in the King's estimation. Excellent Winterfeld; — but then there are also Schmettau, Bevern and others, possibly in private not too well affected to this Winterfeld. In fact, there is rather a multitude of Counsellors; — and an ingenuous fine-spirited Prince, perhaps more capable of eloquence on the Opposition side, than of condensing into real wisdom a multitude of counsels, when the crisis rises, and the affair becomes really difficult. Crisis did rise: the victorious Austrians, after such delay, had finally made up their minds to press this one a little, this one rather than the King, and hang upon his skirts; Daun and Prince Karl set out after him, just about the time of his arrival, — "70,000 strong," the Prince hears, including plenty of Pandours. Certain it is, the poor Prince's mind did flounder a good deal; and his procedures succeeded extremely ill on this occasion. Cer-

tain, too, that they were extremely ill taken at headquarters: and that he even died soon after, — chiefly
of broken heart, said the censorious world. It is well
known how Europe rang with the matter for a long
while; and Books were printed, and Documents, and
Collections by a Master's Hand. * We, who can spend
but a page or two on it, must carefully stand by the
essential part.

"*June 30th — July 3d*, Prince at Jung-Buntzlau, in chief
"command. Besides Winterfeld, the Generals under him
"are Ziethen, Schmettau, Fouquet, Retzow, Goltz, and
"two others who need not be of our acquaintance. Im-
"possible to stay there, thinks the Prince, thinks every-
"body; and they shift to Neuschloss, westward thirty miles.
"July 1st, Daun had crossed the Elbe (Daun let us say for
"brevity, though it is Daun and Karl, or even Karl *and*
"Daun, Karl being chief, and capable of saying so at times,
"though Daun is very splendent since Kolin), — crossed the
"Elbe above Brandeis; Nadasti, with precursor Pandours,
"now within an hour's march of Jung-Buntzlau; — and it was
"time to go.
"*July 3d-6th*, At Neuschloss, which is thought a strong
"position, key of the localities there, and nearer Friedrich
"too, the Prince staid not quite four days; shifted to Böhm
"(Böhm*isch*) Leipa, *July 7th*, — rather off from Leitmeritz,
"but a march towards Zittau, where the provisions are. 'A
"bad change,' said the Prince's friends afterwards; 'change
"advised by Winterfeld, — who never mentioned that
"circumstance to his Majesty, many as he did mention, not
"in the best way!' — Prince gets to Böhm Leipa, July 7th;
"stays there, in questionable circumstances, nine days.
"Böhm Leipa is still not above thirty miles north-east-
"ward of the King; and it is about the same distance south-

* *Lettres Secrètes touchant la Dernière Guerre; de Main de Maitre; divi-
sées en deux parties* (Francfort et Amsterdam, 1772): this is the Prince's
own Statement, Proof in hand. By far the clearest Account is in *Schmettau's Leben* (by his Son), pp. 353-354. See also Preuss, II. 57-61, and especially II. 407.

"westward from Zittau, out of which fine Town, partly by
"cross-roads, the Prince gets his provisions on this march.
"From Zittau hitherward, as far as the little Town of Gabel,
"which lies about half way, there is broad High Road, the
"great Southern *Kaiser-Strasse:* from Gabel, for Böhm
"Leipa, you have to cross south-westward by country roads;
"the keys to which, especially Gabel, the Prince has not
"failed to secure by proper garrison parties. And so, for
"about a week, not quite uncomfortably, he continues at
"Böhm Leipa; getting in his convoys from Zittau. Diligently
"scanning the Pandour stragglings and sputterings round
"him, which are clearly on the increasing hand. Diligently
"corresponding with the King, meanwhile; who much dis-
"courages undue apprehension, or retreat movement till
"the last pinch. 'Edging backward, and again backward,
"you come bounce upon Berlin one day, and will then have
"to halt!'—which is not pleasant to the Prince. But, in-
"disputably, the Pandour spurts on him do become Pandour
"gushings, with regulars also noticeable: it is certain the
"Austrians are out,—pretending first to mean the King and
"Leitmeritz; but knowing better, and meaning the Prince
"and Böhm Leipa all the while."—By way of supplement,
take Daun's positions in the interim:

Daun and Karl were at Podschernitz, 26th June; 1st July,
cross the Elbe, above Brandeis (Nadasti now within an hour's
march of Jung-Buntzlau); 7th July (day while the Prince is
flitting to Böhm Leipa), Daun is through Jung-Buntzlau to
Münchengrätz; thence to Liebenau; 14th, to Niemes, not
above four miles from the Prince's rightmost outpost (rightmost or eastmost, which looks away from his Brother); while
a couple of advanced parties, Beck and Macguire, hover on
his flank Zittau-ward, and Nadasti (if he knew it) is pushing
on to rear.

"*Thursday, 14th July.* About six in the evening, at Böhm
"Leipa, distinct cannon-thunder is heard from north-east:
"'Evidently Gabel getting cannonaded, and our wagon
"convoy' (empty, going to Zittau for meal, General Putt-
"kammer escorting) 'is in a dangerous state!' And by and
"by hussar parties of ours come in, with articulate news to
"that bad effect: 'Gabel under hot attack of regulars; Putt-
"kammer with his 3,000 vigorously defending, will expect to

"be relieved within not many hours!' Here has the crisis
"come. Crisis sure enough; — and the Prince, to meet
"it, summons that refuge of the irresolute, a Council of
"War.

"Winterfeld, who is just come home in these moments,
"did not attend; — not, till three next morning. Winter-
"feld had gone to bed; fairly 'tired dead,' with long
"marching and hurrying about. To the poor Prince there
"are three courses visible. Course *first*, That of joining
"the King at Leitmeritz. Gabel, Zittau lost in that case;
"game given up; — reception likely to be bad at Loitmeritz!
"Course *second*, — the course Friedrich himself would at
"once have gone upon, and been already well a-head with,
"— That of instantly taking measures for the relief of Putt-
"kammer. Dispute Gabel to the last; retreat, on loss of it,
"Parthian-like, to Zittau, by that broad Highway, short
"and broad, whole distance hence only thirty miles. 'Thirty
"miles,' say the multitude of Counsellors: 'Yes; but the
"first fifteen, *to* Gabol, is cross-road, hilly, difficult; they
"have us in flank!' 'We are 25,000,' urges the Prince;
"fifteen miles is not much!' The thing had its difficulties:
"the Prince himself, it appears, faintly thought it feasible:
"'25,000 we; 20,000 they; only fifteen miles,' said he. But
"the variety of Counsellors: 'Cross-roads, defiles, flank-
"march, dangerous,' said they. And so the *third* course,
"which was incomparably the worst, found favour in Council
"of War: That of leaving Gabel and Puttkammer to their
"fate; and of pushing off for Zittau leftwards through the
"safe Hills, by Kamnitz, Kreywitz, Rumburg; — which, if
"the reader look, is by a circuitous, nay quite parabolic
"course, twice or thrice as far: — 'In that manner, let us
"save Zittau and our Main Body!' said the Council of War.
"Yes, my friends; a cannon-ball, endeavouring to get into
"Zittau from the town-ditch, would have to take a parabolic
"course; — and the cannon-ball would be speedy upon it,
"and not have Hill roads to go by! This notable parabolic
"circuit of narrow steep roads may have its difficulties for an
"Army and its baggages!" Enough, the poor Prince adopted
that worst third course; and even made no despatch in getting
into it; and it proved ruinous to Zittau, and to much else,
his own life partly included.

"*July 16th-22d.* Thursday night, or Friday 3 A.M., that
"third and incomparably worst course was adopted: Gabel,
"Puttkammer with his wagons, ensigns, kettledrums, all
"this has to surrender in a day: High Road to Zittau, for
"the Austrians, is a smooth march, when they like to gather
"fully there, and start. And in the Hills, with their jolts
"and precipitous windings, infested too by Pandours, the
"poor Prussian Main Body, on its wide parabolic circuit, has
"a time of it! Loses its pontoons, loses most of its baggage;
"obliged to set fire, not to the Pandours, but to your own
"wagons, and necessaries of army life; encamps on bleak
"heights; no food, not even water; road quite lost, road to
"be rediscovered or invented; Pandours sputtering on you
"out of every bush and hollow, your peasant wagoners
"cutting traces and galloping off: — such are the phenomena
"of that march by circuit leftward, on the poor Prince's part.
"March began, soon after midnight, *Saturday 16th*, Schmettau
"as vanguard; and" —

And, in fine, by *Friday 22d*, after not quite a week
of it, the Prince, curving from northward (in parabolic
course, *less* speedy than the cannon-ball's would have
been) into sight of Zittau, — behold, there *are* the
Austrians far and wide to left of us, encamped impregnable behind the Neisse River there! They have
got the Eckart's Hill, which commands Zittau: — and
how to get into Zittau and our magazines, and how to
subsist if we were in? The poor Prince takes post on
what Heights there are, on his own side of the Neisse;
looks wistfully down upon Zittau, asking How?

About stroke of noon the Austrians, from their
Eckartsberg, do a thing which was much talked of.
They open battery of red-hot balls upon Zittau; kindle
the roofs of it, shingle-roofs in dry July; set Zittau all
on blaze, the 10,000 innocent souls shrieking in vain
to Heaven and Earth; and before sunset Zittau is ashes
and red-hot walls, not Zittau but a cinder-heap, —

Prussian Garrison not hurt, nor Magazine as yet; Garrison busy with buckets, I should guess, but beginning to find the air grow very hot. On the morrow morning, Zittau is a smouldering cinder-heap, hotter and hotter to the Prussian Garrison; and does not exist as a City.

One of the most inhuman actions ever heard of in War, shrieks universal Germany; asks itself what could have set a chivalrous Karl upon this devil-like procedure? "Protestants these poor Zittauers were; shone in commerce; no such weaving, industrying, in all Teutschland elsewhere: Hah! An eye-sorrow, they, with their commerce, their weavings, and industryings, to Austrian Papists, who cannot weave or trade?" that was finally the guess of some persons; — wide of the mark, we may well judge. Prince Xavier of Saxony, present in the Camp too, made no remonstrance, said others. Alas, my friends, what could Xavier probably avail, the foolish fellow, with only three regiments? Prince Karl, it was afterwards evident, could have got Zittau unburnt; and could even have kept the Prussians out of Zittau altogether. Zittau surely would have been very useful to Prince Karl. But overnight (let us try to fancy it so), not knowing the Prussian possibilities, Prince Karl, screwed to the devilish point, had got his furnaces lighted, his red-hot balls ready; and so, hurried on by his Pride and by his other Devils, had — There are devilish things sometimes done in War. And whole cities are made ashes by them. For certain, here is a strange way of commencing your 'Deliverance of Saxony!' And Prince Karl carries, truly, a brandmark from this conflagration, and will till all memory of him cease. As to Zittau, it rebuilt itself. Zittau is alive again; a strong stone city, in our day. On its new-built Townhouse stands again "*Benefacere et male audire regium est,* To do well, and be ill spoken of, is the part of kings" (amazingly true of them, — when they are not shams). What times for Herrnhuth; preparing for its Christian Sabbath, under these omens near by!

The Prince of Prussia tells us, he "early next morning (Saturday, 23d July) had his tents pitched;" which was but an unavailing procedure, with poor Zittau gone such a road. "Bring us bread out of that ruined Zittau," ordered the Prince: his Detachment returns ineffectual, "So hot, we cannot march in." And the Garrison Colonel (one Dierecke and five battalions are garrison) sends out word: "So hot, we cannot stand it." "Stand it yet a very little; and — !" answers the Prince: but Dierocke and battalions cannot, or at least cannot long enough; and set to marching out. In firm order, I have no doubt, and with some modicum of bread: but the tumbling of certain burnt walls parted Colonel and men, in a sad way. Colonel himself, with the colours, with the honours (none of his people, it seems, though they were scattered loose), was picked up by an Austrian party, and made prisoner. A miserable business, this of Zittau!

Next evening, Sunday, after dark, Prince of Prussia strikes his tents again; rolls off in a very unsuccinct condition; happily unchased, for he admits that chase would have been ruinous. Off towards Löbau (what nights for Zinzendorf and Herrnhuth, as such things tumble past them!); thence towards Bautzen; and arrives in the most lugubrious torn condition any Prussian General ever stood in. Reaches Bautzen on those terms; — and is warned that his Brother will be there in a day or two.

One may fancy Friedrich's indignation, astonishment and grief, when he heard of that march towards Zittau through the Hills by a parabolic course; the issue of which is too guessable by Friedrich. He himself instantly rises from Leitmeritz; starts, in fit divisions, by the Pascopol, by the Elbe passes, for Pirna; and, leaving Moritz of Dessau with a 10,000 to secure the Passes about Pirna, and Keith to come on with the Magazines, hastens across for Bautzen, to look into these advancing triumphant Austrians, these strange Prussian proceedings. On first hearing of that side-march, his auguries had been bad enough;* but the event has far surpassed them. Zittau gone; the Army hurrying home, as if in flight, in that wrecked condition; the door of Saxony, door of Silesia left wide open, — Daun has only to choose! Day by day, as Friedrich advanced to repair that mischief, the news of it have grown worse on him. Days rife otherwise in mere bad news. The Russians in Memel, Preussen at their feet; Soubise's French and the Reichs Army pushing on for Erfurt, to "deliver Saxony," on that western side: and from the French-English scene of operations — In those same bad days, Royal Highness of Cumberland has been doing a feat worth notice in the above connexion! Read this, from an authentic source:

"*Hastenbeck, 22d-26th July* 1757. Royal Highness, hitching "back and back, had got to Hameln, a strong place of his on "the safe side of the Weser; and did at last, Hanover itself

* Letter to Wilhelmina, "Linay, 22d July" (second day of the march from Leitmeritz): *Œuvres*, xxvii. t. 298.

"being now nigh, call halt; and resolve to make a stand. July
"22d" (very day while the Prince of Prussia came in sight of
Zittau, with the Austrians hanging over it), "Royal Highness
"took post in that favourable vicinity of Hameln; at perfect
"leisure to select his ground: and there sat waiting D'Estrées,
"— swamps for our right wing, and the Weser not far off;
"small Hamlet of Hastenbeck in front, and a woody knoll for
"our left; — totally inactive for four days long; attempting
"nothing upon D'Estrées and his intricate shufflings, but
"looking idly noonward to the courses of the sun, till D'Estrées
"should come up. Royal Highness is much swollen into
"obesity, into flabby torpor; a changed man since Fontenoy
"times; shockingly inactive, they say, in this post at Hasten-
"beck. D'Estrées, too, is ridiculously cautious, 'has manœuv-
"ered fifteen days in advancing about as many British
"miles.' D'Estrées did at last come up (July 25th), nearly two
'to one of Royal Highness, — 72,000 some count him, but
"considerably anarchic in parts, overwhelmed with Court
"Generals and Princes of the Blood, for one item; — and
"decides on attacking, next morning. D'Estrées duly went to
"reconnoitre, but unluckily 'had mist suddenly falling.' —
"'Well; we must attack, all the same!'

"And so, *26th July*, Tuesday, there ensued a *Battle of
"Hastenbeck:* the absurdest Battle in the world; and which
"ought, in fairness, to have been lost by *both*, though Royal
"Highness alone had the ill luck. Both Captains behaved
"very poorly; and each of them had a subaltern who behaved
"well. D'Estrées, with his 70,000 *versus* 40,000 posted there,
"knows nothing of Royal Highness's position; sees only Royal
"Highness's left wing on that woody Height; and, after hours
"of preliminary cannonading, sends out General Chevert
"upon that. Chevert, his subaltern" (a bit of right soldier-
stuff, the Chevert whom we knew at Prag, in old Belleisle
times), "goes upon it like fury; whom the Brunswick Grena-
"diers resist in like humour, hotter and hotter. Some hard
"fighting there, on Royal Highness's left; Chevert very fiery,
"Grenadiers very obstinate; till, on the centre, westward, in
"Royal Highness's chief battery there, some spark went the
"wrong way, and a powder-wagon shot itself aloft with
"hideous blaze and roar; and in the confusion, the French
"rushed in, and the battery was lost. Which discouraged the

"Grenadiers; so that Chevert made some progress upon them,
"on their woody Height, and began to have confident hope.
  "Had Chevert known, or had D'Estrées known, there was,
"close behind said Height, a Hollow, through which these
"Grenadiers might have been taken in rear. Dangerous
"Hollow, much neglected by Royal Highness, who has only
"General Breitenbach with a weak party there. This Breiten-
"bach, happening to have a head of his own, and finding
"nothing to do in that Hollow or to rightward, bursts out, of
"his own accord, on Chevert's left flank; cannonading, volley-
"ing, horse-charging; — the sound of which ('Hah, French
"there too!') struck a damp through Royal Highness, who
"instantly ordered retreat, and took the road. What singular
"ill luck that *sound* of Breitenbach to Royal Highness! For
"observe, the *effect* of Breitenbach, — which was, to recover
"the lost battery (gallant young Prince of Brunswick, 'Here-
"ditary Prince,' or Duke that is to be, striking in upon it with
"bayonet-charge at the right moment), — made D'Estrées
"too order retreat! 'Battle lost,' thinks D'Estrées; — and with
"good cause, had Breitenbach been supported at all. But no
"subaltern durst; and Royal Highness himself was not over-
"takeable, so far on the road. Royal Highness wept on hear-
"ing; the Brunswick Grenadiers too are said to have wept
"(for rage); and probably Breitenbach and the Hereditary
"Prince."*

  This is the last of Royal Highness's exploits in War. The retreat had been ordered "To Hannover;" but the bagagge by mistake took the road for Minden; and Royal Highness followed thither, — much the same what road he or it takes. Friedrich might still hope he would retreat on Magdeburg; 40,000 good soldiers might find a Captain there, and be valuable against a D'Estrées and Soubise in those parts. But no; it was through Bremen Country, to Stade, into the Sea, that Royal Highness, by ill luck, retreated! He has still one great vexation to give Friedrich, — to us almost a comfort, knowing what followed out of it; — and will have to be mentioned one other time in this History, and then go over our horizon altogether.

---

* Mauvillon, I. 278; Anonymous of Hamburg, L 206 (who gives a Plan and all manner of details, if needed by anybody); Kausler; &c. &c.

Whether Friedrich had heard of Hastenbeck the day his Brother and he met (July 29th, at Bautzen), I do not know: but it is likely enough he may have got the news that very morning; which was not calculated to increase one's good humour! His meeting with the Prince is royal, not fraternal, as all men have heard. Let us give, with brevity, from Schmettau Junior, the exact features of it; and leave the candid reader, who has formed to himself some notion of kingship and its sorrows and stern conditions (having perhaps himself something of kingly, in a small potential way), to interpret the matter, and make what he can of it:

"*Bautzen, 29th July* 1757. The King with reinforcement is "coming hither, from the Dresden side; to take up the reins "of this dishevelled Zittau Army; to speed with it against the "Austrians, and, if humanly possible, lock the doors of Silesia "and Saxony again, and chase the intruders away. Prince of "Prussia and the other Generals have notice, the night before: "'At 4 A.M. to-morrow (29th), wait his Majesty.' Prince and "Generals wait accordingly, all there but Goltz and Winter- "feld; they not, which is noted.

"For above an hour, no King; Prince and Generals ride "forward:—there is the King coming; Prince Henri, Duke "Ferdinand of Brunswick, and others in his train. King "noticing them, at about 300 paces distance, drew bridle; "Prince of Prussia did the like, train and he saluting with "their hats, as did the King's train in return. King did not "salute;—on the contrary, he turned his horse round, and "dismounted, as did everybody else on such signal. King lay "down on the ground, as if waiting the arrival of his Vanguard; "and bade Winterfeld and Goltz sit by him." Poor Prince of Prussia, and battered heavy-laden Generals! "After a minute "or two, Goltz came over and whispered to the Prince. "'Hither, *meine Herren*, all of you; a message from his Ma- "jesty!' cried the Prince. Whereupon, to Generals and "Prince, Goltz delivered, in equable official tone, these

"affecting words: 'His Majesty commands me to inform your
"Royal Highness, That he has cause to be greatly discon-
"tented with you; that you deserve to have a Court-martial
"held over you, which would sentence you and all your
"Generals to death; but that his Majesty will not carry the
"matter so far, being unable to forget that in the Chief
"General he has a Brother!'"*

The Prince answered, He wanted only a Court-martial; and the like, in stiff tone. Here is the Letter he writes next day to his Brother, with the Answer:

Prince of Prussia to the King.

"Bautzen, 30th July 1757.

"MY DEAR BROTHER, — The Letters you have written me,
"and the reception I yesterday met with, are sufficient proof
"that, in your opinion, I have ruined my honour and reputa-
"tion. This grieves, but it does not crush me, as in my own
"mind I am not conscious of the least reproach. I am perfectly
"convinced that I did not act by caprice: I did not follow the
"counsels of people incapable of giving good ones; I have
"done what I thought to be suitablest for the Army. All your
"Generals will do me that justice.

"I reckon it useless to beg of you to have my conduct in-
"vestigated: this would be a favour you would do me; so I
"cannot expect it. My health has been weakened by these
"fatigues, still more by these chagrins. I have gone to lodge
"in the Town, to recruit myself.

"I have requested the Duke of Bevern to present the Army
"Reports; he can give you explanation of everything. Be
"assured, my dear Brother, that in spite of the misfortunes
"which overwhelm me, and which I have not deserved, I shall
"never cease to be attached to the State; and as a faithful
"member of the same, my joy will be perfect when I learn the
"happy issue of your Enterprises. I have the honour to be,"—
AUGUST WILHELM."**

* Schmettau, pp. 334-5.
** Mais de Maître, p. 21.

King's Answer, the same day.

"Camp near Bautzen, 30th July 1757.

"MY DEAR BROTHER, — Your bad guidance has greatly "deranged my affairs. It is not the Enemy, it is your ill-"judged measures that have done me all this mischief. My "Generals are inexcusable; either for advising you so ill, or "in permitting you to follow resolutions so unwise. Your ears "are accustomed to listen to the talk of flatterers only. Daun "has not flattered you; — behold the consequences. In this "sad situation, nothing is left for me but trying the last ex-"tremity. I must go and give battle; and if we cannot conquer, "we must all of us have ourselves killed.

"I do not complain of your heart; but I do of your incapa-"city, of your want of judgment in not choosing better "methods. A man who" (like me; mark the phrase, from such a quarter!) "has but a few days to live need not dissemble. I "wish you better fortune than mine has been; and that all the "miseries and bad adventures you have had may teach you to "treat important things with more of care, more of sense, and "more of resolution. The greater part of the misfortunes "which I now see to be near comes only from you. You and "your Children will be more overwhelmed by them than I. "Be persuaded nevertheless that I have always loved you, "and that with these sentiments I shall die. — FRIEDRICH."*

As the King went off, to the Heights of Weissenberg, Zittau way, to encamp there against the Austrians, that same evening, the Prince did not answer this Letter, — except by asking verbally through Lieutenant-Colonel Lentulus (a mute Swiss figure, much about the King, who often turns up in these Histories), "for leave to return to Dresden by the first escort." — "Depends on himself; — an escort is going this night!" answered Friedrich. And the Prince went accordingly; and, by two stages, got into Dresden with his escort on the morrow. And had, not yet conscious of it,

* *Mais de Maître*, p. 22.

quitted the Field of War altogether; and was soon about to quit the world, and die, poor Prince. Died within a year, 12th June 1758, at Oranienburg, beside his Family, where he had latterly been.* — Winterfeld was already gone, six months before him; Goltz went, shortly after him; the other Zittau Generals all survived this War.

The poor Prince's fate, as natural, was much pitied; and Friedrich, to this day, is growled at for "inhuman treatment" and so on. Into which question we do not enter, except to say that Friedrich too had his sorrows; and that probably his concluding words, "with these sentiments I shall die," were perfectly true. *Main de Maître* went widely abroad over the world. The poor Prince's words and procedures were eagerly caught up by a scrutinising public, — and some of the former were not too guarded. At Dresden, he said, one morning, calling on a General Finck whom we shall hear of again: "Four such disagreeing, thin-skinned, high "pacing (*uneinige, piquirte*) Generals as Fouquet, Schmet- "tau, Winterfeld and Goltz, about you, what was to be "done!" said the Prince to Finck.**

His Wife, when at last he came to Oranienburg, nursed him fondly; that is one comfortable fact. Prince Henri, to the last, had privately a grudge of peculiar intensity, on this score, against all the peccant parties, King not excepted. As indeed he was apt to have, on various scores, the jealous, too vehement little man.

Friedrich's humour at this time I can guess to have been well-nigh desperate. He talks once of "a horse, on too much provocation, getting the bit between its

* Preuss, II. 60 (Ib. 76).   ** Ib. II. 79 n.; see Ib. 60, 78.

teeth; regardless thenceforth of chasms and precipices:"*
— though he himself never carries it to that length;
and always has a watchful eye, when at his swiftest!
From Weissenberg, that night, he drives-in the Pandours
on Zittau and the Eckartsberg; but the Austrians don't
come out. And, for three weeks, in this fierce necessity of being speedy, he cannot get one right stroke at
the Austrians; who sit inexpugnable upon their Eckart's
Hill, bristling with cannon; and can in no way be ma-
nœuvered down, or forced or enticed into Battle. A
baffling, bitterly impatient three weeks; — two of them,
the worst two, he spends at Weissenberg itself, chasing
Pandours, and scuffling on the surface, till Keith and
the Magazine-train come up; — even writing Verses
now and then, when the hours get unendurable otherwise!

The instant Keith and the Magazines are come, he
starts for Bernstadt; 56,000 strong after this junction:
— and a Prussian Officer, dating "Bernstädtel" (Bernstadt on the now Maps), "21st August 1757," sends
us this account; which also is but of preliminary nature:

"*August 15th*, Majesty left Weissenberg, and marched
"hither, much to the enemy's astonishment, who had lain
"perfectly quiet for a fortnight past, fancying they were a
"mastiff on the door-sill of Silesia: little thinking to be
"trampled on in this unceremonious way! General Beck, when
"our hussars of the vanguard made appearance, had to saddle
"and ride as for life, leaving every rag of baggage, and forty
"of his Pandours captive. Our hussars stuck to him, chasing
"him into Ostritz, where they surprised General Nadasti at
"dinner; and did a still better stroke of business: Nadasti
"himself could scarcely leap on horseback and get off; left all

* Letter to Wilhelmina, "Linay, 22d July" (cited above).

"his field-equipage, coaches, horses, kitchen-utensils, flunkies "seventy-two in number, — and, what was worst of all, a "secret box, in which was found certain Dresden Cor- "respondences of a highly treasonous character, which now "the writers there may quake to think of;" — if Friedrich, or we, could take much notice of them, in this press of hurries!*

Next day, August 16th, Friedrich detached five battalions to Görlitz; — Prince Karl (he calls it *Daun*) still camping on the Eckartsberg; — and himself, about 4 P.M., with the main Army, marched up to those Austrians on their Hill, to see if they would fight.** No, they wouldn't: they merely hustled themselves round so as to face him; face him, and even flank him with cannon batteries if he came too near. Steep ground, "precipitous front of rocks," in some places. "A hollow before their front; Village of Wittgenau "there, and three roads through it, *one* of them with width "for wheels;" Daun sitting inaccessible, in short. Next day, Winterfeld, with a detached Division, crossed the Neisse, tried Nadasti: "Attack Nadasti, on his woody knoll at Hirschfeld yonder; they will have to rise and save him!" In vain, that too; they let Nadasti take his own luck: for four days (16th-20th August) everything was tried, in vain.

No Battle to be had from these Austrians. And it would have been so infinitely convenient to us: Reichs Army and Soubise's French are now in the actual pre- cincts of Erfurt (August 25th, Soubise took quarter there); Royal Highness of Cumberland is staggering back into the Sea; Richelieu's French (not D'Estrées's any more, D'Estrées being superseded in this strange way) are aiming, it is thought, towards Magdeburg,

* *Helden-Geschichte,* iv. 596-599.   ** *Œuvres de Frédéric,* iv. 157.

had they once done with Royal Highness; Swedes are getting hold of Pommern; Russians, in huge force, of Preussen: how comfortable to have had our Austrians finished before going upon the others! For four days more (August 20th-24th), Friedrich arranges his Army for watching the Austrians, and guarding Silesia; — Bevern and Winterfeld to take command in his absence: — and, August 25th, has to march, with a small Division, which, at Dresden, he will increase by Moritz's, now needless in the Pirna Country; towards Thüringen; to look into Soubise and the Reichs Army, as a thing that absolutely cannot wait. Arrives in Dresden, Monday, August 29th; and — Or let the old Newspaper report it, with the features of life:

"*Dresden*, *29th August* 1757. This day, about noon, his "Majesty, with a part of his Army from the Upper Lausitz, "arrived at the Neustadt here. Though the kitchen had been "appointed to be set up at what they call The Barns (*Die* "*Scheunen*), his Majesty was pleased to alight in Königsbrück "Street, at the new House of Brühl's Chamberlain, Haller; "and there passed the night. Tuesday evening, 30th, his "Majesty the King, with his Lifeguards of Horse and of Foot, "also with the Gens d'Armes and other Battalions, marched "through the City, about a mile out on the Freiberg road, "and took quarter in Klein Hamberg. The 31st, all the Army "followed," — a poor 23,000, Moritz and he, that was all!* — "the King's field-equipage, which had been taken from the "Brühl Palace and packed in twelve wagons, went with "them."**

* "22,560" (Tempelhof, i. 228).
** Rödenbeck, p. 315; Preuss, ii. 64 n.; Mitchell's Interview (*Memoirs and Papers*, i. 270).

CHAPTER VI.

DEATH OF WINTERFELD.

BEFORE going upon this forlorn march of Friedrich's, one of the forlornest a son of Adam ever had, we must speak of a thing which befel to rearward, while the march was only half-done, and which greatly influenced it and all that followed. It was the seventh day of Friedrich's march, not above eighty miles of it yet done, when Winterfeld perished in fight. No Winterfeld now to occupy the Austrians in his absence; to stand between Silesia and them, or assist him farther in his lonesome struggle against the world. Let us spend a moment on the exit of that brave man: Bernstadt-Görlitz Country, September 7th, 1757.

The Bevern Army, 36,000 strong, is still there in its place in the Lausitz, near Görlitz; Prince Karl lies quiet in his near Zittau, ever since he burnt that Town, and stood four days in arms unattackable by Friedrich with prospect of advantage. The Court of Vienna cannot comprehend this state of inactivity: "Two to one, and a mere Bevern against you, the King far away in Saxony upon his desperate Anti-French mission there: why not go in upon this Bevern? The French, whom we are by every courier passionately importuning to sweep Saxony clear, what will they say of this strange mode of sweeping Silesia clear?" Maria Theresa and her Kriegs-Hofrath are much exercised with these thoughts, and with French and other remonstrances that come. Maria Theresa and her Kriegs-Hofrath at length despatch their supreme Kaunitz, Graf Kaunitz in person, to stir up Prince Karl, and look into the matter with his own wise eyes and great heart. Prince Karl, by way of treat to this high gentleman, determines on doing something striking upon Bevern.

Bevern lies with his main body about Görlitz, in and to westward of Görlitz, a pleasant Town on the left bank of the Neisse (readers know there are Four Neisses, and which of them this is), with fine hilly country all round, bulky solitary Heights and Mountains rising out of fruitful plains, — two Hochkirchs (*High-Kirks*), for example, are in this region, one of which will become extremely notable next year: — Bevern has a strong camp leaning on the due Heights here, with Görlitz in its lap; and beyond Görlitz, on the right bank of the Neisse, united to him by a Bridge, he has placed Winterfeld with 10,000, who lies with his back to Görlitz, proper brooks and fencible places flanking him, has a Dorf (*Thorp*) called Moys in *his* lap; and, some short furlong beyond Moys, a 2,000 of his grenadiers planted on the top of a Hill called the Moysberg, called also the Holzberg (*Woodhill*) and Jäkelsberg, of which the reader is to take notice. Fine outpost, with proper batteries atop, with hussar squadrons and hussar pickets sprinkled about; which commands a far outlook towards Silesia, and in marching thither, or in continuing here, is useful to have in hand, — were it not a little too distant from the main body. It is this Jäkelsberg, capable of being snatched if one is sudden enough, that Prince Karl decides on: it may be good for much or for little to Prince Karl; and, if even for nothing, it will be a brilliant affront upon

10*

Winterfeld and Bevern, and more or less charming to Kaunitz.

Winterfeld, the ardent enterprising man, King's other self, is thought to be the mainspring of affairs here (small thanks to him privately from Bevern, add some): and is stationed in the extreme van, as we see; Winterfeld is engaged in many things besides the care of this post; and indeed where a critical thing is to be done, we can imagine Winterfeld goes upon it. "We must try to stay here till the King has finished in Saxony!" says Winterfeld always. To which Bevern replies, "Excellent, truly; but how?" Bevern has his provender at Dresden, sadly far off; has to hold Bautzen garrisoned, and gets much trouble with his convoys. Better in Silesia, with our magazines at hand, thinks Bevern, less mindful of other considerations.

Tuesday, September 6th, Prince Karl sends Nadasti to the right bank of the River, forward upon Moys, to do the Jäkelsberg before day tomorrow: only some 2,000 grenadiers on it; Nadasti has with him 15,000, some count 20,000 of all arms, artillery in plenty; surely sufficient for the Jäkelsberg; and Daun advances, with the main body, on the other side of the River, to be within reach, should Moys lead to more serious consequences. Nadasti diligently marches all day; posts himself at night within few miles of Moys; gets his cannon to the proper Hills (*Gallows* Hill and others), his Croats to the proper Woods; and, before daylight on the morrow, means to begin upon the Moys Hill and its 2,000 grenadiers.

Wednesday morning, at the set hour, Nadasti, with artillery bursting out and quivering battle-lines, is at work accordingly; hurls up 1,000 Croats, for one item, and regulars to the amount of "forty companies in three lines." The grenadiers, somewhat astonished, for the morning was misty and their hussar-posts had come hastily in, stood upon their guard, like Prussian men; hurled back the 1,000 Croats fast enough; stubbornly repulsed the regulars too, and tumbled them down hill with bullet-storm for accompaniment; gallantly foiling this first attempt of Nadasti's. Of course Nadasti will make another, will make ever others: capture of the Jäkelsberg can hardly be doubtful to Nadasti.

Winterfeld was not at Moys, he was at Görlitz, just got in from escorting an important meal-convoy hither out of Bautzen; and was in conference with Bevern, when rumour of these Croat attacks came in at the gallop from Moys. Winterfeld made little of the rumours: he had heard of some attack intended, but it was to have been overnight, and has not been. "Mere foraging of Croat rabble, like yesterday's!" said Winterfeld, and continued his present business. In few minutes the sound of heavy cannonading convinced him. "Haha, there are my guests," said he; "we must see if we cannot entertain them right!" sprang to horseback, ordered on, double-quick, the three regiments nearest him, and was off at the gallop, — too late; or, alas, too *early* we might rather say! Arriving at the gallop, Winterfeld found his grenadiers and their insufficient reinforcements rolling back, the Hill lost; Winterfeld "sprang to a fresh horse," shot his lightning glances and energies to this hand and that; stormfully rallied the matter, recovered the Hill; and stormfully defended it, for, I should guess, an hour or more; and might still have done one knows not what, had not a bullet struck him through the breast, and suddenly ended all his doings in this world.

Three other reasons the Prussians give for loss of their Hill, which are of no consequence to them or to us in comparison. First, that Bevern, on message after message, sent no reinforcement; that Winterfeld was left to his own 10,000, and what he and they could make of it. Bevern is jealous of Winterfeld, hint they, and willing to see his impetuous audacity checked. Perhaps only cautious of getting into a general action for what was intrinsically nothing? Second, that two regiments of Infantry, whom Winterfeld detached double-quick to seize a couple of villages (Leopoldshayn, Hermsdorf) on his right, and therefrom fusillade Nadasti on flank, found the villages already occupied by thousands of Croats, with regular foot and cannon-batteries, and could in no wise seize them. This was a great reverse of advantage. Third, that an Aide-de-Camp made a small misnomer, misreport of one word, which was terribly important! "Bring me hither Regiment Manteuffel!" Winterfeld had ordered. The Aide-de-Camp reported it "Grenadiers Manteuffel:" upon which, the grenadiers, who were posted in a walled garden, an important point to Winterfeld's right, came instantly to order; and Austrians instantly rushed in to the vacant post, and galled Winterfeld's other flank by their fire.*

Enough, Winterfeld lay bleeding to death, the Hill was lost, Prussians drawing off slowly and backforemost, about two in the afternoon; upon which the

* Abundant Accounts in Seyfarth, II. (Beylagen), 162-163; Helden-Geschichte, IV. 615-633; Retiow, I. 216-221.

Austrians also drew off, leaving only a small party on the Hill, who voluntarily quitted it next morning. Next morning, likewise, Winterfeld had died. The Hill was, except as bravado, and by way of comfort to Kaunitz, nothing for the Austrians; but the death of Winterfeld, which had come by chance to them in the business, was probably a great thing. Better than two pitched battles gained: who shall say? He was a shining figure, this Winterfeld; dangerous to the Austrians. The most shining figure in the Prussian Army, except its Chief; and had great thoughts in his head. Prussia is not skilful to celebrate her Heroes, — the Prussian Muse of History, choked with dry military pipeclay, or with husky cobwebbery and academic pedantry, how can she? — but if Prussia can produce heroes worth celebrating, that is the one important point. Apart from soldiership, and the outward features which are widely different, there is traceable in Winterfeld some kinship in soul to English Chatham his contemporary; though he has not had the fame of Chatham.

Winterfeld was by no means universally liked; as what brave man is or can be? Too susceptible to flattery; too this, too that. He is, one feels always, except Friedrich only, the most shining figure in the Prussian Army; and it was not unnatural he should be Friedrich's one friend, — as seems to have been the case. Friedrich, when this Job's-message reached him (in Erfurt Country, eight days hence), was deeply affected by it. To tears, or beyond tears, as we can fancy. "Against my multitude of enemies, I may "contrive resources," he was heard to say; "but I shall find no Winterfeld again!" Adieu, my one friend, real Peer, sole companion to my lonely pilgrimage in these perilous high regions.

"The Prince of Prussia, contrariwise" (says a miserable little Note, which must not be withheld) "brightened up at the "news: 'I shall now die much more content, knowing that "'there is one so bad and dangerous man fewer in the Army!' "And, six months after, in his actual death-moments, he ex- "claimed: 'I end my life, the last period of which has cost me "so much sorrow; but Winterfeld is he who shortened my "days!'"* — Very bitter Opposition humours circulating, in their fashion, there as elsewhere in this world!

Bevern, the millstone of Winterfeld being off his neck, has become a more responsible, though he feels himself a much-delivered man. Had not liked Winterfeld, they say; or had even hated him, since those bad Zittau times. Can now, at any rate, make for Schlesien and the meal-magazines, when he sees good. He will find meal readier there; may be find other things corresponding! Nobody now to keep him painfully manœuvering in these parts; with the King's Army nearer to him, but meal not.

On the third day after (September 10th), Bevern, having finished packing, took the road for Schlesien; Daun and Karl attending him; nothing left of Daun and Karl in those Saxon Countries, — except, at Stolpen, out Dresden-wards, some Reserve-post or Rearguard of 15,000, should we chance to hear of that again. And from the end of September onwards, Bevern's star, once somewhat bright at Reichenberg, shot rapidly downwards, under the horizon altogether; and there came, post after post, such news out of Schlesien, — to say nothing of that Stolpen Party, — as Friedrich had never heard before.

* Preuss, ii. 78; citing Retzow.

CHAPTER VII.

FRIEDRICH IN THÜRINGEN, HIS WORLD OF ENEMIES ALL COME.

The Soubise-Hildburghausen people had got rendezvoused at Erfurt about August 25th; 50,000 by account, and no Enemy within 200 miles of them; and in the Versailles circles it had been expected they would proceed to the "Deliverance of Saxony" straightway. What is to hinder? — Friedrich, haggling with the Austrians at Bernstadt, could muster but a poor 23,000, when he did march towards Erfurt. In those same neighbourhoods, within reach of Soubise, is the Richelieu, late D'Estrées, Army; elated with Hastenbeck, comfortably pushing Royal Highness of Cumberland, who makes no resistance, step by step, into the sea; victoriously plundering, far and wide, in those countries, Hanover itself the Headquarter. In the Versailles circles, it is farther expected that Richelieu, "Conqueror of Minorca," will shortly besiege and conquer Magdeburg, and so crown his glories. Why not; were the "Deliverance of Saxony" complete?

The whole of which turned out greatly otherwise, and to the sad disappointment of Versailles. The Conqueror of Minorca is probably aware that the conquering of Magdeburg, against one whose platforms are not rotten, and who does *not* "lie always in his bed," as poor old Blakeney did, will be a very different matter. And the private truth is, Maréchal de Richelieu never turned his thoughts upon Magdeburg at all, nor upon any point of war that had difficulties, but solely upon collecting plunder for himself in those Countries. One of the most magnificent marauders on record; in no danger, he, of becoming monitory and a pendulum, like the 1,000 that already swing in that capacity to rear of him! And he did manage, in this Campaign, which was the last of his military services, so as to pay off at Paris "above 50,000 *l.* of debts; "and to build for himself a beautiful Garden Mansion "there, which the mocking populations called 'Hanover "Pavilion (*Pavillon d'Hanovre*);'" a name still sticking to it, I believe.* Of the Richelieu Campaign we are happily delivered from saying almost anything: and the main interest for us turns now on that Soubise-Hildburghausen wing of it, — which also is a sufficiently contemptible affair; not to be spoken of, beyond the strictly unavoidable.

Friedrich with his 23,000 setting out from Dresden, August 30th, has a march of about 170 miles towards Erfurt. He may expect to find, — counting Richelieu, if Royal Highness of Cumberland persist in acting *zero* as hitherto, — a confused mass of about 150,000 Enemies, of one sort and other, waiting him ahead; not to think of those he has just left behind; — and he cannot well be in a triumphant humour! Behind, before, around, it is one gathering of Enemies: one point only certain, that he must beat them, or else die. Readers would fain follow him in this forlorn march; him, the one point of interest now in it: and readers shall, if we can manage, though it is extremely difficult. For, on getting to Erfurt, he finds his Soubise-Hildburg-

* Barbier, iii. 264, 271.

hausen Army off on retreat among the inaccessible Hills still farther westward; and has to linger painfully there, and to detach, and even to march personally against other Enemies; and then, these finished, to march back towards his Erfurt ones, who are taking heart in the interim: — and, in short, from September 1st to November 5th, there are two months of confused manœuvering and marching to and fro in that West-Saxon region, which are very intricate to readers. November 5th is a day unforgettable: but anterior to that, what can we do? Here, dated, are the Three grand Epochs of the thing; which readers had better fix in mind as a preliminary:

1º. *September 13th*, Friedrich has got to Erfurt neighbourhood; but Soubise and Company are off westward to the Hills of Eisenach, won't come down; Friedrich obliged to linger thereabouts, painfully waiting almost a month, till

2º. *October 11th*, hearing that "15,000 Austrians" (that Stolpen Party, left as rearguard at Stolpen; Croats mainly, under a General Haddick) are on march for Berlin, he rises in haste thitherward, through Leipzig, Torgau, say 100 miles; hears that Haddick *has* been in Berlin (16th-17th October) for one day, and that he is off again full speed with a ransom of 30,000'., which they have had to pay him: upon which Friedrich calls halt in the Torgau country; — and would have been uncertain what to do, had not

3º. Soubise and Company, extremely elated with this Haddick Feat, come out from their Hills, intent to deliver Saxony after all. So that Friedrich has to turn back (October 26th-30th) through Leipzig again; towards, — in fact towards *Rossbach* and *November 5th,* in his old Saale Country, which does not prove so wearisome as formerly!

These are the cardinal dates; these let the reader recur to, if necessary, and keep steadily in mind: it will then perhaps be possible to intercalate, in a manner intelligible to him, what other lucent phenomena there are; and these dismal wanderings, and miserablest two months of Friedrich's life, will not be wholly a provoking blotch of enigmatic darkness, but in some sort a thing with features in the twilight of the Past.

I. *Friedrich's March to Erfurt from Dresden* (31st August—13th September 1757).

The march to Erfurt was of twelve days, and without adventure to speak of. Mayer and Free-Battalion had the vanguard, Friedrich there as usual; main body, under Keith with Ferdinand and Moritz, following in several columns: straight towards their goal; with steady despatch; for twelve days; — weather often very wet.* Seidlitz, with cavalry, had gone ahead, in search of one Turpin, a mighty hunter and Hussar among the French, who was threatening Leipzig, threatening Halle: but Turpin made off at sound of him, without trying fight; so that Seidlitz had only to halt, and rejoin, hoping better luck another time.

A march altogether of the common type, — the stages of it not worth marking except for special readers; — and of memorable to us offers only this, if even this: at Rötha, in Leipzig Country, the eighth stage from Dresden, Friedrich writes, willing to try for Peace if it be possible,

* Tempelhof, i. 229; Rödenbeck, i. 317 (not very correct); in Westphalen (n. 20 &c.) a personal Diary of this March, and of what followed on Duke Ferdinand's part.

To the Maréchal Duc de Richelieu.

"Rötha, 7th September 1757.

"I feel, M. le Duc, that you have not been put in the post "where you are for the purpose of Negotiating. I am per-"suaded, however, that the Nephew of the great Cardinal "Richelieu is made for signing treaties no less than for "gaining battles. I address myself to you from an effect of "the esteem with which you inspire even those who do not "intimately know you.

"'Tis a small matter, Monsieur (*Il s'agit d'une bagatelle*): "only to make Peace, if people are pleased to wish it! I know "not what your Instructions are: but, in the supposition that "the King your Master, now assured by your successes, will "have put it in your power to labour in the pacification of "Germany, I address to you the Sieur d'Elcheset" (Sieur Balbi is the real name of him, an Italian Engineer of mine, who once served with you in the Fontenoy times, — and some say he has privately a 15,000*l*. for your Grace's acceptance, — "the Sieur d'Elcheset), in whom you may place complete con-"fidence.

"Though the events of this Year afford no hope that your "Court still entertains a favourable disposition for my in-"terests, I cannot persuade myself that a union which has "lasted between us for sixteen years may not have left some "trace in the mind. Perhaps I judge others by myself. But, "however that may be, I, in short, prefer putting my interests "into the King your Master's hands rather than into any "other's. If you have not, Monsieur, any Instructions as to "the Proposal hereby made, I beg of you to ask such, and to "inform me what the tenor of them is.

"He who has merited statues at Genoa" (ten years ago, in those *Anti*-Austrian times, when Genoa burst up in revolt, and the French and Richelieu beautifully intervened against the oppressors); "he who conquered Minorca in spite of im-"mense obstacles; he who is on the point of subjugating "Lower Saxony, — can do nothing more glorious than to "restore Peace to Europe. Of all your laurels, that will be "the fairest. Work in this Cause, with the activity which has "secured you such rapid progress otherwise; and be per-

"suaded that nobody will feel more grateful to you than,
"Monsieur le Duc, — Your faithful Friend, — FRÉDÉRIC."*

Richelieu, it appears by any evidence there is, went willingly into this scheme; and applied at Versailles, as desired; with a peremptory negative for result. Nothing came of the Richelieu attempt there; nor of "*ce M. de Mirabeau,*" if he ever went; nor of any other on that errand. Needless to apply for Peace at Versailles (and a mere waste of your "sum of 15,000*l.*," which one hopes is fabulous in the present scarcity of money): — nor should we perhaps have mentioned the thing at all, except for the sake of Wilhelmina, whose fond scheme it is in this extremity of fate; scheme which she tries in still other directions, as we shall see; her Brother willing too, but probably with much less hope. If a civil Letter and a bribe of Money will do it, these need not be spared.

This at Rötha is the day while Winterfeld, on Moys Hill, is meeting his death. Today at Pegau, in this neighbourhood, Seidlitz, who could not fall in with Turpin, has given the Hussars of Loudon a beautiful slap; the first enemy we have seen on this march; and the last, — nothing but Loudon and Hussars visibly about, the rest of those Soubise-Reichs people dormant, as would seem. "D'Elcheset," Balbi, or whoever he was, would not find Richelieu at Hanover; but at a place called Kloster-Zeven, in Bremen Country, fifty or sixty miles farther on. There, this day, are Richelieu with one Sporcken a Hanoverian, and Lynar a Dane,

* Given in *Rödenbeck*, I. 813 (doubtless from *Mémoires de Richelieu*, Paris, 1793, IX. 175, the one fountain-head in regard to this small affair): for "the 15,000*l.*" and other rumoured particulars, see Retzow, I. 197; Preuss, II. 84; *Œuvres de Frédéric*, IV. 145.

rapidly finishing a thing they were pleased to call "Convention of Kloster-Zeven;" which Friedrich regarded as another huge misfortune fallen on him, — though it proved to have been far the reverse a while after. Concerning which take this brief Note; cannot be too brief on such a topic:

"Never was there a more futile Convention than that of Klos-
"ter-Zeven; which filled all Europe with lamentable noises, in-
"dignations and anxieties, during the remainder of that Year;
"and is now reduced, for Europe and the Universe, to a silent
"mathematical point, or mere mark of position, requiring
"still to be attended to in that character, though itself zero
"in any other. Here are the main particulars, in their
"sequence.

"August 3d, towards midnight, '11 P.M.' say the Books,
"Maréchal de Richelieu arrives in the D'Estrées Camp
"('Camp of Oldendorf,' still only one march west of Hasten-
"beck); to whom D'Estrées on the instant, loftily, delivers up
"his Army; explains with loyalty, for a few days more, all
"things needful to the new Commander; declines to be him-
"self Second; and loftily withdraws to the Baths of Aachen
"'for his health.'

"Royal Highness of Cumberland is, by this time, well on
"Elbe-ward, Ocean-ward. Till August 1st, for one week,
"Royal Highness of Cumberland lay at Minden, some thirty
"odd miles from Hastenbeck; deploring that sad mistake;
"but unpersuadable to stand, and try amendment of it·
"August 1st, the French advancing on him again, he moved
"off northward, sea-ward. By Nienburg, Verden, Rotenburg,
"Zeven, Bremenvörde, Stade; — arrived at Stade, on the
"tidal Waters of the Elbe, August 5th; and by necessity did
"halt there. From Minden onwards, Richelieu, not D'Estrées,
"has had the chasing of Royal Highness: one of the simplest
"functions; only that the country is getting muddy, difficult
"for artillery-carriage (thinks Richelieu), with an Army so
"dilapidated, hungry, short of pay; and that Royal Highness,
"a very furious person to our former knowledge, might turn
"on us like a boar at bay, endangering everything; and

9th Sept. 1757.

"finally, that one's desire is not for battle, but for a fair "chance of plunder to pay one's debts.

"Britannic Majesty, in this awful state of his Hanover "Armaments, has been applying at the Danish Court; "Richelieu too sends off an application thither: 'Mediate "between us, spare useless bloodshed!'"* — Whereupon "Danish Majesty (Britannic's son-in-law) cheerfully under- "takes it; bids one Lynar bestir himself upon it. Count "Lynar, an esteemed Official of his, who lives in those neigh- "bourhoods; Danish Viceroy in Oldenburg, — much con- "cerned with the Scriptures, the Sacred Languages, and "other seraphic studies, — and a changed man, since we saw "him last in the Petersburg regions, making love to Mrs. "Anton Ulrich long ago! Lynar, feeling the axis of the world "laid on his shoulder in this manner, loses not a moment; "invokes the Heavenly Powers; goes on it with an alacrity "and a despatch beyond praise. Runs to the Duke of Cum- "berland at Stade; thence to Richelieu at Zeven: back to "the Duke, back to Zeven: 'Won't you; and won't *you?*' "and in four short days has the once world-famed 'Conven- "tion of Kloster-Zeven' standing on parchment, — signed, "ready for ratifying: 'Royal Highness's Army to go home to "'their countries again' (routes, methods, times: when, how, "and what next, all left unsettled), 'and noise of War to cease "'in those parts.' Signed cheerfully on both sides, 9th Sep- "tember 1757; and Lynar striking the stars with his sublime "head.**

"Unaccountable how Lynar had managed such a diffi- "culty. He says seraphically, in a Letter to a friend, which "the Prussian hussars got hold of, 'The idea of it was inspired "'by the Holy Ghost:' — at which the whole world haha'd "again. For it was a Convention vague, absurd, not capable "of being executed; ratification of it refused by both Courts, "by the French Court first, if that was any matter: — and the "only thing now memorable of it is, that *it* was a total Futi- "lity; but that there ensued from it a Fact still of importance; "namely:

* Valfons, p. 291.
** Büsching (who alone is exact in the matter), *Beiträge*, IV. 187-8, § *Lynar*: see Schöll, III. 49; Valfons, pp. 292-3; *Œuvres de Frédéric*, IV. 143 (with correction of Preuss's Note there).

"That on the 5th of October following, Royal Highness "quitted Stade, and his wrecked Army hanging sorrowful "there, like a flight of plucked cranes in mid-air;—arrived at "Kensington, October 12th; heard the paternal Majesty say, "that evening, 'Here is my son who has ruined me, and dis- "'graced himself!'—and thereupon indignantly laid down "his military offices, all and sundry; and ceased altogether "to command Armies, English or other, in this world.*
"Whereby, in the then and now diagram of things, Kloster- "Zeven, as a mathematical point, continues memorable in "History, though shrunk otherwise to zero!
"Pitt's magnanimity to Royal Highness was conspicuous. "Royal Highness, it is said, had been very badly used in this "matter by his poor peddling Father and the Hanover "Ministers; the matter being one puddle of imbecilities from "beginning to end. He was the soul of honour; brave as a "Welf lion; but of dim poor head; and had not the faintest "vestige" (allergeringste, says Mauvillon) "of military skill: "awful in the extreme to see in command of British Armies! "Adieu to him, forever and a day."

Ever since July 29th, three days after Hastenbeck, Pitt had been in Office again; such the bombardment by Corporation-Boxes and Events impinging on Britannic Majesty: but not till now, as I fancy, had Pitt's way, in regard to those German matters, been clear to him. The question of a German Army, if you must have a No-General at the top of it, might well be problematical to Pitt. To equip your strong fighting man, and send him on your errand, regardless of expense; and, by way of preliminary, cut the head off him, before saying "Good-speed to you, strong man!" But with a General, Pitt sees that it can be different; that perhaps "America can be conquered in Germany," and that, with a Britannic Majesty so disposed, there is no other way of trying it. To this course, Pitt stands

* In *Walpole* (m. 59-64) the amplest minuteness of detail.

henceforth, heedless of the gazetteer cackle, "Hah, our Pitt too become German, after all his talking!" — like a seventy-four under full sail, with sea, wind, pilot all of one mind, and only certain waterfowl objecting. And is King of England, for the next Four Years; the one King poor England has had, this long while; — his hand felt shortly at the ends of the Earth. And proves such a blessing to Friedrich, among others, as nothing else in this War; pretty much his one blessing, little as he expected it. Before long, Excellency Mitchell begins consulting about a General, — and Friedrich dimly sees better things in the distance, and that Kloster-Zeven had not been the misfortune he imagined, but only "The darkest hour," which, it is said, lies "nearest to the dawn."

II. *The Soubise-Hildburghausen People take into the Hills; Friedrich in Erfurt Neighbourhood, hanging on, Week after Week, in an Agony of Inaction* (13th September —10th October).

Friedrich's march has gone by Döbeln, Grimma, to Pegau and Rötha, Leipzig way, but with Leipzig well to right: it just brushes Weissenfels to rightward, next day after Rötha; crosses Saale River near Naumburg, whence straight through Weimar Country, Weimar City on your left, to Erfurt on the northern side; — and,

"*Erfurt, Tuesday, 13th September 1757*, About 10 in the "morning" (listen to a faithful Witness), "there appeared "Hussars on the heights to northward: — 'Vanguard of his "Prussian Majesty!' said Erfurt with alarm, and our French "guests with alarm. And scarcely were the words uttered, "when said Vanguard, and gradually the whole Prussian "Army" (only some 9,000, though we all thought it the whole), "came to sight; posting itself in half-moon shape "round us there; French and Reichs folk hurrying off what "they could from the Cyriaksberg and Petersberg, by the "opposite gates,"—towards Gotha, and the Hills of Eisenach.

"Think what a dilemma for Erfurt, jammed between two "horns in this way, should one horn enter before the other got "out! Much parleying and supplicating on the part of Erfurt: "Till at last, about 4 P.M., French being all off, Erfurt flung "its gates open; and the new Power did enter, with some due "state: Prussian Majesty in person (who could have hoped "it!) and Prince Henri beside him; Cavalry with drawn "swords; Infantry with field-pieces, and the band playing" — Prussian grenadier march, I should hope, or something equally cheering. "The rest of the Vanguard, and, in suc- "cession, the Army altogether, had taken Camp outside, look- "ing down on the Northern Gate, over at Ilgertshofen, a "village in the neighbourhood, about two miles off.*

That is the first sight Friedrich has of "*La Dauphine*," as the Versailles people call this Bellona, come to "deliver Saxony;" and she is considerably coyer than had been expected. Many sad days, and ardent vain vows of Friedrich, before he could see the skirt of her again! From Ilgertshofen, north-westward to Dittelstädt, Gamstädt, and other poor specks of villages in Gotha Territory, is ten or fifteen miles; from Dittelstädt eastward to Buttstädt and Buttelstädt, in Weimar Country, may be twenty-five: in this area, Friedrich, shifting about, chiefly for convenience of quarters, — headquarter Kirschleben for a while, Buttelstädt finally and longest, — had to wander impatiently to and fro, for four weeks and more; no work procurable, or none worth mentioning: — in the humour of a man whose House is on fire, flaming out of every

* *Helden-Geschichte,* iv. 636-7.

window, front and rear; who *has* run up with quenching apparatus; and cannot, being spell-bound, get the least bucket of it applied. And is by nature the rapidest soul now alive. Figure his situation there, as it gradually becomes manifest to him! —

For the present, *Dauphiness* Bellona, hurrying to the Hills, has left some tagrag of remnant in Gotha. Whereupon, the second day, here is an "Own Correspondent" again, — not going by electric telegraph, but (what is a sensible advantage) credible in every point, when he does come:

"*Gotha, Thursday, 15th September*. Grand-Duke and "Duchess, like everybody else, have been much occupied all "morning with the fact, that the Prussian Army" (Seidlitz and a regiment or two, nothing more) "is actually here; took "possession of the Town-Gates and Main Guard, this morn-"ing, — certain Hungarian-French hussar rabble, hateful to "every one in Gotha, having made off in time, rapidly towards "Eisenach and the Hills.

"Towards noon, his Royal Majesty in highest person, with "his Lord Brother the Prince Henri's Royal Highness, arrived "in Gotha; sent straightway, by one of his Officers, a com-"pliment to the Grand-Duke; and 'would have the pleasure "to come and dine, if his Serene Highness permitted.' Serene "Highness, self and Household always cordially Friedrich's, "was just about sitting down to dinner; and answered with "exuberantly glad surprise, — or was answering, when Royal "Majesty himself stept in with smiling face; and embracing "the Duke, said: "I timed myself to arrive at this moment, "'thinking your Durchlaucht would be at dinner, that I might "'be received without ceremony, and dine like a neighbour "'among you.' Unexpected as this visit was, the joy of Duke "and Duchess," always fast friends to Friedrich, and the latter ever afterwards his correspondent, "may be conceived, "but not adequately expressed; as both the Serenities were "touched, in the most affecting manner, by the honour of so "great a King's sudden presence among them.

"His Majesty requested that the Frau von Buchwald, our

"Most Gracious Duchess's Hof-Dame, whose qualities he
"much valued, might dine with them," — being always fond
of sensible people, especially sensible women. "The whole
"Highest and High company" (Royal, that is, and Ducal)
"was, during table, uncommonly merry. The King showed
"himself altogether content; and his bright clever talk and
"sprightly sallies, awakening everybody to the like, left not
"the last trace visible of the weighty toils he was then
"engaged in; — as if the weightier these were, the less should
"they fetter the noble openness (*Freymüthigkeit*) of this high
"soul, which is not to be cast down by the heaviest burden.
"His Majesty having taken leave of Duke and Duchess,
"and graciously permitted the chiefest persons of the Gotha
"Court to pay their respects, withdrew to his Army."* Slept,
I find elsewhere, "at Gamstädt, on the floor of a little Inn;"
meaning to examine Posts in that part, next morning.

Here has been a cheerful little scene for Friedrich;
the last he has in these black weeks. A laborious Predecessor, striving to elucidate, leaves me this Note:

"What a pity one knows nothing, nor can know, about
"this Duke and Duchess, though their names, especially the
"latter's name, are much tossed to and fro in the Books! We
"heard of them, favourably, in Voltaire's time; and may
"again, at least of the Lady, who is henceforth a Correspond-
"ent of Friedrich's. The above is a dim direct view of them,
"probably our last as well as first. Duke's name is Fried-
"rich III.; I do believe, a man of solidity, honour, and polite
"dignified sense, a highly respectable Duke of Sachsen-
"Gotha, contented to be obscure, and quietly do what was
"still doable in that enigmatic situation. He is Uncle to our
"George III.; — his Sister is the now Princess-Dowager of
"Wales, with a Lord Bute, and I know not what questionable
"figures and intrigues, or suspicions of intrigue, much about
"her. His Duchess, Louisa Dorothee, is a Princess of dis-
"tinguished qualities, literary tastes, — Voltaire's Hostess,
"Friedrich's Correspondent: a bright and quietly shining
"illumination to the circle she inhabits. Duke is now fifty-
"eight, Duchess forty-seven; and they lost their eldest Son

* *Letter in Helden-Geschichte,* IV. 638-9.

"last year. There has been lately a considerable private "brabble as to Tutorage of the Duke of Weimar (Wilhel-"mina's maddish Duke, who is dead lately; and a Prince left, "who soon died also, but left a Son, who grew to be Goethe's "friend); Tutorage claimed by various Cousins, has been "adjudged to this one, King Friedrich cooperating in such "result.

"As to the famed Grand-Duchess, she is a Sachsen-"Meiningen Princess, come of Ernst the Pious, of Johann the "Magnanimous, as her Husband and all these Sachsens are: "when Voltaire went precipitant, with such velocity, from "the Potsdam Heaven, she received him at Gotha; set him on "writing his *History of the Empire*, and endeavoured to break "his fall. She was noble to Voltaire, and well honoured by "that uncertain Spirit. There is a fine Library at Gotha; "and the Lady bright loves Books, and those that can write "them; — a friend of the Light, a Daughter of the Sun and "the Empyrean, not of Darkness and the Stygian Fens."*

Friedrich's first Letter to her Highness was one of thanks, above a year ago, for an act of kindness, act of justice withal, which she did to one of his Official people. Here, on the morrow of that dinner, is the second Letter, much more aerial and cordial, in which style they all continue, now that he has seen the admired Princess.

To the Most Serene Grand-Duchess of Sachsen-Gotha.

Dittelstädt, "16th September 1757.

"MADAME, — Yesterday was a Day I shall never forget; "which satisfied a just desire I have had, this long while, to "see and hear a Princess whom all Europe admires. I am "not surprised, Madame, that you subdue people's hearts; "you are made to attract the esteem and the homage of all "who have the happiness to know you. But it is incompre-"hensible to me how you can have enemies; and how men "representing Countries that by no means wish to pass for "barbarous, can have been so basely *(indignement)* wanting

* Michaelis, L. 517; &n. &c.

"in the respect they owe you, and in the consideration which "is due to all sovereigns" (French not famous for their refined demeanour in Saxony this time). "Why could not I fly to "prevent such disorders, such indecency! I can only offer "you a great deal of good will; but I feel well that, in present "circumstances, the thing wanted is effective results and "reality. May I, Madame, be so happy as to render you some "service! May your fortune be equal to your virtues! I am "with the highest consideration, Madame, your Highness's "faithful Cousin. — F."*

To Wilhelmina he says of it, next day, still gratified, though sad news have come in the interim; — death of Winterfeld, for one black item:

* * "The day before yesterday I was in Gotha. It was "a touching scene to see the partners of one's misfortunes, "with like griefs and like complaints. The Duchess is a "woman of real merit, whose firmness puts many a man to "shame. Madame de Buchwald appears to me a very estim- "able person, and one who would suit you much: intelligent, "accomplished, without pretensions, and good-humoured. "My Brother Henri is gone to see them today. I am so "oppressed with grief, that I would rather keep my sadness "to myself. I have reason to congratulate myself much on "account of my Brother Henri; he has behaved like an angel, "as a soldier, and well towards me as a Brother. I cannot, "unfortunately, say the same of the elder. He sulks at me "(*il me boude*), and has sulkily retired to Torgau, from whence, "I hear, he is gone to Wittenberg. I shall leave him to his "caprices and to his bad conduct; and I prophesy nothing "good for the future, unless the younger guide him."† * *

This is part of a long sad Letter to Wilhelmina; parts of which we may recur to, as otherwise illustrative. But before going into that tragic budget of bad

* *Œuvres de Frédéric*, XVIII. 168.

† "Kirschleben, near Erfurt, 17th September 1757" (*Œuvres de Frédéric*, XXVII. l. 306).

news, let us give the finale of Gotha, which occurred the next day, — tragi-comic in part, — and is the last of action in those dreary four weeks.

Gotha, 18th September. "Since Thursday 15th, Major-"General Seidlitz," youngest Major-General of the Army, but a rapidly rising man, "has been Commandant in Gotha, "under flourishing circumstances; popular and supreme, "though only with a force of 1,500, dragoons and hussars. "Monday morning early, Seidlitz's scouts bring word that the "Soubise-Hildburghausen people are in motion hitherward; "French hussars and Austrian, Turpin's, Loudon's, all that "are; grenadiers in mass; — total, say, 8,000 horse and foot, "with abundance of artillery; — have been on march all "night, to retake Gotha; with all the Chief Generals and "Dignitaries of the Army following in their carriages, for "some hours past, to see it done. Seidlitz, ascertaining these "things, has but one course left, that of clearing himself out, "which he does with orderly velocity: and at 9 A.M., the "Dignitaries and their 8,000 find open gates, Seidlitz clean "off; occupy the posts, with due emphasis and flourish; and "proceed to the Schloss in a grand triumphant way, — where "privately they are not very welcome, though one puts the "best face on it, and a dinner of importance is the first thing "imperative to be set in progress. A flurried Court that of "Gotha, and much swashing of French plumes through it, all "this morning, since Seidlitz had to flit.

"Seidlitz has not flitted very far. Seidlitz has ranked his "small dragoon-hussar force in a hollow, two miles off; has "got warning sent to a third regiment within reach of him, "'Come towards me, and in a certain defile, visible from "'Gotha eastward, spread yourselves so and so!' — and "judges by the swashing he hears of up yonder, that perhaps "something may still be done. Dinner, up in the Schloss, is "just being taken from the spit, and the swashing at its "height, when — 'Hah, what is that, though?' and all "plumes pause. For it is Seidlitz, artistically spread into "single files, on the prominent points of vision; advancing "again, more like 15,000 than 1,500: 'And in the Defile "yonder, that regiment, do you mark it; the King's vanguard, "I should say? — To horse!'"

"That is Seidlitz's fine Bit of Painting, hung out yonder, "hooked on the sky itself, as temporary background to Gotha, "to be judged of by the connoisseurs. For pictorial effect, "breadth of touch, truth to Nature, and real power on the con- "noisseur, I have heard of nothing equal by any artist. The "high Generalcy, Soubise, Hildburghausen, Darmstadt, "mount in the highest haste; everybody mounts, happy he "who has anything to mount; the grenadiers tumble out of "the Schloss; dragoons, artillery tumble out; Dauphiness "takes wholly to her heels, at an extraordinary pace: so that "Seidlitz's hussars could hardly get a stroke at her; caught "sixty and odd, nine of them Officers not of mark; did kill "thirty; and had such a haul of equipages and valuable "effects, cosmetic a good few of them, habilatory, artistic, as "caused the hussar heart to sing for joy. Among other "plunder, was Loudon's Commission of Major-General, just "on its road from Vienna" (poor Mannstein's death the suggesting cause, say some); — "undoubtedly a shining "Loudon; to whom Friedrich, next day, forwarded the Docu- "ment with a polite Note." *

The day after this bright feat of Seidlitz's, which was a slight consolation to Friedrich, there came a Letter from the Duchess, not of compliment only; the Letter itself had to be burnt on the spot, being, as would seem, dangerous for the High Lady, who was much a friend of Friedrich's. Their Correspondence, very polite and graceful, but for most part gone to the unintelligible state, and become vacant and spectral, figures considerably in the Books, and was, no doubt, a considerable fact to Friedrich. His Answer on this occasion may be given, since we have it, — lest there should not elsewhere be opportunity for a second specimen.

* *Helden-Geschichte,* iv. 640; Westphalen, ii. 37; *Œuvres de Frédéric* iv. 147.

Friedrich to the Grand-Duchess of Sachsen-Gotha.

"Kirschleben, near Erfurt, 20th September 1757.

"MADAME, — Nothing could happen more glorious to my "troops than that of fighting, Madame, under your eyes and "for your defence. I wish their help could be useful to you; "but I foresee the reverse. If I were obstinately to insist on "maintaining the post of Gotha with Infantry, I should ruin "your City for you, Madame, by attracting thither and fixing "there the theatre of the War; whereas, by the present "course, you will only have to suffer little rubs *(passades)*, "which will not last long.

"A thousand thanks that you could, in a day like yester-"day, find the moment to think of your Friends, and to "employ yourself for them." (Seidlitz's attack was brisk, quite sudden, with an effect like Harlequin's sword in Pantomimes; and Gotha in every corner, especially in the Schloss below and above stairs, — dinner cooked for A, and eaten by B, in that manner, — must have been the most agitated of little Cities.) "I will neglect nothing of what you "have the goodness to tell me; I shall profit by these notices. "Heaven grant it might be for the deliverance and the "security of Germany!

"The most signal mark of obedience I can give you con-"sists unquestionably in doing your bidding with this Letter." (Burn it, so soon as read.) "I should have kept it as a monu-"ment of your generosity and courage: but, Madame, since "you dispose of it otherwise, your orders shall be executed; "persuaded that if one cannot serve one's friends, one must at "least avoid hurting them; that one may be less circumspect "for one's own interest, but that one must be prudent and "even timid for theirs. I am with the highest esteem and the "most perfect consideration, Madame, your Highness's most "faithful and affectionate Cousin, — F."*

From Erfurt, on the night of his arrival, finding the Dauphiness in such humour, Friedrich had ordered Ferdinand of Brunswick with his Division, and Prince Moritz with his, both of whom were still at Naumburg,

* *Œuvres de Frédéric,* XVIII. 167.

to go on different errands, — Ferdinand out Halberstadt-Magdeburg way whither Richelieu, vulture-like, if not eagle-like, is on wing; Moritz to Torgau to secure our magazine and be on the outlook there. Both of them marched on the morrow (November 14th): and are sending him news, — seldom comfortable news; mainly that, in spite of all one can do (and it is not little on Ferdinand's part), the Richelieu vultures, 80,000 of them, floating onward, leagues broad, are not to be kept out of Halberstadt, well if out of Magdeburg itself; — and that, in short, the general conflagration, in those parts too, is progressive.* Moritz, peaceable for some weeks in Torgau Country, was to have an eye on Brandenburg withal, on Berlin itself; and before long Moritz will see something noticeable there!

From Preussen, Friedrich hears of mere ravagings and horrid cruelties, Cossack-Calmuck atrocities, which make human nature shudder:** "Fight those monsters; go into them, at all hazards!" he writes to Lehwald peremptorily. Lehwald, 25,000 against 80,000, does so; draws up, in front of Wehlau, not far east of Königsberg, among woody swamps, *August 30th*, at a Hamlet called *Gross-Jägersdorf*, with his best skill; fights well, though not without mistakes; and is beaten by cannon and numbers.*** Preussen now lies at Apraxin's discretion. This bit of news too is on the road for Erfurt Country. Such a six weeks for the swift

---

* In Orlich's *Fürst Moritz*, pp. 71-89; and in *Westphalen*, ii. 23-148 (about Ferdinand): interesting Documentary details, Autographs of Friedrich, &c., in regard to both these Expeditions.

** In *Helden-Geschichte*, iv. 417-437, the hideous details.

*** Tempelhof, i. 299; Retzow, i. 212; &c. &c. ("Russians lost about 9,000," by their own tale 5,000; "the Prussians 3,000" and the Field).

man, obliged to stand spell-bound, — idle posterity never will conceive it; and description is useless.

Let us add here, that Apraxin did not advance on Königsberg, or farther into Preussen at all; but, after some loitering, turned, to everybody's surprise, and wended slowly home. "Could get no provision," said Apraxin for himself. "Thought the Czarina was dying," said the world; "and that Peter her successor would take it well!" Plodded slowly home, for certain; Lehwald following him, not too close, till over the border. Nothing left of Apraxin, and his huge Expedition, but Memel alone; Memel, and a great many graves and ruins. So that Lehwald could be recalled, to attend on the Swedes, before Winter came. And Friedrich's worst forebodings did not take effect in this case; — nor in some others, as we shall see.

Lamentation-Psalms of Friedrich.

Meanwhile, is it not remarkable that Friedrich wrote more Verses, this Autumn, than almost in any other three months of his life? Singular, yes; though perhaps not inexplicable. And if readers could fairly understand that fact, instead of running away with the shell of it, and leaving the essence, it would throw a great light on Friedrich. He is not a brooding inarticulate man, then; but a bright-glancing, articulate; not to be struck dumb by the face of Death itself. Flashes clear-eyed into the physiognomy of Death, and Ruin, and the Abysmal Horrors opening; and has a sharp word to say to them. The explanation of his large cargo of Verses this Autumn is, That always, alternating with such fiery velocity, he had intolerable periods of waiting till things were ready. And took to verses, by way of expectorating himself, and keeping down his devils. Not a bad plan, in the circumstances, — especially if you have so wonderful a turn for expectoration by speech. "All bad as Poetry, those Verses?" asks the reader. Well, some of them are not of first-rate goodness. Should have been burnt; or the time marked which they took up, and whether it was good time wasted (which I suppose it almost never was), or bad time skilfully got over. Time, that is the great point; and the heart-truth of them, or mere lip-truth, another. We must give some specimens, at any rate.

Especially that notable Specimen from the Zittau Countries: the "Epistle to Wilhelmina (*Epître à ma Sœur* *);" which is the keynote, as it were; the fountain-head of much other verse, and of much prose withal, and Correspondencing not with Wilhelmina alone, of which also some taste must be given. Primary *Epître;* written, I perceive, in that interval of waiting for Keith and the magazines, — though the final date is "Bernstadt, August 24th." Concerning which, Smelfungus takes, over-hastily, the liberty to say: "Strange, is it "not, to be on the point of fighting for one's existence; "overwhelmed with so many businesses; and disposed "to go into verse in addition! *Conceive* that form of "mind; it would illuminate something of Friedrich's "character: I cannot yet rightly understand such an "aspect of structure, and know not what to say of it, "except "'Strange!'" —

Understand it or not, we do gather by means of it some indisputable glimpses, nearly all the direct insight allowed us out of any source, into Friedrich's inner

* *Œuvres de Frédéric,* xii. 36-42.

man; what his thoughts were, what his humour was in that unique crisis; and to readers in quest of that, these Pieces, fallen obsolete and frosty to all other kinds of readers, are well worth perusing, and again perusing. Most veracious Documents, we can observe; nothing could be truer; Confessions they are, in the most emphatic sense; no truer ever made to a Priest in the name of the Most High. Like a soliloquy of Night-Thoughts, accidentally becoming audible to us. Mahomet, I find, wrote the Koran in this manner. From those poor Poems, which are voices *De Profundis*, there might, by proper care and selection, be constructed a Friedrich's Koran; and, with commentary and elucidation, it would be pleasant to read. The Koran of Friedrich, or the Lamentation-Psalms of Friedrich! But it would need an Editor, — other than Dryasdust! Mahomet's Koran, treated by the Arab Dryasdust (merely turning up the bottom of that Box of Shoulder-blades, and printing them), has become dreadfully tough reading, on this side of the Globe; and has given rise to the impossiblest notions about Mahomet! Indisputable it is, Heroes, in their affliction, Mahomet and David, have solaced themselves by snatches of Psalms, by Suras, bursts of Utterance rising into Song; — and if Friedrich, on far other conditions, did the like, what has History to say of blame to him?

Wilhelmina comes out very strong, in this season of trouble; almost the last we see of our excellent Wilhelmina. Like a lioness; like a shrill mother when her children are in peril. A noble sisterly affection is in Wilhelmina; shrill Pythian vehemence trying the impossible. That a Brother, and such a Brother, the most heroic now breathing, brave and true, and the soul of honour in all things, should have the whole world rise round him, like a delirious Sorcerer's-Sabbath, intent to hurl the mountains on him, — seems such a horror and a madness to Wilhelmina. Like the broodhen flying in the face of wild dogs, and packs of hounds in full trail! Most Christian Pompadour Kings, enraged Czarinas, implacable Empress-Queens; a whole world in armed delirium rushes on, regardless of Wilhelmina. Never mind, my noble one; your Brother will perhaps manage to come up with this leviathan or that, among the heap of them, at a good time, and smite into the fifth rib of him. Your Brother does not the least shape towards giving in; thank the Heavens, he will stand to himself at least; his own poor strength will all be on his own side.

Wilhelmina's hopes of a Peace with France; mission of her Mirabeau, missions and schemes not a few, we have heard of on Wilhelmina's part with this view; but the notablest is still to mention: that of stirring up, by Voltaire's means, an important-looking Cardinal de Tencin to labour in the business. Eminency Tencin lives in Lyon, known to the Princess on her Italian Tour; — shy of asking Voltaire to dinner on that fine occasion; — but, except Officially, is not otherwise than well-affected to Voltaire. Was once Chief Minister of France, and would fain again be; does not like these Bernis novelties and Austrian Alliances, had he now any power to overset them. Let him correspond with Most Christian Majesty, at least; plead for a Peace with Prussia, Prussia being so ready that way. Eminency Tencin, on Voltaire's suggestion, did so, perhaps is even now doing so; till ordered to hold *his* peace on such subjects. This is certain and well known; but nothing else is known, or to us knowable, about it; Voltaire, in vague form, being our one authority, through whom it is vain to hunt, and again hunt.* The Dates, much more the features and circumstances, all lie buried from us, and, — till perhaps the *Lamentation-Psalms* are well edited, — must continue lying. As a fact certain, but undeniably vague.

Voltaire's procedure, one can gather, is polite, but two-faced; not sublime on this occasion. In fact, is intended to serve himself. To the high Princess he writes devotionally, ready to obey in all things; and then to his Eminency Cardinal Tencin, it rather seems as if the tone were: "Pooh! yes, your Eminency; such are the poor Lady's notions. But does your Eminency take notice how high my connections are; what service a poor obscure creature might perhaps do the State some day?" Friedrich himself is, in these ways, brought into correspondence with Voltaire again; and occasionally writes to him in this War, and ever afterwards: Voltaire responds with fine sympathy, always prettily, in the enthusiasm of the moment; — and at other times he writes a good deal about Friedrich, oftenest in rather a mischievous dialect. "The traitor!" exclaim some Prussian writers, not many or important, in our time. In fact, there is a considerable touch of grinning malice (as of Monkey *versus* Cat, who had once burnt *his* paw, instead of getting his own burnt), in those utterances of Voltaire: some of which the reader will grin over too, without much tragic feeling, — the rather as they did our Felis Leo no manner of

---

* Œuvres (*Mémoires*), II. 92-98; ib. L 143: Preuss, II. 84.

ill, and show our incomparable *Singe* with a sparkle of the *Tigre* in him; theoretic sparkle merely and for moments, which makes him all the more entertaining and interesting at the domestic hearth.

Of Friedrich's Lamentation-Psalms we propose to give the First and the Last: these, with certain Prose Pieces, intermediate and connecting may perhaps be made intelligible to readers, and throw some light on these tragic weeks of the King's History:

1°. *Epître à ma Sœur* (First of the Lamentation-Psalms). — This is the famed "Epistle to Wilhelmina," already spoken of; which the King despatched from Bernstadt, "August 24th," just while quitting those parts, on the Erfurt Errand; — though written before, in the tedium of waiting for Keith. The Piece is long, vehement, altogether sincere; lyrically sings aloud, or declaims in rhyme, what one's indignant thought really is on the surrounding woes and atrocities. We faithfully abridge, and condense into our briefest Prose; — readers can add water, and the jingle of French rhymes *ad libitum*. It starts thus:

"O sweet and dear hope of my remaining days; O Sister, "whose friendship, so fertile in resources, shares all my "sorrows, and with a helpful arm assists me in the gulf! It "is in vain that the Destinies have overwhelmed me with "disasters: if the crowd of Kings have sworn my ruin; if the "Earth have opened to swallow me, — you still love me, noble "and affectionate Sister: loved by you, what is there of "misfortune?" (Branches off into some survey of it, nevertheless.)

"Huge continents of thunder-cloud, plots thickening "against me" (in those Menzel Documents), "I watched with "terror; the sky getting blacker, no covert for me visible: on "a sudden, from the deeps of Hell, starts forth Discord" (with capital-letter), "and the tempest broke.

"*Ce fut dans ton Sénat, O fougueuse Angleterre!*
"*Où ce monstre inhumain fit éclater la guerre:*

"It was from thy Senate, stormful England, that she first "launched out War. In remote climates first; in America, "far away; — between France and thee. Old Ocean shook with it; Neptune, in the depths of his caves *(ses grottes profondes)*, saw the English subjecting his waves *(ses ondes)*: the wild Iroquois, prize of these crimes *(forfaits)*, bursts out, detesting the tyrants who disturb his Forests" — and scalping Braddock's people and the like.

"Discord, charmed to see such an America, and feeble mortals crossing the Ocean to exterminate one another, addresses the European Kings: 'How long will you be slaves to what are called laws? Is it for you to bend under worn-out notions of justice, right? Mars is the one God: Might is Right. A King's business is to do something famous in this world.'

"O Daughter of the Cæsars," Maria Theresa, "how, at these words, ambition, burning in thy soul, breaks out uncontrollable! Probity, honour, treaties, duty: feeble considerations these, to a heart letting loose its flamy passions; determining to rob the generous Germans of their liberties; to degrade thy equals; to extinguish 'Schism' (so called), and set up despotism on the wrecks of all."

"Huge project" — "*fier Triumvirat*," — what not: "From Roussillon and the sunny Pyrenees to frozen Russia, all arm for Austria, and march at her bidding. They concert my downfall, trample on my rights.

"The Daughter of the Cæsars, proudly certain of victory, — 'tis the way of the Great, whose commonplace virtue, pusillanimous in reverses, overbearing in success, cannot bridle their cupidity, — designates to the Triumvirate what Kings are to be proscribed" (Britannic George and me, Reich busy on us both even now), "and those ungrateful tyrants, by united crime, immolate to each other, without remorse, their dearest allies." For instance:

"*O jour digne d'oubli! Quelle atroce imprudence!*
"*Thérèse, c'est l'Anglais que tu rends à la France:*

"Theresa! it is England thou art selling to France;" — Yes, a thing worth noting. "Thy generous support in thy first adversities; thy one friend then, when a world had risen to devour thee. Thou reignest now: — but it was England alone that saved thee anything to reign over!

"*Tu régnes, mais lui seul a sauvé tes états:*
"*Les bienfaits chez les rois ne sont que des ingrats.*

"And thou, lazy Monarch," — stupid Louis, let us omit him: — "Pompadour, selling her lover to the highest bidder, "makes France, in our day, Austria's slave!" We omit Koliu Battle, too, spoken of with a proud modesty (Prag is not spoken of at all); and how the neighbouring ravenous Powers, onlookers hitherto, have opened their throats with one accord to swallow Prussia, thinking its downfall certain: "Poor mercenary Sweden, once so famous under its soldier "Kings, now debased by a venal Senate;" — Sweden, "what "say I? my own kindred" (foolish Anspach and others), "driven, by perverse motives, join in the plot of horrors, and "become satellites of the prospering Triumvirs.

"And thou, loved People" (my own Prussians), "whose "happiness is my charge" (notable how often he repeats this), "it is thy lamentable destiny, it is the danger which "hangs over thee, that pierces my soul. The pomps of my "rank I could resign without regret. But to rescue thee, in "this black crisis, I will spend my heart's blood. Whose *is* "that blood but thine? With joy will I rally my warriors to "avenge thy affront; defy death at the foot of the ramparts" (of Daun and his Eckartsberg, ahead yonder), "and either "conquer, or be buried under thy ruins." Very well; but ah, —

"Preparing with such purpose, ye Heavens, what mourn-"ful cries are those that reach us: 'Death has laid low thy "Mother!' — Hah, that was the last stroke, then, which "angry Fate had reserved for me. — — O Mother, Death flies "my misfortunes, and spreads his livid horrors over thee!" (Very tender, very sad, what he says of his Mother; but must be omitted and imagined. General finale is:)

"'Thus Destiny with a deluge of torments fills the poisoned "remnant of my days. The present is hideous to me, the "future unknown: what, you say I am the creature of a *Bene-*"*ficent* Being? —

"*Quoi! serais-je formé par un Dieu bienfaisant!*
"*Ah! s'il était si bon, tendre pour son ouvrage*" —

— Hush, my little Titan!

"And now, ye promoters of sacred lies, go on leading "cowards by the nose, in the dark windings of your labyrinth: "— to me the enchantment is ended, the charm disappears. "I see that all men are but the sport of Destiny. And that, if

"there do exist some Gloomy and Inexorable Being, who
"allows a despised herd of creatures to go on multiplying
"here, he values them as nothing; looks down on a Phalaris
"crowned, on a Socrates in chains; on our virtues, our
"misdeeds, on the horrors of war, and all the cruel plagues
"which ravage Earth, as a thing indifferent to him. Where-
"fore, my sole refuge and only haven, loved Sister, is in the
"arms of death:

"*Ainsi mon seul asile et mon unique port
"Se trouve, chère sœur, dans les bras de la mort.*" *

20. *Wilhelmina to Voltaire, with something of Answer* (First of certain intercalary Prose Pieces). — Wilhelmina has been writing to Voltaire before, and getting consolations since Kolin; but her Letters are lost, till this the earliest that is left us:

Baireuth, 19th August 1757 (To Voltaire). — "One first "knows one's friends when misfortunes arrive. The Letter "you have written does honour to your way of thinking. I "cannot tell you how much I am sensible to what you have "done" (set Cardinal Tencin astir, with result we will hope). "The King, my Brother, is as much so as I. You will find a "Note here, which he bids me transmit to you" (Note lost). "That great man is still the same. He supports his mis- "fortunes with a courage and a firmness worthy of him. He "could not get the Note transcribed. It began by verses. "Instead of throwing sand on it, he took the inkbottle; that "is the reason why it is cut in two."

— This Note, we say, is lost to us; — all but accidentally thus: Voltaire, 12th September, writes twice to friends. Writing to his D'Argentals, he says: "The affairs of this "King" (Friedrich) "go from bad to worse. I know not if I "told you of the Letter he wrote to me about three weeks ago" (say August 17th-18th: the Note through Wilhelmina, evidently): "'I have learned,' says he, 'that you had interested "yourself in my successes and misfortunes. There remains "to me nothing but to sell my life dear,' &c. His Sister "writes me one much more lamentable;" the one we are now reading: —

"I am in a frightful state; and will not survive the de- "struction of my House and Family. That is the one con-

* *Œuvres,* XII. 36-42; is sent off to Wilhelmina, 24th August.

13th Sept. — 10th Oct. 1757.

"solution that remains to me. You will have fine subjects
"for making Tragedies of. O times! O manners! You will,
"by the illusory representation, perhaps draw tears; while
"all contemplate with dry eyes the reality of these miseries:
"the downfall of a whole House, against which, if the truth
"were known, there is no solid complaint. I cannot write
"farther of it: my soul is so troubled that I know not what I
"am doing. But whatever happen, be persuaded that I am
"more than ever your friend, — WILHELMINA." *

Friedrich, while Wilhelmina writes so, is at the foot of the
Eckartsberg, eagerly manœuvring with the Austrians, in
hopes of getting battle out of them, — which he cannot.
Friedrich, while he wrote that Note to Voltaire, and instead of
sandbox shook the inkbottle over it, was just going out on that
errand.

Voltaire, 12th September (to a Lady whose Son is in the
D'Estrées wars).** — "Here are mighty revolutions, Madame;
"and we are not at the end yet. They say there have
"18,000 Hanoverians been disposed of at Stade" (Convention
of Kloster-Zeven). "That is no small matter. I can hope
"M. Richelieu" (who is '*mon héros*,' when I write to himself)
"will adorn his head with the laurels they have stuck in his
"pocket. I wish Monsieur your Son abundance of honour
"and glory without wounds, and to you Madame unalterable
"health. The King of Prussia has written me a very
"touching Letter" (one line of which we have read); "but I
"have always Madame Denis's adventure on my heart," at
Frankfurt yonder. "If I were well, I would take a run to
"Frankfurt myself on the business," — now that Soubise's
reserves are in those parts, and could give Freytag and
Schmidt such a dusting for me, if they liked! Shall I write to
Collini on it? Does write, and again write, the second year
hence, as still better chances rise. ***

3º. *Wilhelmina to Voltaire again, with Answer* (Second of
the Prose Pieces). — Not a very zealous friend of Friedrich's,
after all, this Voltaire! Poor Wilhelmina, terrified, by that
Epître of her Brother's, and his fixed purpose of seeking
Death, has, in her despair (though her Letter is lost), been urg-

* In *Œuvres de Voltaire*, LXXVII. 30.   ** Ib. LXXVII. 55-56.
*** Collini, pp. 208-211 ("January—May 1759").

ing Voltaire to write dissuading him; — as Voltaire does. Of which presently. Her Letter to Voltaire on this thrice-important subject is lost. But in the very hours while Voltaire sat writing what we have just read, "always with Madame "Denis's adventure on my heart," Wilhelmina, at Baireuth, is again writing to him as follows:

Baireuth, 12th September 1757 (To Voltaire). — "Your "Letter has sensibly touched me; that which you addressed "to me for the King" (both Letters lost to us) "has produced "the same effect on him. I hope you will be satisfied with his "Answer as to what concerns yourself; but you will be as "little so as I am with the resolutions he has formed. I had "flattered myself that your reflections would make some im- "pression on his mind. You will see the contrary by the "Letter adjoined.

"'To me there remains nothing but to follow his destiny if "it is unfortunate. I have never piqued myself on being a "philosopher; though I have made my efforts to become so. "The small progress I made did teach me to despise "grandeurs and riches: but I could never find in philosophy "any cure for the wounds of the heart, except that of getting "done with our miseries by ceasing to live. The state I am "in is worse than death. I see the greatest man of his age, "my Brother, my friend, reduced to the frightfullest ex- "tremity. I see my whole Family exposed to dangers and "perhaps destruction; my native Country torn by pitiless "enemies; the Country where I am" (Reichs Army, Anspach, what not) "menaced by perhaps similar misfortune. Would "to Heaven I were alone loaded with all the miseries I have "described to you! I would suffer them, and with firmness.

"Pardon these details. You invite me, by the part you "take in what regards me, to open my heart to you. Alas, "hope is well-nigh banished from it. Fortune, when she "changes, is as constant in her persecutions as in her favours. "History is full of those examples: — but I have found none "equal to the one we now see; nor any War as inhuman and "as cruel among civilised nations. You would sigh if you "knew the sad situation of Germany and Preussen. The "cruelties which the Russians commit in that latter Country "make nature shudder.*. How happy you in your Hermi-

* Details, horrible but authentic, in *Helden-Geschichte*, already cited.

"tage; where you repose on your laurels, and can philo"sophise with a calm mind on the deliriums of men! I wish "you all the happiness imaginable. If Fortune ever favour "us again, count on all my gratitude. I will never forget the "marks of attachment which you have given; my sensibility "is your warrant; I am never half-and-half a friend, and "I shall always be wholly so of Brother Voltaire. — WIL-"HELMINA.

"Many compliments to Madame Denis. Continue, I pray "you, to write to the King." *

Voltaire to Wilhelmina (Day uncertain: *The Délices*, *September 1757*). — "Madame, my heart is touched more than "ever by the goodness and the confidence your Royal High"ness deigns to show me. How can I be but melted by "emotion! I see that it is solely your nobleness of soul that "renders you unhappy. I feel myself born to be attached "with idolatry to superior and sympathetic minds, who think "like you.

"You know how much I have always, essentially and at "heart, been attached to the King your Brother. The more "my old age is tranquil, and come to renounce everything, "and make my retreat here a home and country, the more am "I devoted to that Philosopher-King. I write nothing to him "but what I think from the bottom of my heart, nothing that I "do not think most true; and if my Letter" (dissuasive of seeking Death; wait, reader) "appears to your Royal High"ness to be suitable, I beg you to protect it with him, as you "have done the foregoing." **

40. *Friedrich to Wilhelmina, and, by anticipation, her Answer* (Third of the Prose Pieces). — "*Kirschleben, near Erfurt, "17th September 1757*. My dearest Sister, I find no other "consolation but in your precious Letters. May Heaven "reward so much virtue and such heroic sentiments!

"Since I wrote last to you, my misfortunes have but gone "on accumulating. It seems as though Destiny would dis"charge all its wrath and fury upon the poor Country which "I had to rule over. The Swedes have entered Pommern. "The French, after having concluded a Neutrality humiliat-

* In *Voltaire*, II, 197-199; LXXVII. 57.
** Voltaire, LXXVII. 37, 59.

"ing to the King of England and themselves" (Kloster-Zeven, which we know), "are in full march upon Halberstadt "and Magdeburg. From Preussen I am in daily expectation "of hearing of a battle having been fought: the proportion of "combatants being 25,000 against 80,000" (was fought, Gross-Jägersdorf, 30th August, and lost accordingly). "The "Austrians have marched into Silesia, whither the Prince of "Bevern follows them. I have advanced this way to fall "upon the corps of the allied Army; which has run off, and "intrenched itself, behind Eisenach, amongst hills, whither to "follow, still more to attack them, all rules of war forbid. "The moment I retire towards Saxony, this whole swarm will "be upon my heels. Happen what may, I am determined, at "all risks, to fall upon whatever corps of the enemy ap-"proaches me nearest. I shall even bless Heaven for its "mercy, if it grant me the favour to die sword in hand.

"Should this hope fail me, you will allow that it would be "too hard to crawl at the feet of a company of traitors, to "whom successful crimes have given the advantage to pre-"scribe the law to me. How, my dear, my incomparable "Sister, how could I repress feelings of vengeance and of "resentment against all my neighbours, of whom there is not "one who did not accelerate my downfall, and will not share "in our spoils? How can a Prince survive his State, the glory "of his Country, his own reputation? A Bavarian Elector, in "his nonage" (Son of the late poor Kaiser, and left ship-wrecked in his seventeenth year), "or rather in a sort of sub-"jection to his Ministers, and dull to the biddings of honour, "may give himself up as a slave to the imperious domination "of the House of Austria, and kiss the hand which oppressed "his Father: I pardon it to his youth and his ineptitude. But "is that the example for me to follow? No, dear Sister, you "think too nobly to give me such mean (*lâche*) advice. Is "Liberty, that precious prerogative, to be less dear to a "Sovereign in the eighteenth century than it was to Roman "Patricians of old? And where is it said, that Brutus and "Cato should carry magnanimity farther than Princes and "Kings? Firmness consists in resisting misfortune: but only "cowards submit to the yoke, bear patiently their chains, and "support oppression tranquilly. Never, my dear Sister, could "I resolve upon such ignominy." —

"If I had followed only my own inclinations, I should have ended it (*je me serais dépêché*) at once, after that unfortunate Battle which I lost. But I felt that this would be weakness, and that it behoved me to repair the evil which had happened. My attachment to the State awoke; I said to myself, It is not in seasons of prosperity that it is rare to find defenders, but in adversity. I made it a point of honour with myself to redress all that had got out of square; in which I was not unsuccessful; not even in the Lausitz" (after those Zittau disasters) "last of all. But no sooner had I hastened this way to face new enemies, than Winterfeld was beaten and killed near Görlitz, than the French entered the heart of my States, than the Swedes blockaded Stettin. Now there is nothing effective left for me to do: there are too many enemies. Were I even to succeed in beating two armies, the third would crush me. The enclosed Note" (in cipher) "will show you what I am still about to try: it is the last attempt.

"The gratitude, the tender affection, which I feel towards you, that friendship, true as the hills, constrains me to deal openly with you. No, my divine Sister, I shall conceal nothing from you that I intend to do; all my thoughts, all my resolutions shall be open and known to you in time. I will precipitate nothing: but also it will be impossible for me to change my sentiments."

"As for you, my incomparable Sister, I have not the heart to turn you from your resolves. We think alike, and I cannot condemn in you the sentiments which I daily entertain (*éprouve*). Life has been given to us as a benefit: when it ceases to be such — ! I have nobody left in this world, to attach me to it, but you. My friends, the relations I loved most, are in the grave; in short, I have lost everything. If you take the resolution which I have taken, we end together our misfortunes and our unhappiness; and it will be the turn of them who remain in this world, to provide for the concerns falling to their charge, and to bear the weight which has lain on us so long. These, my adorable Sister, are sad reflections, but suitable to my present condition.

"The day before yesterday I was at Gotha" (yes, see

above;—and tomorrow, if I knew it, Seidlitz with pictorial effects will be there). * *

"But it is time to end this long, dreary Letter; which "treats almost of nothing but my own affairs. I have had "some leisure, and have used it to open on you a heart filled "with admiration and gratitude towards you. Yes, my "adorable Sister, if Providence troubled itself about human "affairs, you ought to be the happiest person in the Universe. "Your not being such, confirms me in the sentiments ex-"pressed at the end of my *Epître*. In conclusion, believe "that I adore you, and that I would give my life a thousand "times to serve you. These are the sentiments which will "animate me to the last breath of my life; being, my beloved "Sister, ever,"—Your—F.*

Wilhelmina's Answer,—by anticipation, as we said: "written 15th September," while Friedrich was dining at Gotha, in quest of Soubise.

"*Baireuth, 15th September 1757*. My dearest Brother, "your Letter and the one you wrote to Voltaire, my dear "Brother, have almost killed me. What fatal resolutions, "great God! Ah, my dear Brother, you say you love me; "and you drive a dagger into my heart. Your *Epître*, which "I did receive, made me shed rivers of tears. I am now "ashamed of such weakness. My misfortune would be so "great" in the issue there alluded to, "that I should find "worthier resources than tears. Your lot shall be mine: I "will not survive either your misfortunes or those of the "House I belong to. You may calculate that such is my firm "resolution.

"But, after this avowal, allow me to entreat you to look "back at what was the pitiable state of your Enemy when you "lay before Prag! It is the sudden whirl of Fortune for both "parties. The like can occur again, when one is least ex-"pecting it. Cæsar was the slave of Pirates; and he became "the master of the world. A great genius like yours finds "resources even when all is lost; and it is impossible this "frenzy can continue. My heart bleeds to think of the poor "souls in Preussen" (Apraxin and his Christian Cossacks there,—who, it is noted, far excel the Calmuck worshippers of the Dalai-Lama). "What horrid barbarity, the detail of

* *Œuvres*, xxvii. t. 303-307.

14th Sept. — 10th Oct. 1757.

"cruelties that go on there! I feel all that you feel on it, my
"dear Brother. I know your heart, and your sensibility for
"your subjects.
  "I suffer a thousand times more than I can tell you;
"nevertheless hope does not abandon me. I received your
"Letter of the 14th by W." (who W. is, no mortal knows).
"What kindness to think of me, who have nothing to give
"you but a useless affection, which is so richly repaid by
"yours! I am obliged to finish; but I shall never cease to
"be, with the most profound respect (*très-profond respect*)," —
that, and something still better, if my poor pen were not
embarrassed), "your," — WILHELMINA.

  5⁰. *Friedrich's Response to the Dissuasives of Voltaire* (Last
of the Lamentation-Psalms: "Buttstädt, October 9th"). —
Voltaire's Dissuasive Letter is a poor Piece;* not worth
giving here. Remarkable only by Friedrich's quiet reception
of it; which readers shall now see, as Finis to those Lamentation-Psalms. There is another of them, widely known,
which we will omit: the *Epître to D'Argens;*** passionate
enough, wandering wildly over human life, and sincere
almost to shrillness, in parts; which Voltaire has also got
hold of. Omissible here; the fixity of purpose being plain
otherwise to Voltaire and us. Voltaire's counter-arguments
are weak, or worse: "That Roman-death is not now ex-
"pected of the Philosopher; that your Majesty will, in the
"worst event, still have considerable Dominions left, all
"that your Great-Grandfather had; still plenty of resources;
"that, in Paris Society, an estimable minority even now
"thinks highly of you; that in Paris itself your Majesty"
(does not say expressly, as dethroned and going on your
travels) "would have resources!" To which beautiful considerations Friedrich answers, not with fire and brimstone,
as one might have dreaded, but in this quiet manner (*Réponse
au Sieur Voltaire*):

  "Je suis homme, il suffit, et né pour la souffrance ;
  "Aux rigueurs du destin j'oppose ma constance.***

---

  * *Œuvres de Voltaire*, LXXVII. 60-83 (*Les Délices*, early in September
1757; no date given).
  ** In *Œuvres de Frédéric*, XII. 50-56 ("Erfurt, 23d September 1757").
  *** "I am a man, and therefore born to suffer; to destiny's rigours my
"stedfastness must correspond." — Quotation from I know not whom.

"But with these sentiments, I am far from condemning Cato
"and Otho. The latter had no fine moment in his life, except
"that of his death." (Breaks off into Verse:)

> "Croyez que si j'étais Voltaire,
> "Et particulier comme lui,
> "Me contentant du nécessaire,
> "Je verrais voltiger la fortune légère," — Or,

to wring the water and the jingle out of it, and give the
substance in Prose:

"Yes, if I were Voltaire and a private man, I could with
"much composure leave Fortune to her whirlings and her
"plungings; to me, contented with the needful, her mad
"caprices and sudden topsy-turvyings would be amusing
"rather than tremendous.

"I know the ennui attending on honours, the burdensome
"duties, the jargon of grinning flatterers, those pitiabilities
"of every kind, those details of littleness, with which you
"have to occupy yourself if set on high on the stage of things.
"Foolish glory has no charm for me, though a Poet and
"King: when once Atropos has ended me forever, what will
"the uncertain honour of living in the Temple of Memory
"avail? One moment of practical happiness is worth a
"thousand years of imaginary in such Temple. — Is the lot
"of high people so very sweet, then? Pleasure, gentle
"ease, true and hearty mirth, have always fled from the
"great and their peculiar pomps and labours.

"No, it is not fickle Fortune that has ever caused my
"sorrows; let her smile her blandest, let her frown her fiercest
"on me, I should sleep every night, refusing her the least
"worship. But our respective conditions are our law; we are
"bound and commanded to shape our temper to the employ-
"ment we have undertaken. Voltaire in his hermitage, in a
"Country where is honesty and safety, can devote himself in
"peace to the life of the Philosopher, as Plato has described
"it. But as to me, threatened with shipwreck, I must con-
"sider how, looking the tempest in the face, I can think, can
"live and can die as a King:

> "Pour moi, menacé du naufrage,
> "Je dois, en affrontant l'orage,
> "Penser, vivre et mourir en roi."*

* Œuvres, LXIII. 14.

This is of October 9th; this ends, worthily, the Lamentation-Psalms; work having now turned up, which is a favourable change. Friedrich's notion of suicide, we perceive, is by no means that of puking up one's existence, in the weak sick way of *felo de se;* but, far different, that of dying, if he needs must, as seems too likely, in uttermost spasm of battle for self and rights to the last. From which latter notion nobody can turn him. A valiantly definite, lucid and shiningly practical soul, — with such a power of always expectorating himself into clearness again. If he do frankly wager his life in that manner, beware, ye Soubises, Karls, and flaccid trivial persons, of the stroke that may chance to lie in him! —

III. *Rumour of an Inroad on Berlin suddenly sets Friedrich on March thither: Inroad takes Effect, — with important Results, chiefly in a left-hand Form.*

October 11th, express arrived, important express from General Finck (who is in Dresden, convalescent from Kolin, and is even Commandant there, of anything · there is to command), "That the considerable Austrian Brigade or Outpost, which was left at Stolpen when the others went for Silesia, is all on march for Berlin." Here is news! "The whole 15,000 of them," report adds; — though it proved to be only a Detachment, picked Tolpatches mostly, and of nothing like that strength; shot off, under a swift General Haddick, on this errand. Between them and Berlin is not a vestige of force; and Berlin itself has nothing but palisades, and perhaps a poor 4,000 of garrison. "March "instantly, you Moritz, who lie nearest; cross Elbe at

"Torgau; I follow instantly!" orders Friedrich;* — and, that same night, is on march, or has cavalry pushed ahead for reinforcement of Moritz.

Friedrich, not doubting but there would be captaincy and scheme among his Enemies, considered that the Swedes, and perhaps the Richelieu French, were in concert with this Austrian movement, — from east, from north, from west, three Invasions coming on the core of his Dominions; — and that here at last was work ahead, and plenty of it! That was Friedrich's opinion, and most other people's, when the Austrian inroad was first heard of: "mere triple ruin coming to "this King," as the Gazetteers judged; — great alarm prevailing among the King's friends; in Berlin, very great. Friedrich, glad, at any rate, to have done with that dismal lingering at Buttelstädt, hastens to arrange himself for the new contingencies; to post his Keiths, his Ferdinands, with their handfuls of force, to best advantage; and push ahead after Moritz, by Leipzig, Torgau, Berlin-wards, with all his might. At Leipzig, in such press of business and interest, — judge by the following phenomenon, what a clear-going soul this is, and how completely on a level with whatever it may be that he is marching towards:

"*Leipzig, 15th October 1757* (Interview with Gottsched). — "At 11 this morning, Majesty came marching into Leipzig; "multitudes of things to settle there; things ready, things "not yet ready, in view of the great events ahead. Seeing "that he would have time after dinner, he at once sent for "Professor Gottsched, a gigantic gentleman, Reigning King "of German Literature for the time being, to come to him "at 8 P.M. Reigning King at that time; since gone wholly to

---

* His Message to Moritz, *Orlich*, p. 75: Rödenbeck, p. 322 (dubious, or wrong).

"the Dustbins,— 'Popular Delusion,' as Old Samuel defines
"it, having since awakened to itself, with scornful hahas
"upon its poor Gottsched, and rushed into other roads worse
"and better; its poor Gottsched become a name now signify-
"ing Pedantry, Stupidity, learned Insanity, and the Worship
"of Coloured Water, to every German mind.

"At 3 precise, the portly old gentleman (towards sixty
"now, huge of stature, with a shrieky voice, and speaks
"uncommonly fast) bowed himself in; and a Colloquy ensued,
"on Literature and so forth, of the kind we may conceive.
"Colloquy which had great fame in the world; Gottsched
"himself having,— such the inaccuracy of rumour and Dutch
"Newspapers, on the matter,— published authentic Report
"of it;* now one of the dullest bits of reading, and worth no
"man's bit of time. Colloquy which lasted three hours, with
"the greatest vivacity on both sides; King impugning, for
"one principal thing, the roughness of German speech;
"Gottsched, in swift torrents (far too copious in such com-
"pany), ready to defend. 'Those consonants of ours,' said
"the King, 'they afflict one's ear: what Names we have;
"all in mere k's and p's: *Knap—*, *Knip—*, *Klop—*, *Krotz—*,
"*Krok—*; — your own Name, for example!'" — Yes, his
own Name, unmusical Gott*sched*, and signifying God's-
Damage (God's-*skaith*) withal. "Husht, don't take a Holy
Name in vain; call the man *Sched* ('Damage' by itself),
can't we!" said a wit once.** — "'Five consonants together,
"*ttsch, ttsch*, what a tone!' continued the King. 'Hear, in
"contrast, the music of this Stanza of Rousseau's' (Repeats
"a stanza). 'Who could express that in German with such
"melody?' And so on; branching through a great many
"provinces: King's knowledge of all Literature, new and
"ancient, 'perfectly astonishing to me;' and I myself, the
"swift-speaking Gottsched, rather copious than otherwise.
"Catastrophe, and summary of the whole, was: Gottsched
"undertook to translate the Rousseau Stanza into German of
"moderate softness; and, by the aid of water did so, that

* Next Year, in a principal Leipzig Magazine, with name signed: given in *Helden-Geschichte*, iv. 728-739, (with multifarious commentaries and flourishings, denoting an attentive world). Nicolai, *Anekdoten*, iii. 286-290.

** Nicolai, *Anekdoten*, iii. 287.

"very night;* sent it next day, and had 'within an hour' a
"gracious Royal Answer in verse; calling one, incidentally,
"'Saxon Swan, *Cygne Saxon*,' though one is such a Goose!
"'Majesty to march at seven tomorrow morning,' said a
"Postscript, — no Interviewing more, at present.

"About ten days after" (not to let this thing interrupt us
again), "Friedrich, on his return to Leipzig, had another
"Interview with Gottsched; of only one hour, this time; —
"but with many topics: Reading of some Gottsched Ode
"(*Ode*, very tedious, frothy, watery, *of Thanks* to Majesty
"for such goodness to the Saxon Swan; reading, too, of
"'some of Madam Gottsched's Pieces'). Majesty confessed
"afterwards, Every hour from the very first had lowered his
"opinion of the Saxon Swan, till at length Gooschood became
'too apparent. Friedrich sent him a gold snuffbox by and
"by, but had no further dialoguing.

"A saying of Excellency Mitchell's to Gottsched, — for
"Gottsched, on that second Leipzig opportunity, went swash-
"ing about among the King's Suite as well, — is still re-
"membered. They were talking of Shakespeare: 'Genial,
"if you will,' said Gottsched, 'but the Laws of Aristotle;
"Five Acts, unities strict!' — 'Aristotle? What is to hinder
"a man from making his Tragedy in Ten acts, if it suit
"him better?' 'Impossible, your Excellency!' — 'Pooh,'
"said his Excellency; 'suppose Aristotle, and general
"Fashion too, had ordered that the clothes of every man
"were to be cut from five ells of cloth: how would the Herr
"Professor like' (with these huge limbs of his) 'if he found
"there were no breeches for him, on Aristotle's account?'
"Adieu to Gottsched; most voluminous of men; — who wrote
"a Grammar of the German Language, which, they say,
"did good. I remember always his poor Wife with some
"pathos; who was a fine, graceful, loyal creature, of ten
"times his intelligence; and did no end of writing and
"translating and compiling (Addison's *Cato*, Addison's
"*Spectator*, thousands of things from all languages), on
"order of her Gottsched, till life itself sank in such enter-
"prises; never doubting, tragically faithful soul, but her

* Copied duly in *Helden-Geschichte*, iv. 728.

[17th Oct. 1757.]

"Gottsched was an authentic Seneschal of Phœbus and the "Nine."*

Monday 17th, at seven, his Majesty pushed off accordingly; cheery he in the prospect of work, whatever his friends in the distance be. Here, from Eilenburg, his first stage Torgau way, are a Pair of Letters in notable contrast.

Wilhelmina to the King (on rumour of Haddick, swoln into a Triple Invasion, Austrian, Swedish, French).

Bairenth, "15th October 1757.

"MY DEAREST BROTHER, — Death and a thousand torments "could not equal the frightful state I am in. There run reports "that make me shudder. Some say you are wounded; others, "dangerously ill. In vain have I tormented myself to have "news of you; I can get none. Oh, my dear Brother, come "what may, I will not survive you. If I am to continue in this "frightful uncertainty, I cannot stand it; I shall sink under it, "and then I shall be happy. I have been on the point of "sending you a courier; but" (environed as we are) "I durst "not. In the name of God, bid somebody write me one word.
"I know not what I have written; my heart is torn in "pieces; I feel that by dint of disquietude and alarms I am "losing my wits. Oh, my dear, adorable Brother, have pity "on me. Heaven grant I be mistaken, and that you may scold "me; but the least thing that concerns you pierces me to the "heart, and alarms my affection too much. Might I die a "thousand times, provided you lived and were happy!
"I can say no more. Grief chokes me; and I can only "repeat that your fate shall be mine; being, my dear Brother, "your —   "WILHELMINA."

What a shrill penetrating tone, like the wildly weeping voice of Rachel; tragical, painful, gone quite to falsetto and

* Her *Letters*, collected by a surviving Lady-Friend, "*Briefe der Frau Luise Adelgunde Viktorie Gottsched*, born *Kulmus* (Dresden, 1771-1772, 6 vols. 8vo)," are, I should suppose, the only Gottsched Piece which anybody would now think of reading.

above pitch; but with a melody in its dissonance like the singing of the stars. My poor shrill Wilhelmina!—

King to Wilhelmina (has not yet received the Above).

"Ellenburg, 17th October 1757.

"MY DEAREST SISTER,— What is the good of philosophy "unless one employ it in the disagreeable moments of life? "It is then, my dear Sister, that courage and firmness "avail us.

"I am now in motion; and having once got into that, you "may calculate I shall not think of sitting down again, except "under improved omens. If outrage irritates even cowards, "what will it do to hearts that have courage?

"I foresee I shall not be able to write again for perhaps six "weeks: which fails not to be a sorrow to me: but I entreat "you to be calm during these turbulent affairs, and to wait "with patience the month of December; paying no regard to "the Nürnberg Newspapers nor to those of the Reich, which "are totally Austrian.

"I am tired as a dog (*comme un chien*). I embrace you with "my whole heart; being with the most perfect affection "(*tendresse*), my dearest Sister, your"— FRIEDRICH.

* * (*at some other hour, same place and day.*) "'No possi-"bility of Peace,' say your accounts" (Letter lost); "'the "French won't hear my name mentioned.' Well; from me "they shall not farther. The way will be, to speak to them "by action, so that they may repent their impertinences and "pride."*

The Haddick affair, after all the rumour about it, proved to be a very small matter. No Swede or Richelieu had dreamt of coöperating; Haddick, in the end, was scarce 4,000 with four cannon; General Rochow, Commandant of Berlin, with his small garrison, had not Haddick skilfully slidden through woods, and been so magnified by rumour, might have marched out, and beaten a couple of Haddicks. As it was, Haddick skil-

* *Œuvres de Frédéric*, XXVII. i. 308, 309, 310.

fully emerging, at the Silesian Gate of Berlin, 16th October, about eleven in the morning, demanded ransom of 300,000 thalers (45,000 *l.*); was refused; began shooting on the poor palisades, on the poor drawbridge there; "at the third shot brought down the drawbridge;" rushed into the suburb; and was not to be pushed out again by the weak party Rochow sent to try it. Rochow, ignorant of Haddick's force, marched off thereupon for Spandau with the Royal Family and effects; leaving Haddick master of the suburb, and Berlin to make its own bargain with him. Haddick, his Croats not to be quite kept from mischief, remained master of the suburb, minatory upon Berlin, for twelve hours or more: and after a good deal of bargaining, — ransom of 45,000 *l.*, of 90,000 *l.*, finally of 27,000 *l.* and "two dozen pair of gloves to the Empress Queen," — made off about five in the morning; wind of Moritz's advance adding wings to the speed of Haddick.*

Moritz did arrive next evening (18th); but with his tired troops there was no catching of Haddick, now three marches ahead. Royal Family and effects returned from Spandau the day following; but in a day or two more, removed to Magdeburg till the Capital were safe from such affronts. Much grumbling against Rochow. "What could I do? How could I know?" answered Rochow, whose eyesight indeed had been none of the best. Berlin smarts to the length of 27,000 *l.* and an alarm; but asserts (not quite mythically, thinks Retzow), that "the two dozen pair of gloves were all gloves for the left hand," — Berlin having wit, and a touch of *absinthe* in it, capable of such things! Friedrich heard the news

* *Helden-Geschichte*, iv. 715-722 (Haddick's own Account, and the Berlin one).

at Annaburg, a march beyond Torgau; and there paused, again uncertain, for about a week coming; after which, he discovered that Leipzig would be the place; and returned thither, appointing a general rendezvous and concentration there.

Scene at Regensburg in the Interim.

Just while Haddick was sliding swiftly through the woods, Berlin now nigh, there occurred a thing at Regensburg; tragic thing, but ending in farce, — Finale of *Reichs-Acht*, in short; — about which all Regensburg was loud, wailing or haha-ing according to humour; while Berlin was paying its ransom and left-hand gloves. One moment's pause upon this, though our haste is great.

"Reichs Diet had got its Ban of the Reich ready for "Friedrich; *Citatio* (solemn Summons) and all else complete; "nothing now wanted but to serve Citatio on him, or 'in-"sinuate' it into him, as their phrase is; — which latter "essential point occasions some shaking of wigs. Dangerous, "serving Citatio in that quarter: and by what art, try to "smuggle it into the hands of such a one? 'Insinuate it into "Plotho's hand; that is the method, and that will suffice!' say "the wigs, and choose an unfortunate Reichs Notary, Dr. "Aprill, to do it; who, in ponderous Chancery-style gives the "following affecting report, — wonderful, but intelligible "(when abridged):

"*Citatio*" to come and receive your Ban, — a very solemn-sounding Document, commencing (or perhaps it is Aprill himself that so commences, no matter which), 'In the Name of 'the Most High God, the Father, Son and Holy Ghost, Amen,' — "was given, Wednesday 12th October, in the Year after "Christ our dear Lord and Saviour's Birth, 1757 Years, To "me Georgius Mathias Josephus Aprill, sworn Kaiserlich "Notarius Publicus; In my Lodging, first floor fronting south, "in Jacob Virnrohr the Innkeeper's House here at Regens-"burg, called the Red-Star," for insinuation into Plotho:

With which solemn Piece, Aprill proceeded next day, Thursday, half-past 2 P.M., to Plotho's dwelling-place, described with equal irrefragability; and, continues Aprill, "did "there, by a servant of the Herr Ambassador von Plotho's, "announce myself; adding that I had something to say to his "Excellency, if he would please to admit me. To which the "Herr Ambassador by the same servant sent answer, that he "was ill with a cold, and that I might speak to his Secretarius "what I had to say. But, as I replied that my message was to "his Excellenz in person, the same servant came back with "intimation that I might call again tomorrow at noon."

Tomorrow, at the stroke of noon, Friday 14th October, Aprill punctually appears again, with recapitulation of the pledge given him yesterday; and is informed that he can walk up stairs. "I proceeded thereupon, the servant going before, "up one pair of stairs, or with the appurtenances (*Gezeugen*) "rather more than one pair, into the Herr Ambassador Frei- "herr von Plotho's Ante-room; who, just as we were entering, "stept-in himself, through a side-door; in his dressing-gown, "and with the words, 'Speak now what you have to say.'

"I thereupon slipt into his hand *Citatio Fiscalis*, and said" —said at first nothing, Plotho avers; merely mumbled, looked like some poor caitiff, come with Law-papers on a trifling Suit we happen to have in the Courts here; — and only by degrees said (let us abridge; *Scene*, Aprill and Plotho, Ante-room in Regensburg, first-floor and rather higher):

Aprill. "'I have to give your Excellenz this Writing,'" — (which privately, could your Excellenz guess it, is) "'*Citatio* "'*Fiscalis* from the Reichstag, summoning his Majesty to show "'cause why Ban of the Reich should not pass upon him!' His "Excellenz at first took the *Citatio* and adjuncts from me; and "looking into them to see what they were, his Excellenz's face "began to colour, and soon after to colour a little more; and "on his looking attentively at *Citatio Fiscalis* he broke into "violent anger and rage, so that he could not stand still any "longer; but with burning face, and both arms held aloft, "rushed close to me, *Citatio* and adjuncts in his right hand, "and broke out in this form:

"*Plotho.* 'What; insinuate (*insinuieren*), you scoundrel!'

"*Aprill.* 'It is my Notarial Office; I must do it.' In spite of

"which the Freiherr von Plotho fell on me with all rage;
"grasped me by the front of the cloak, and said:

"*Plotho.* 'Take it back, wilt thou!' And as I resisted doing
"so, he stuck it in upon me, and shoved it down with all
"violence between my coat and waistcoat; and, still holding
"me by the cloak, called to the two servants who had been
"there, 'Fling him down stairs!'—which they, being discreet
"fellows, and in no flurry, did not quite, nor needed quite to
"do ('Must, sir, you see, unless!'), and so forced me out of the
"house; Excellenz Plotho retiring through his Ante-room,
"and his Body-servant, who at first had been on the stairs,
"likewise disappearing as I got under way,"—and have to
report, in such manner, to the Universe and Reichs Diet, with
tears in my eyes.*

What became of Reichs Ban after this, ask not. It fell
dead by Friedrich's victories now at hand; rose again into life
on Friedrich's misfortunes (August 1758), threatening to include George Second in it; upon which the *Corpus Evangelicorum* made some counter-mumblement;—and, I have heard,
the French privately advised: "Better drop it; these two Kings
are capable of walking out of you, and dangerously kicking
the table over as they go!"— Whereby it again fell dead,
positively for the last time, and, in short, is worth no mention
or remembrance more.

Corpus Evangelicorum had always been against Reichs
Ban; a few Dissentients, or Half-Dissentients excepted,—as
Mecklenburg wholly and with a will; foolish Anspach wholly;
and the Anhalts haggling some dissent, and retracting it (why,
I never knew);— for which Mecklenburg and the Anhalts,
lying within clutch of one, had to repent bitterly in the years
coming! Enough of all that.

The Haddick invasion, which had got its gloves,
left-hand or not, and part of its road expenses, brought
another consequence much more important on the *per
contra* side. The triumphing, *te-deum*-ing and jubilation over it,—"His Metropolis captured; Royal Family
in flight!"— raised the Dauphiness Army, and espe-

* Preuss, ii. 397-401; in *Helden-Geschichte,* iv. 745-9, Plotho's Account.

cially Versailles, into such enthusiasm, that Dauphiness came bodily out (on order from Versailles); spread over the Country, plundering and insulting beyond example; got herself reinforced by a 15,000 from the Richelieu Army; crossed the Saale; determined on taking Leipzig, beating Friedrich, and I know not what. Keith, in Leipzig with a small Party, had summons from Soubise's vanguard (October 24th): Keith answered, He would burn the suburbs; — upon which, said vanguard, hearing of Friedrich's advent withal, took itself rapidly away. And Soubise and it would fain have recrossed Saale, I have understood, had not Versailles been peremptory.

In a word, Friedrich arrived at Leipzig, October 26th; Ferdinand, Moritz, and all the others, coming or already come: and there is something great just at hand. Friedrich's stay in Leipzig was only four days. Cheering prospect of work now ahead here; — add to this, assurance from Preussen that Apraxin is fairly going home, and Lehwald coming to look after the Swedes. Were it not that there is bad news from Silesia, things generally are beginning to look up.

Of the hour spent on Gottsched, in these four days, we expressly take no notice farther; but there was another visit much less conspicuous, and infinitely more important: that of a certain Hanoverian Graf von Schulenburg, not in red or with plumes, like a Major-General as he was, but "in the black suit of a Country Parson," — coming, in that unnoticeable guise, to inform Friedrich officially, "That the Hanoverians and Majesty of England have resolved to renounce the Convention of Kloster-Zeven; to bring their poor Stade Army into the field again; and do now request him, King Friedrich, to grant them Duke Ferdinand of Brunswick to be General of the same."*

Here is an unnoticeable message, of very high moment indeed. To which Friedrich, already prepared, gives his cheerful consent; nominations and practicalities to follow, the instant these present hurries are over. Who it was that had prepared all this, whose suggestion it first was, Friedrich's, Mitchell's, George's, Pitt's, I do not know, — I cannot help suspecting Pitt; Pitt and Friedrich together. And certainly of all living men, Ferdinand, — related to the English and Prussian royalties, a soldier of approved excellence, and likewise a noble-minded, prudent, patient and invincibly valiant and stedfast man, — was, beyond comparison, the fittest for this office. Pitt is now fairly in power; and perceives, — such Pitt's originality of view, — that an Army *with* a Captain to it may differ beautifully from one without. And in fact we may take this as the first twitch at the reins, on Pitt's part; whose delicate strong hand, all England running to it with one heart, will be felt at the ends of the earth before many months go. To the great and unexpected joy of Friedrich, for one. "England has taken long to produce a great man," he said to Mitchell; "but here is one at last!"

---

* Mauvillon, i. 256; Westphalen, i. 315; indistinct both, and with slight variations. Mitchell Papers (in British Museum), likewise indistinct: Additional Mss., 6815, pp. 96 and 106 ("Lord Holderness to Mitchell," doubtless on Pitt's instigation, "10th October 1757," is the *beginning* of it, — two days before Royal Highness got home from Stade); see ib. 6806, pp. 241-252.

CHAPTER VIII.

BATTLE OF ROSSBACH.

FRIEDRICH left Leipzig, Sunday October 30th; encamped, that night, on the famous Field of Lützen; with the vanguard, he (as usual, and Mayer with him, who did some brisk smiting home of what French there were); Keith and Duke Ferdinand following, with main body and rear.

Movements on the Soubise-Hildburghausen part are all retrograde again; — can Dauphiness Bellona do nothing, then, except shuttle forwards and then backwards according to Friedrich's absence or presence? The Soubise-Hildburghausen Army does immediately withdraw on this occasion, as on the former; and makes for the safe side of the Saale again, rapidly retreating before Friedrich, who is not above one to two of them, — more like one to three, now that Broglio's Detachment is come to hand. Broglio got to Merseburg, October 26th, — guess 15,000 strong; — considerably out of repair, and glad to have done with such a march, and be within reach of Soubise. This is the Second Son of our old Blusterous Friend; a man who came to some mark, and to a great deal of trouble, in this War; and ended, readers know how, at the Siege of the Bastille forty years afterwards!

So soon as rested, Broglio, by order, moves leftwards to Halle, to guard Saale Bridge there; Soubise himself edging after him to Merseburg, on a similar errand; and leaving Hildburghausen to take charge of Weissenfels and the Third Saale Bridge. That is Dauphiness's posture while Friedrich encamps at Lützen: — let impatient human nature fix these three places for itself, and hasten to the catastrophe of wretched Dauphiness. Soubise, it ought to be remembered, is not in the highest spirits; but his Officers in over-high, "Doing "this *petit* Marquis de Brandebourg the honour to have "a kind of War with him (*de lui faire une espèce de* "*guerre*)," as they term it. Being puffed up with general vanity, and the newspaper rumour about Haddick's feat, — which, like the gloves it got, is going all to left-hand in this way. Hildburghausen and the others overrule Soubise; and indeed there is no remedy: "Provision almost out; — how retreat to our magazines and our fastnesses, with Friedrich once across Saale, and sticking to the skirts of us?" Here, from eye-witnesses where possible, are the successive steps of Dauphiness towards her doom, which is famous in the world ever since.

"Monday, 31st October 1757," as the Town-Syndic of Weissenfels records, "about eight in the morning,[*] "the King of Prussia, with his whole Army" (or what seemed to us the whole, though it was but a half; Keith with the other half being within reach to northward, marching Merseburg way), "came before this Town." Has been here before; as Keith has, as Soubise and others have: a town much agitated lately by transit of troops. It was from the eastern, or high landward side, where the so-called Castle is, that Friedrich came:

[*] Müller, *Schlacht bei Rossbach* ("a Centenary Piece," Berlin, 1857, — containing several curious Extracts), p. 44; *Holden-Geschichte,* iv. 643, 651-669.

Castle built originally on some "White Crag (*Weisse Fels*," not now conspicuous), from which the town and whilom Duchy take their name.

"We have often heard of Weissenfels, while the poor old "drunken Duke lived, who used to be a Suitor of Wilhelmina's, "liable to hard usage; and have marched through it, with the "Salzburgers, in peaceable times. A solid pleasant-enough "little place (6,000 souls or so); lies leant against high ground "(White Crags, or whatever it once was) on the eastern or "right bank of the Saale; a Town in part flat, in part very "steep; the streets of it, or main street and secondaries, "running off level enough from the River and Bridge; rising "by slow degrees, but at last rapidly against the high ground "or cliffs, just mentioned; a stiff acclivity of streets, till "crowned by the so-called Castle, the 'Augustus Burg' in "those days, the 'Friedrich-Wilhelm Barrack' in ours. It "was on this crown of the cliffs that his Prussian Majesty "appeared.

"Saale is of good breadth here; has done perhaps two "hundred miles, since he started, in the Fichtelgebirge (*Pine "Mountains*), on his long course Elbe-ward; received, only ten "miles ago, his last big branch, the wide-wandering Unstrut, "coming in with much drainage from the northern parts: — "in breadth, Saale may be compared to Thames, to Tay or "Beauley; his depth not fordable, though nothing like so deep "as Thames's; main cargo visible is rafts of timber: banks "green, definite, scant of wood: river of rather dark com- "plexion, mainly noiseless, but of useful pleasant qualities "otherwise."

From this Castle or landward side come Friedrich and his Prussians, on Monday morning about eight. "The garrison, some 4,000 Reichs folk and a French "Battalion or two, shut the Gates, and assembled in "the Market-place," — a big square, close at the foot of the Heights; "on the other hand, from the top of "the Heights (*Klammerk*, the particular spot), the Prus- "sians cannonaded Town and Gates; to speedy bursting "open of the same; and rushed in over the walls of "the Castle-court, and by other openings into the Town: "so that the Garrison above-said had to quit, and roll "with all speed across the Saale Bridge, and set the "same on fire behind them." This was their remedy for all the Three Bridges, when attacked; but it succeeded nowhere so well as here.

"The fire was of extreme rapidity; prepared be-"forehand:" Bridge all of dry wood coated with pitch — "fire reinforced too, in view of such event, by all "the suet, lard and oleaginous matter the Garrison "could find in Weissenfels; some hundredweights of "tallow-dips, for one item, going up on this occasion." Bridge "worth 100,000 thalers," is instantly ablaze: some 400 finding the Bridge so flamy, and the Prussians at their skirts, were obliged to surrender; — Feldmarschall Hildburghausen, sleeping about two miles off, gets himself awakened in this unpleasant manner. Flying garrison halt on the other side of the River, where the rest of their Army is; plant cannon there, against quenching of the Bridge; and so keep firing, answered by the Prussians, with much noise and no great mischief, till 3 P.M., when the Bridge is quite gone (Tollkeeper's Lodge and all), and the enterprise of crossing there had plainly become impossible.

Friedrich quickly, about a mile farther down the River, has picked out another crossing-place, in the interim, and founded some new adequate plank or raft bridge there; which, by diligence all night, will be crossable tomorrow. So that, except for amusing the enemy, the cannonading may cease at Weissenfels. A certain Duc de Crillon, in command at this Weissenfels Bridge-burning and cannonade, has a chivalrous Anecdote (amounting nearly to zero when well examined) about saving or sparing Friedrich's life on this interesting occasion: How, being now on the safe side of the River, he Crillon with his staff taking some refection of breakfast after the furious flurry there had been; there came to him one of his Artillery Captains, stationed in an Island in the River, asking, "Shall I shoot the King of Prussia, Monseigneur? He is down reconnoitering his end of the Bridge: shan't I then?" To whom Crillon gives a glass of wine, and smilingly magnanimous answer to a negative effect.* Concerning which, one has to remark, Not only *first*, that the Artillery Captain's power of seeing Friedrich (which is itself uncertain) would indeed mean the power of aiming at him, but differs immensely from that of hitting him with shot; so that this "Shall I kill the King?" was mainly thrasonic wind from Captain Bertin. But *secondly*, that there is no "Island" in the River thereabouts, for Captain Bertin to fire from! So that probably the whole story is wind or little more: dreamlike, or at best, some idle thrasonic-theoretic question, on the part of Bertin; proper answer thereto (consisting mainly in a glass of wine) from Monseigneur: — all which, on retrospection, Monseigneur feels, or would fain feel, to have been not theoretic-thrasonic but practical, and of a rather godlike nature. Zero mainly, as we said; Friedrich thanks you for zero, Monseigneur.

"The Prussians were billeted in the Town that "night," says our Syndic; "and in many a house there "came to be twenty men, and even thirty and above "it, lodged. All was quiet through the night, the

* "*Mémoires militaires de Louis &c. Duc de Crillon* (Paris, 1791), p. 166;"
— as cited by Preuss, II. 88.

"French and the Reichs folk were drawn back upon "the higher grounds, about Burgwerben and on to "Tagwerben; and we saw their watchfires burning." Friedrich's Bridge meanwhile, unmolested by the enemy, is getting ready.

Keith, looking across to Merseburg on the morrow morning (Tuesday, Nov. 1st), whither he had marched direct with the other Half of the Army, finds Merseburg Bridge destroyed, or broken; and Soubise with batteries on the farther side, intending to dispute the passage. Keith despatches Duke Ferdinand to Halle, another twelve miles down, who finds Halle Bridge destroyed in like manner, and Broglio intending to dispute; which, however, on second thoughts, neither of them did. Friedrich's new Bridge at Herren-Mühle (*Lordships' Mill*) is of course an important point to them; Friedrich's passage now past dispute! "Let us fall back," say they, "and rank ourselves a little; we are 50 or 60,000 strong; ill off for provisions, but well able to retreat; and have permission to fight on this side of the River."

The combined Army, "Dauphiness," or whatever we are to call it, does on Wednesday morning (November 2d) gather-in its cannon and outskirts, and give up the Saale question; retire landwards to the higher grounds some miles; and diligently get itself united, and into order of battle better or worse, near the Village of Mücheln (which means Kirk *Michael*, and is still written "*Sanct Michel*" by some on this occasion). There Dauphiness takes post, leaning on the heights, not in a very scientific way; leaving Keith and Ferdinand to rebuild their Bridges unmolested, and all Prussians to come across at discretion. Which they have diligently done (2d-3d November), by their respective Bridges; and on Thursday afternoon are all across, encamped at Bedra, in close neighbourhood to Mücheln; which Friedrich has been out reconnoitering, and finds that he can attack next morning very early.

Next morning, accordingly, "by two o'clock, with a bright moon shining," Friedrich is on horseback, his Army following. But on examining by moonlight, the enemy have shifted their position; turned on their axis, more or less, into new wood-patches, new batteries and bogs; which has greatly mended their affair. No good attacking them so, thinks Friedrich; and returns to his Camp; slightly cannonaded, one wing of him, from some battery of the enemy; and immoderately crowed over by them: "Dare not, you see! Tried, and was defeated!" cry their newspapers and they, — for one day. Friedrich lodges again in Bedra this night, others say in Rossbach; shifts his own Camp a little; left wing of it now at Rossbach (*Horse-Brook* or *Beck*, soon to be a world-famous Hamlet): the effects of hunger on the Dauphiness, so far from her supplies, will, he calculates, be stronger than on him, and will bring her to better terms shortly. Dauphiness needs bread; one may have fine clipping at the skirts of her, if she try retreat. That Dauphiness would play the prank she did next morning, Friedrich had not ventured to calculate.

Catastrophe of Dauphiness (Saturday, 5th November 1757).

Meandering Saale is on one of his big turns, as he passes Weissenfels; turning, pretty rapidly here, from south-eastward, which he was a dozen miles ago, round to north-eastward or northward altogether, which he gets to be at Merseburg, a dozen farther down. Right across from Weissenfels, lapped in this crook of the Saale, or washed by it on south side and on east, rises, with extreme laziness, a dull circular lump of country, six or eight miles in diameter; with Rossbach and half-a-dozen other scraggy sleepy Hamlets scattered on it; — which, till the morning of Saturday 5th November 1757, had not been notable to any visitor. The topmost point or points, for there are two (not discoverable except by tradition and guess), the country-people do call Hills, *Janus-Hügel*, *Pölzen-Hügel*, — Hill sensible to wagon-horses in those bad loose tracks of sandy mud, but unimpressive on the Tourist, who has to admit that there seldom was so flat a Hill. Rising, let us guess, forty yards in the three or four miles it has had. Might be called a perceptibly potbellied plain, with more propriety; flat country, slightly puffed up; — in shape not steeper than the mould of an immense tea-saucer would be. Tea-saucer 6 miles in diameter, 100 feet in depth, and of irregular contour, which indeed will sufficiently represent it to the reader's mind.

Saale, at four or five miles distance, bounds this scraggy lump on the east and on the south. Westward and northward, springing about Mücheln on each hand, and setting off to right and to left Saale-ward, are what we take to be two brooks; at least are two hollows: and behind these, the country rises higher; undulating still on lazy terms, but now painted azure by the distance, not unpleasant to behold, with its litter all lapped out of sight, and its poor brooks tinkling forward (as we judge) into the Saale, Merseburg way, or reverse-wise into the Unstrut, the last big branch of Saale. Southward from our Janus Height, eight or nine miles off, may be seen some vestige of Freiburg; steeple or gilt weathercock faintly visible, on the Unstrut yonder; — which I take to be Soubise's bread-basket at present. And farther off, and opposite the *mouth* of the Unstrut, well across the Saale, lies another nameable Town (visible in clear weather, as a smoke-cloud at certain hours, about meal-time, when the kettles are on boil), the Town of Naumburg, — one of several German Naumburgs, — the Naumburg of Gustaf Adolf; where his slain body lay, on the night of Lützen Battle, with his poor Queen and others weeping over it. Naumburg is on the other side of Saale, not of importance to Soubise in such posture.

This is the circular block or lump of country, on the north or north-west side of which Friedrich now lies, and which will become, he little thinks how memorable on the morrow. Over the heights, immediately eastward of Friedrich, there is a kind of hollow, or scooped-out place; shallow valley of some extent, which deserves notice against tomorrow; but in general the ground is lazily spherical, and without noticeable hollows or valleys when fairly away from the River. A dull blunt lump of country; made of sand and mud, — may have been grassy once, with broom on it, in the pastoral times; is now under poor plough-husbandry, arable or scratchable in all parts, and looks rather miserable in winter-time. No vestige of hedge on it, of shrub or bush; one tree, ugly but big, which may have been alive in Friedrich's time, stands not far from Rossbach Hamlet; one, and no more discoverable in these areas.

Various Hamlets lie sprinkled about: very sleepy, rusty, irregular little places; huts and cattle-stalls huddled down, as if shaken from a bag; much straw, thick thatch and crumbly mud-brick; but looking warm and peaceable; for the Fourfooted and the Twofooted; which latter, if you speak to them, are solid reasonable people, with energetic German eyes and hearts, though so ill-lodged. These Hamlets, needing shelter and spring water, stand generally in some slight hollow, if well up the Height, as Rossbach is; sometimes, if near the bottom, they are nestled in a sudden dell or gash, — work of the primeval rains, accumulating from above, and ploughing out their way. The rains, we can see, have been busy; but there is seldom the least stream visible, bottom being too sandy and porous. On the western slope, there is in our time a kind of coal, or coal-dust, dug up; in the way of quarrying, not of mining; and one or two big chasms of this sort are confusedly busy; the natives mix this valuable coal-dust with water, mould into bricks, and so use as fuel: one of the features of these hamlets is the strange black bricks, standing on edge about the cottage-doors, to drip, and dry in the sun. For this or for other reasons, the westward slope appears to be the best; and has a major share of hamlets on it: Rossbach is high up, and looks over upon Mücheln, and its dim belfry and appurtenances, which lie safe across the hollow, perhaps two miles off, — safe from Friedrich, if there were eatables and lodging to be had in such a place. Friedrich's left wing is in Rossbach. Bedra where Friedrich's right wing is; Branderode where the Soubise right is, then Gröst, Schevenroda, Zeuchfeld, Pettstädt, Lunstädt, — especially Reichartswerben, where Soubise's right will come to be: these the reader may take note of in his Map. Several of them lie in ashes just then; plundered, replundered, and at last set fire to; so busy have Soubise's hungry people been, of late, in the Country they came to "deliver." The Freiburg road, the Naumburg road, both towards Merseburg, cross this Height; straight like the string, Saale by Weissenfels being the bow.

The *Herrenhaus* (Squire's Mansion) still stands in Rossbach, with the littery Hamlet at its flank: a high, pavilion-roofed, and though dilapidated, pretentious kind of House; some kind of court round it, some kind of hedge or screen of brushwood and brickwall: terribly in need of the besom, it and its environment throughout. King, I suppose, did lodge there overnight: certain it is the Squire was absent; and the Squire's Man, three days afterwards, reported to him as follows: * * "Satur-"day the 5th, about 8 A.M., his Majesty mounted to "the roof of the Herrenhaus here, some tiles having "been removed" (for that end, or by accident, is not said), "and saw how the French and Reichs Army "were getting in movement," — wriggling out of their Camp leftwards, evidently aiming towards Gröst. "In "about an hour, near half their Army was through "Gröst, and had turned southward, rather south-east-"ward, from Gröst, out in the Rossbach and Almsdorf "region, and proceeding still towards Pettstädt," — towards Schevenroda more precisely, not towards Pettstädt yet. "His Majesty looked always through the "perspective: and to me was the grace done to be ever "at his side, and to name for him the roads the French "and Reichs Army was marching." *

* Müller, p. 50; Rödenbeck, p. 326.

The King had heard of this phenomenon hours before, and had sent out hussars and scouts upon it; but now sees it with his eyes: — "Going for Freiburg, and their bread-cupboard," thinks the King; who does not as yet make much of the movement; but will watch it well, and calculates to have a stroke at the rear end of it, in due season. With which view, the cavalry, Seidlitz and Mayer, are ordered to saddle; foot regiments, and all else, to be in readiness. This French-Reichs Dauphiness is not rapid in her field-exercise; and has a great deal of wriggling and unwinding before she can fairly pick herself out, and get forward towards Schevenroda on the Freiburg road. In three or in two parallel columns, artillery between them, horse ahead, horse arear; haggling along there; — making for their breadbaskets, thinks the King. A body of French, horse chiefly, under St. Germain, come out, in the Schortau-Almsdorf part, with some salvoing and prancing, as if intending to attack about Rossbach, where our left wing is: but his Majesty sees it to be a pretence merely: and St. Germain, motionless, and doing nothing but cannonade a little, seems to agree that it is so. Dauphiness continues her slow movements; King, in this Squire's Mansion of Rossbach, sits down to dinner, dinner with Officers at the usual hour of noon, — little dreaming what the Dauphiness has in her head.

Truth is, the Dauphiness is in exultant spirits, this morning; intending great things against a certain "little Marquis of Brandenburg," to whom one does so much honour. Generals looking down yesterday on the King of Prussia's Camp, able to count every man in it (and half the men being invisible, owing to bends of the ground), counted him to 10,000 or so; and had said, "Pshaw, are not we above 50,000; let us end it! Take him on his left. Round yonder, till we get upon his left, and even upon his rear withal, St. Germain coöperating on the other side of him: on left, on rear, on front, at the same moment, is not that a sure game?" A very ticklish game, answers surly sagacious Lloyd: "No general will permit himself to be taken in flank "with his eyes open; and the King of Prussia is the "unlikeliest you could try it with!"

Trying it meanwhile they are; marching along by the low grounds here, intending to sweep gradually leftwards towards Janus-Hill quarter; there to sweep home upon him, coil him up, left and rear and front, in their boa-constrictor folds, and end his trifle of an Army and him. "Why not, if we do our duty at all, annihilate his trifle of an Army; take himself prisoner, and so end it?" Report says, Soubise had really, in some moment of enthusiasm lately, warned the Versailles populations to expect such a thing; and that the Duchess of Orleans, forgetful of poor King Louis's presence, had, in *her* enthusiasm, exclaimed: "*Tant mieux*, I shall at last see a King, then!" But perhaps it is a mere French epigram, such as the winds often generate there, and put down for fact. — Friedrich's retreat to Weissenfels is cut off for Friedrich: an Austrian party has been at the Herren-Mühle Bridge this morning, has torn it up and pitched it into the river; planks far on to Merseburg by this time. And, in fact, unless Friedrich be nimble — But that he usually is.

Friedrich's dinner had gone on with deliberation for about two hours, Friedrich's intentions not yet known to any, but everybody, great and small, waiting eagerly for them, like greyhounds on the slip, — when Adjutant Gaudi, who had been on the Housetop the while, rushes into the Dining-room faster than he ought, and, with some tremor in his voice and eyes, reports hastily: "At Schevenroda, at Pettstädt yonder! Enemy has turned to left. Clearly for the left." — "Well, and if he do? No flurry needed, Captain!" answered Friedrich, — (*not* in these precise words; but rebuking Gaudi, with a look not of laughter wholly, and with a certain question, as to the state of Gaudi's stomachic part, which is still known in traditional circles, but is not mentionable here); — and went, with due gravity, himself to the roof, with his Officers. "To the left, sure enough; meaning to attack us there:" the thing Friedrich had despaired of is voluntarily coming, then; — and it is a thing of stern qualities withal; a wager of life, with glorious possibilities behind.

Friedrich earnestly surveys the phenomenon for some minutes; in some minutes, Friedrich sees his way through it, at least into it, and how he will do it. Off, eastward; march! Swift are his orders; almost still swifter the fulfilment of them. Prussian Army is a nimble article in comparison with Dauphiness! In half an hour's time, all is packed and to the road; and, except Mayer and certain Free-Corps or Light-Horse, to amuse St. Germain and his Almsdorf people, there is not a Prussian visible in these localities to French eyes. "At half-past two," says the Squire's Man, — or let us take him a sentence earlier, to lose nothing of such a Document: "At noon his Majesty took dinner; sat till "about two o'clock; then again went to the roof; and "perceived that the Enemy's Army at Pettstädt were "turning about the little Wood there north-eastward, "as if for Lunstädt" (into the Lunstädt road); — "such "cannonading, too," from those Almsdorf people, "that "the balls flew over our heads," — or I tremulously thought so. "At half-past two, the word was given, "March! And good speed they made about it, in this "Herrenhaus, and out of doors too, striking their tents, "and cording up and trimly shouldering everything "with incredible brevity," as if machinery were doing it; "and at three, on the Prussian part, all was packed "and out into the court for being carried off; and, in "fact, the Prussian Army was on march at three." Seidlitz, with all his Horse, vanishing round the corner of the Height; speeding along, invisible on his northern slope there, straight for the Janus-Pölzen Hill part; the Infantry following, double-quick; — well knowing, each, what he has got to do.

But at this interesting point, the Editors, — small thanks to them, authentic but thrice-stupid mortals, — cut short our Eye-witness, not so much as telling us his name, some of them not even his date or whereabouts; and so the curtain tumbles down (as if its string had been cut, or suddenly eaten by unwise animals), and we are left to gray hubbub, and our own resources at secondhand. Except only that a French Officer, — one of those cannonading from Almsdorf, no doubt, — declares that "it was like a change of "scene in the Opera (*décoration d'Opéra*),"* so very rapid; and that "they all rolled off eastward at quick "time." At extremely quick time; and soon, in the slight hollow behind Janus Hügel, vanished from sight

---

* Letter in *Müller*, p. 60. In *Westphalen* (n. 128-183) is a much superior French Letter, intercepted somewhere, and fallen to Duke Ferdinand; well worth reading, on Rossbach and the previous Affairs.

of these Almsdorf French, and of the Soubise-Hildburghausen Army in general. Which latter is agreeably surprised at the phenomenon; and draws a highly flattering conclusion from it. "Gone, then; off at double-quick for Merseburg; aha!" think the Soubise-Hildburghausen people: "Double-quick you too, my pretty men, lest they do whisk away, and we never get a stroke at them!" —

Seidlitz, meanwhile, with his cavalry (thirty-eight squadrons, about 4,000 horse), is rapidly doing the order he has had. Seidlitz at a sharp military trot, and the infantry at double-quick to keep up near him, which they cannot quite do, are, as we have said, making right across for the Pölzen-Hill and Janus-Hill quarter; their route the string, French route the bow; and are invisible to the French, owing to the heights between. Seidlitz, when he gets to the proper point eastward, will wheel about, front to southward, and be our left wing; infantry, as centre and right, will appear in like manner; and — we shall see!

The exultant Dauphiness, or Soubise-Hildburghausen Army (let us call it, for brevity's sake, Dauphiness or French, which it mainly was), on that rapid disappearance of the Prussians, never doubted but the Prussians were off on flight for Merseburg, to get across by the Bridge there. Whereat Dauphiness, doubly exultant, mended her own pace, cavalry at a sharp trot, infantry double-quick, but unable to keep up, — for the purpose of capturing or intercepting the runaway Prussians. Speed, my friends, — if you would do a stroke upon Friedrich, and show the Versailles people a King at last! Thus they, hurrying on, in two parallel columns, — infantry, long floods of it, coming double-quick but somewhat fallen behind; cavalry 7,000 or so, as vanguard, — faster and faster; sweeping forward on their southern side of the Janus-and-Pölzen slope, and now rather climbing the same.

Seidlitz has his hussar pickets on the top, to keep him informed as to their motions, and how far they are got. Seidlitz, invisible on the south slope of the Pölzen Hügel, finds about half-past 3 P. M., that he is now fairly ahead of Dauphiness; Seidlitz halts, wheels, comes to the top, "Got the flank of them, sure enough!" — and without waiting signal or farther orders, every instant being precious, rapidly forms himself; and plunges down on these poor people. "Compact as a wall, and with an incredible velocity (*d'une vitesse incroyable*)," says one of them. Figure the astonishment of Dauphiness; of poor Broglio, who commands the horse here. Taken in flank, instead of taking other people; intercepted, not in the least needing to intercept! Has no time to form, though he tried what he could. Only the two Austrian regiments got completely formed; the rest very incompletely; and Seidlitz, in the blaze of rapid steel, is in upon them. The two Austrian regiments, and two French that are named, made what debate was feasible; — courage nowise wanting, in such sad want of captaincy; nay Soubise in person galloped into it, if that could have helped. But from the first, the matter was hopeless; Seidlitz slashing it at such a rate, and plunging through it and again through it, thrice, some say four times: so that, in the space of half an hour, this luckless cavalry was all tumbling off the ground: plunging down hill, in full flight, across its own infantry or whatever obstacle, Seidlitz on the hips of it; and galloping madly over the horizon, towards Freiburg as it proved; and was not again heard of that day.

In about half an hour, that bit of work was over; and Seidlitz, with his ranks trimmed again, had drawn himself southward a little, into the Hollow of Tageswerben, there to wait impending phenomena. For Friedrich with the Infantry is now emerging over Janus Hill, in a highly thunderous manner, — eighteen pieces of artillery going, and "four big guns taken from the walls of Leipzig;" and there will be events anon. It is said, Hildburghausen, at the first glimpse of Friedrich over the hill-top, whispered to Soubise, "We are lost, Royal Highness!" — "Courage!" Soubise would answer; and both, let us hope, did their utmost in this extremely bad predicament they had got into.

Friedrich's artillery goes at a murderous rate; had come in view, over the hill-top, before Seidlitz ended, — "nothing but the muzzles of it visible" (and the fire-torrents from it) to us poor French below. Friedrich's lines; or rather his one line, mere tip of his left wing, — only seven battalions in it, five of them under Keith from the second or reserve line; whole centre and right wing standing "refused," in oblique rank, invisible, *behind* the Hill, — Friedrich's line, we say, the artillery to its right, shoots out in mysterious Prussian rhythm, in echelons, in potences, obliquely down the Janus-Hill side; straight, rigid, regular as iron clockwork; and strides towards us, silent, with the lightning sleeping in it: — Friedrich has got the flank of Dauphiness, and means to keep it. Once and again and a third time, poor Soubise, with his poor regiments much in an imbroglio, here heaped on one another, there with wide gaps, halt being so sudden, — attempts to recover the flank, and pushes out this regiment and the other, rightward, to be even with Friedrich. But sees with despair that it cannot be; that Friedrich with his echelons, potences and mysterious Prussian resources, pulls himself out like the pieces of a prospect-glass, piece after piece, hopelessly fast and seemingly no end to them; and that the flank is lost, and that — Unhappy Generals of Dauphiness, what a phenomenon for them! A terrible Friedrich, not fled to Merseburg at all; but mounted there on the Janus Hill, as on his saddle-horse, with face quite the other way; — and for holster-pistol, has plucked out twenty-two cannon. Clad verily in fire; Chimæra-like, *riding* the Janus Hill, in that manner; left leg (or wing) of him spurning us into the abysses, right one ready to help at discretion!

Hildburghausen, I will hope, does his utmost; Soubise, Broglio for certain do. The French line is in front, next the Prussians: poor Generals of Dauphiness are panting to retrieve themselves. But with regiments jammed in this astonishing way, and got collectively into the lion's throat, what can be done? Steady, rigid as iron clockwork, the Prussian line strides forward; at forty-paces distance, delivers its first shock of lightning, bursts into platoon fire; and so continues, steady at the rate of five shots a minute, — hard to endure by poor masses all in a coil. "The artillery tore down "whole ranks of us," says the Würtemberg Dragoon;* "the Prussian musketry did terrible execution."

Things began to waver very soon, French reeling back from the Prussian fire, Reichs troops rocking very uneasy, torn by such artillery; when, to crown the

* His Letter in *Müller*, p. 83.

matter, Seidlitz, seeing all things rock to the due extent, bursts out of Tageswerben Hollow, terribly compact and furious, upon the rear of them. Which sets all things into inextricable tumble; and the Battle is become a rout and a riding into ruin, no Battle ever more. Lasted twenty-five minutes, this second act of it, or till half-past four: after which, the curtains rapidly descending (Night's curtain, were there no other) cover the remainder; the only stage-direction, *Exeunt Omnes.* Which for a 50 or 60,000, ridden over by Seidlitz Horse, was not quite an easy matter! They left, of killed and wounded, near 3,000; of prisoners, 5,000 (Generals among them 8, Officers 300): in sum, about 8,000; not to mention cannon, 67 or 72; with standards, flags, kettledrums and meaner baggages *ad libitum* in a manner. The Prussian loss was, 165 killed, 376 wounded; — between a sixteenth and a fifteenth part of theirs: in number the Prussians had been little more than one to three; 22,000 of all arms, — not above half of whom ever came into the fire; Seidlitz and seven battalions doing all the fighting that was needed. St. Germain tried to cover the retreat; but "got broken," he says, — Mayer bursting in on him, — and soon went to slush like the others.

Seldom, almost never, not even at Crecy or Poictiers, was any Army better beaten. And truly, we must say, seldom did any better deserve it, so far as the Chief Parties went. Yes, Messieurs, this is the *petit Marquis de Brandebourg;* you will know this one, when you meet him again! The flight, the French part of it, was towards Freiburg Bridge; in full gallop, long after the chase had ceased; crossing of the Unstrut there, hoarse, many-voiced, all night; burning of the

Bridge; found burnt, when Friedrich arrived next morning. He had encamped at Obschütz, short way from the field itself. French Army, Reichs Army, all was gone to staves, to utter chaotic wreck. Hildburghausen went by Naumburg; crossed the Saale there; bent homewards through the Weimar Country; one wild flood of ruin, swift as it could go; at Erfurt "only one "regiment was in rank, and marched through with "drums beating." His Army, which had been disgustingly unhappy from the first, and was now fallen fluid on these mad terms, flowed all away in different rills, each by the course straightest home; and Hildburghausen arriving at Bamberg, with hardly the ghost or mutilated skeleton of an Army, flung down his truncheon, — "A murrain on your Reichs Armies and regimental chaoses!" — and went indignantly home. Reichs Army had to begin at the beginning again; and did not reappear on the scene till late next Year, under a new Commander, and with slightly improved conditions.

Dauphiness Proper was in no better case; and would have flowed home in like manner, had not home been so far, and the way unknown. Twelve thousand of them rushed straggling through the Eichsfeld; plundering and harrying, like Cossacks or Calmucks: "Army "blown asunder, over a circle of forty miles radius," writes St. Germain: "had the Enemy pursued us, after "I got broken" (burst in upon by Mayer and his Free-Corps people), "we had been annihilated. Never did "Army behave worse; the first cannon salvo decided "our rout and our shame." *

In two-days time (November 7th), the French had

---

* St. Germain to Verney: different Excerpts of Letters in the two weeks after Rossbach and before (given in Preuss, ii. 97).

got to Langensalza, fifty-five miles from the Battlefield of Rossbach; plundering, running, *sacre-dieu*-ing; a wild deluge of molten wreck, filling the Eichsfeld with its waste noises, making night hideous and day too;— in the villages, Placards were stuck up, appointing Nordhausen and Heiligenstadt for rallying-place.*

Soubise rode, with few attendants, all night towards Nordhausen, — eighty miles off, foot of the Brocken Country, where the Richelieu resources are; — Soubise with few attendants, face set towards the Brocken; himself, it is like, in a somewhat hag-ridden condition.

"The joy of poor Teutschland at large," says one of my Notes, "and how all Germans, Prussian and Anti-Prussian "alike, flung up their caps, with unanimous *Lebe-hoch*, at the "news of Rossbach, has often been remarked; and indeed is "still almost touching to see. The perhaps bravest Nation in "the world, though the least braggart, very certainly *ein* "*tapferes Volk* (as their Goethe calls them); so long insulted, "snubbed and trampled on, by a luckier, not a braver: — has "not your exultant Dauphiness got a beautiful little dose ad- "ministered her; and is gone off in foul shrieks, and pangs of "the interior, — let no man ask whitherward! '*Si un Allemand* "*peut avoir de l'esprit* (Can a German possibly have sharpness "of wits)?' Well, yes, it would seem: here is one German "graduate who understands his medicine-chest, and the "quality of patients! — Dauphiness got no pity anywhere; "plenty of epigrams, and mostly nothing but laughter even in "Paris itself. Napoleon long after, who much admires Fried- "rich, finds that this Victory of Rossbach was inevitable; 'but "what fills me with astonishment and shame,' adds he, 'is that "it was gained by six battalions and thirty squadrons' (seven "properly, and thirty-eight) 'over such a multitude!'**—It is "well known, Napoleon, after Jena, as if Jena had not been

* Müller, p. 73.
** Montholon, *Mémoires &c. de Napoléon* (Napoleon's *Précis des Guerres de Frédéric II*, vii. 210).

"enough for him, tore down the first Monument of Rossbach, "some poor ashlar Pyramid or Pillar, raised by the neigh- "bourhood, with nothing more afflictive inscribed on it than a "date; and sent it off in carts for Paris (where no stone of it "ever arrived, the Thüringen Carmen slinking off, and leaving "it scattered in different places over the face of Thüringen "in general); so that they had the trouble of a new one "lately."*

From Friedrich the "Army of the Circles," that is, Dauphiness and Company, — called *Hoopers* or "Coopers"(*Tonneliers*), with a desperate attempt at wit by pun, — get their Adieu in words withal. This is the famed *Congé de l'Armée des Cercles et des Tonneliers;* a short metrical Piece; called by Editors the most profane, most indecent, most &c.; and printed with asterisk veils thrown over the worst passages. Who shall dare, searching and rummaging for insight into Friedrich, and complaining that there is none, to lift any portion of the veil; and say "See — Faugh!" The cynicism, truly, but also the irrepressible honest exultation, has a kind of epic completeness, and fulness of sincerity; and, at bottom, the thing is nothing like so wicked as careless commentators have given out. Dare to look a little:

'*Adieu, grands écraseurs de rois,*' so it starts: "Adieu, grand "crushers of Kings; arrogant windbags, Turpin, Broglio, "Soubise, — Hildburghausen with the gray beard, foolish "still as when your beard was black in the Turk-War time:— "brisk journey to you all!" That is the first stanza; unexceptionable, had we room. The second stanza is, — with the veils partially lifted; with probably "*Mouse*" put into the first blank; and into the third, something of or belonging to "*César*," —

> " *Je vous ai vu comme* . . .
> " *Dans des ronces en certain lieu*
> " *Ent l'honneur de voir* . . .
> " *Ou comme au gré de sa luxure*
> " *Le bon Nicomède à l'écart*
> " *Aiguillonnait sa flamme impure*
> " *Des* . . . . . . "

Enough to say, the Author, with a wild burst of spiritual enthusiasm, sings the charms of the rearward part of certain

* Rödenbeck, *Beiträge*, i. 298; ib p. 885, Lithograph of the poor extinct Monument itself.

men; and what a royal ecstatic felicity there sometimes is in indisputable survey of the same. He rises to the heights of Anti-Biblical profanity, quoting Moses on the Hill of Vision; sinks to the bottomless of human or ultra-human depravity, quoting King Nicomedes's experiences on Cæsar (happily known only to the learned); and in brief, recognises that there is, on occasion, considerable beauty in that quarter of the human figure, when it turns on you opportunely. A most cynical, profane affair: yet, we must say by way of parenthesis, one which gives no countenance to Voltaire's atrocities of rumour about Friedrich himself in this matter; the reverse rather, if well read; being altogether theoretic, scientific; sings with gusto the glow of beauty you find in that unexpected quarter, — while *kicking* it deservedly and with enthusiasm. "To see the" — what shall we call it: seat of honour, in fact, "of your enemy:" has it not an undeniable charm? "I own to "you in confidence, O Soubise and Company, this fine laurel "I have got, and was so in need of, is nothing more or other "than the sight of your"—*four asterisks*. "Oblige me, when- "ever clandestine Fate brings us together, by showing me that" — always that, if you would give me pleasure when we meet. "And oh," next stanza says, "to think what our glory is founded "on,"—on view of that unmentionable object, I declare to you! — And through other stanzas, getting smutty enough (though in theory only), which we need not prosecute farther.* A certain heartiness and epic greatness of cynicism, life's naked- ness grown almost as if innocent again; an immense suppress- ed insuppressible Haha, on the part of this King. Strange *Te-Deum* indeed. Coming from the very heart, truly, as few of them do; but not, in other points, recommendable at all! — Here, of the night before, is something better:

To Wilhelmina.

"Near Weissenfels" (Obschütz, in fact; does not yet know what the Battle will be *called*), "5th November 1757.

"At last, my dear Sister, I can announce you a bit of good "news. You were doubtless aware, that the Coopers with "their circles had a mind to take Leipzig. I ran up, and

* *(Œuvres de Frédéric,* XIX. 70-78 (written at Freiburg, 6th November, when his Majesty got thither, and found the Bridge burnt).

"drove them beyond Saale. The Duc de Richelieu sent "them a reinforcement of twenty battalions and fourteen "squadrons" (say 15,000 horse and foot); "they then called "themselves 63,000 strong. Yesterday I went to reconnoitre "them; could not attack them in the post they held. This "had rendered them rash. Today they came out with the in- "tention of attacking me; but I took the start of them *(les ai* "*prévenu).* It was a Battle *en douceur* (soft to one's wish). "Thanks to God I have not a hundred men killed; the only "General ill wounded is Meinecke. My Brother Henri and "General Seidlitz have slight hurts" (gunshots, not so slight, that of Seidlitz) "in the arm. We have all the Enemy's "cannon, all the" * * "I am in full march to drive them "over the Unstrut" (already driven, your Majesty; bridge burning).

"You, my dear Sister, my good, my divine and af- "fectionate Sister" (faithful to the bone, in good truth, poor Wilhelmina), "who deign to interest yourself in the fate of a "Brother who adores you, deign also to share in my joy. The "instant I have time, I will tell you more. I embrace you "with my whole heart. Adieu. F." *

Ulterior Fate of Dauphiness; flies over the Rhine in bad Fashion; Dauphiness's Ways with the Saxon Populations in her Deliverance-Work.

Friedrich had no more fighting with the French. November 9th, at Merseburg, in all stillness, Duke Ferdinand got his Britannic Commission, his Full Powers, from Friedrich and the parties interested; in all still- ness, made his arrangements, as if for Magdeburg and his Governorship there, — Friedrich hastening off for Silesia the while. Duke Ferdinand did stay six days in Magdeburg, inspecting or pretending to inspect; very pleasant with his Sister and the Royalties that are now there; but at midnight of day sixth, shot off

* *Œuvres de Frédéric,* xxvii. 1. 010.

silently on wider errand. And, in sum, on Wednesday, 24th November 1757, appeared in Stade, on horseback at morning parade there; intimating, to what joy of the poor Brunswick Grenadiers and others, That he was come to take command; that Kloster-Zeven is abolished; that we are not an 'Observation Army,' rotting here in the parish pound, any longer, but an 'Allied Army' (such now our title), intending to strike for ourselves, and get out of pound straightway! —

"*Wednesday 24th November — Monday 29th.* Duke Fer-
"dinand did accordingly pick up the reins of this distracted
"Affair; and, in a way wonderful to see, shot sanity into
"every fibre of it; and kept it sane and road-worthy for the
"Five Years coming. With a silent velocity, an energy, an
"imperturbable stedfastness, and clear insight into cause and
"effect; which were creditable to the school he came from;
"and were a very joyful sight to Pitt and others concerned.
"So that from next Monday, 'November 29th, before day-
"light,' when Ferdinand's batteries began playing upon
"Harburg (French Fortress nearest to Stade), the reign of
"the French ceased in those Countries; and an astonished
"Richelieu and his French, lying scattered over all the West
"of Germany, in readiness for nothing but plunder, had to
"fall more or less distracted in their turn; and do a number of
"astonishing things. To try this and that, of futile, more or
"less frantic nature; be driven from post after post; be
"driven across the Aller first of all; — Richelieu to go
"home thereupon, and be succeeded by one still more in-
"competent.

"*December 13th*, a fortnight after Ferdinand's appearance,
"Richelieu had got to the safe side of the Aller (burning of
"Zelle Bridge and Zelle Town there, his last act in Ger-
"many); Ferdinand's quarters now wide enough; and
"vigorous speed of preparation going on for farther chase,
"were the weather mended. *February 17th (1758)*, Fer-
"dinand was on foot again; Prince de Clermont, the still
"more incompetent successor of Richelieu, gazing wide-eyed
"upon him, but doing nothing else: and for the next six

CHAP. VIII.] BATTLE OF ROSSBACH. 227
9th Nov. 1757 — 31st March 1758.

"weeks, there was seen a once triumphant Richelieu-
"D'Estrées French Army, much in rags, much in disorder, in
"terror, and here and there almost in despair, — winging
"their way; like clouds of draggled poultry, caught by a
"mastiff in the corn. Across Weser, across Ems, finally
"across the Rhine itself, every feather of them, — their long-
"drawn cackle, of a shrieky type, filling all Nature in those
"months; the mastiff steadily following.* To the astonish-
"ment of Pitt and mankind. Can this be the same Army that
"Royal Highness led to the Sea and the Parish Pound? The
"same identically, wasted to about two-thirds by Royal High-
"ness; not a drum in it changed otherwise, only One Man
"different, — and he is the important one!

"Pitt, when the news of Rossbach came, awakening the
"bonfires and steeple-bells of England to such a pitch, had
"resolved on an emphatic measure: that of sending English
"Troops to reinforce our Allied Army, and its new General;
"— such an Ally as that Rossbach one being rare in the eyes
"of Pitt. 'Postpone the meeting of Parliament, yet a few
"days, your Majesty,' said Pitt, 'till I get the estimates
"ready!'** To which Majesty assented, and all England
"with him: 'England's own Cause,' thinks Pitt, with con-
"fidence: 'our way of Conquering America, — and, in the
"circumstances, our one way!' English did land, ac-
"cordingly; first instalment of them, a 12,000 (in August
"next), increased gradually to 20,000; with no end of
"furnishings to them and everybody; with results again satis-
"factory to Pitt; and very famous in the England that then
"was, dim as they are now grown."

The effect of all which was that Pitt, with his
Ferdinands and reinforcements, found work for the
French ever onwards from Rossbach; French also turn-
ing as if exclusively upon perfidious Albion: and the

* Mauvillon, i. 252-254 ("9th November 1757-1st April 1758"); Westphalen, i. 316-503 (abundantly explicit, authentic, and even entertaining,—
with the ample Correspondences, Ib. II. 147-250); Schaper, Vie militaire du
Maréchal Prince Ferdinand (2 tomes, 8vo, Magdebourg, 1796, 1798), i. 7-100
(a careful Book; of an official exactitude, like Westphalen's, — and appears
to be left incomplete like his).
** Thackeray, i. 310.

15*

thing became, in Teutschland, as elsewhere, a duel of life and death between these natural enemies,—Teutschland the centre of it, — Teutschland and the accessible French Sea-Towns, — but the circumference of it going round from Manilla and Madras to Havannah and Quebec again. Wide-spread furious duel; prize, America and life. By land and sea; handsomely done by Pitt on both elements. Land part, we say, was always mainly in Germany, under Ferdinand, — in Hessen and the Westphalian Countries, as far east as Minden, as far west as Frankfurt-on-Mayn, generally well north of Rhine, well south of Elbe: that was, for five years coming, the cockpit or place of deadly fence between France and England. Friedrich's arena lies eastward of that, occasionally playing into it a little, and played into by it, and always in lively sympathy and consultation with it: but, except the French subsidisings, diplomatisings and great diligence against him in foreign Courts, Friedrich is, in practical respects, free of the French; and ever after Rossbach, Ferdinand and the English keep them in full work, — growing yearly too full. A heavy Business for England and Ferdinand; which is happily kept extraneous to Friedrich thenceforth; to him and us; which is not on the stage of his affair and ours, but is to be conceived always as vigorously proceeding along-side of it, close beyond the scenes, and liable, at any time, to make tragic entry on him again: — of which we shall have to notice the louder occurrences and cardinal phases, but, for the future, nothing more.

Soubise, who had crept into the skirts of the Richelieu Army in Hanover or Hessen Country, had of course to take wing in that general flight before the mastiff. Soubise did not cross the Rhine with it; Soubise made off eastward;[*] — found new roost in Hanau-Frankfurt Country; and had thoughts of joining the Austrians in Bohemia next Campaign; but got new order, — such the pinches of a winged Clermont with a mastiff Ferdinand at his poor draggled tail; — and came back to the Ferdinand scene, to help there; and never saw Friedrich again. Both Broglio and he had a good deal of fighting (mostly beating) from Ferdinand; and a great deal of trouble and sorrow in the course of this War; but after Rossbach it is not Friedrich or we, it is Ferdinand and the Destinies that have to do with them. Poor Soubise, except that he was the creature of Generalissima Pompadour, which had something radically absurd in it, did not deserve all the laughter he got: a man of some chivalry, some qualities. As for Broglio, I remember always, not without human emotion, the two extreme points of his career as a soldier: Rossbach and the Fall of the Bastille. He was towards forty, when Friedrich bestrode the Janus Hill in that fiery manner; he was turned of eighty when, from the pavements of Paris, the Chimæra of Democracy rose on him, in fire of a still more horrible description.

Dauphiness-Bellona, in her special and in her widest sense, has made exit, then. Gone, like clouds of draggled poultry home across the Rhine. She was the most marauding Army lately seen, also the most gasconading, and had the least capacity for fighting: three worse qualities no army could have. How she fought, we have seen sufficiently. Before taking leave of her forever, readers, as she is a paragon in her kind, would

[*] Westphalen, i. 601 ("end of March 1758").

perhaps take a glance or two at her marauding qualities, — by a good opportunity that offers. Plotho at Regensburg, that a supreme Reichs Diet may know what a 'deliverance of Saxony' this has been, submits one day the following irrefragable Documents, "which have happened," not without good industry of my own, "to fall into my" (Plotho's) "hands." They are Documents partly of epistolary, partly of a Petitionary form, presented to Polish Majesty, out of that Saxon Country; and have an *affidavit* quality about them, one and all.

1º. *Big Dauphiness* (that is, D'Estrées) *in the Wesel Countries, at an early Stage, — while still endeavouring what she could to behave well, hanging 1,000 marauders and the like* (A private Letter):

"*County Mark, 20th June 1757*. The French troops are "going on here in a way to utterly ruin us. Schmidt, their "President of Justice, whom they set up in Cleve, has got "orders to change all the Magistracies of the Country" (Protestant by nature), "so as that half the members shall be "Catholic. Bielefeld was openly plundered by the French "for three hours long. You cannot by possibility represent "to yourself what the actual state of misery in these Countries "is. A *scheffel* of rye costs three thalers sixteen groschen" (who knows how many times its natural price!). "And now "we are to be forced to eat the spoiled meal those French "troops brought with them; which is gone to such a state no "animal would have it. This poisoned meal we are to buy "from them, ready money, at the price they fix; and that "famine may induce us, they are about to stop the mills, and "forcibly take away what little bread-corn we have left. God "have pity on us, and deliver us soon! Next week we are to "have a transit of 6,000 Pfalzers" (Kur-Pfalz, foolish idle fellow, and Kur-Baiern too, are both in subsidy of France, as usual; 6,000 Pfalzers just due here); "these, I suppose, will "sweep us clean bare." *

* *Helden-Geschichte*, IV. 399.

Wesel Fortress, Gate of the Rhine, could not be defended by Friedrich: and the Hanover Incapables, and England still all in St. Vitus, would not hear of undertaking it; left it wide-open for the French; never could recover it, or get the Rhine-Gate barred again during the whole War. One hopes they repented; — but perhaps it was only Pitt and Duke Ferdinand that did so, instead! The Wesel Countries were at once occupied by the French; 'a conquest of her Imperial Majesty's;' continued to be administered in Imperial Majesty's name, — and are thriving as above.

2⁰. *Dauphiness Proper* (that is, Soubise) *in Thüringen, at a late Stage:*

Letter from Freiburg, shortly after Rossbach. — "It was on "the 23d October, a Sunday, that we of Freiburg had our "first billeting of French; a body of cavalry from different "regiments" (going to take Leipzig, take Torgau, what not): "and from that day, Freiburg never emptied of French, who "kept marching through it in extraordinary quantities. The "marching lasted fourteen days, namely, till the 6th No-"vember" (day *after* Rossbach; when they burnt our poor Bridge, and marched for the last time); "and often the "billeting was so heavy, that in a single house there were "forty or fifty men. Who at all times had to be lodged and "dieted gratis; nay many householders, over and above the "ordinary meal, were obliged to give them money too; and "many poor people, who can scarcely get their own bit of "bread, had to run and bring at once their sixteen or eighteen "groschen" (pence) "worth of wine, not to speak of coffee "and sugar. And a great increase of the mischief it was "always, that the soldiers and common people did not under-"stand one another's language." — Heavy billeting; but what was that? * * "Vast, nearly impossible quantities "of forage and provision," were wrung from us, as from all the other Towns and Villages about, "under continual "threatening to burn and rase us from the earth. Often did "our French Colonel threaten, 'He would have the cannon "opened on Freiburg straightway.' Nay, had it stood by "foraging, we might have reckoned ourselves lucky. But "our straits increased day by day; and sheer plundering be-"came more and more excessive.

"The robbing and torturing of travellers, the plundering "and burning of Saxon Villages" — "Almost all the Towns "and Villages hereabouts are so plundered out, that many a "one now has nothing but what he carries on his body. "Plundering was universal: and no sooner was one party "away, than another came, and still another; and often the "same house was three or four times plundered. Branderode, "a Village two leagues from this" (stands on the Field of Rossbach, if we look), "is so ruined out, that nobody almost "has anything left: Chief-Inspector Baron von Rose's Schloss "there, with its splendid appointments, they ruined utterly; "took all money, victuals, valuables, furniture, clothes, linen "and beds, all they could carry; what could not be carried "away, they cut, hewed and smashed to pieces; broke the "wine-casks; and even tore up the documents and letters "they found lying in the place. Branderode Dorf was twice "set fire to by them; and was, at last, with Zeuchfeld, which "is an Amtsdorf, — after both had been plundered, — "reduced to ashes. The Churches of Branderode and Zeuch-"feld, with several other Churches, were plundered; the "altars broken, the altar-cloths and other vestures cut to "pieces, and the sacred vessels and cups carried away, — "except" (for we have a notarial exactness, and will exaggerate nothing) "that in the case of Branderode they sent "the cup back. Of the pollution of the altars, and of the "blasphemous songs these people sang in the churches, one "cannot think without horror.

"And it was merely our pretended Allies and Protectors "that have desecrated our divine service, utterly wasted our "Country, reduced the inhabitants to want and desperation, "and, in short, have so behaved that you would not know this "region again. Truly these troops have realised for us most "of the infamies we heard reported of the Cossacks, and their "ravagings in Preussen lately.

"It is one of their smallest doings that they robbed a "Saxon Clergyman" (name and circumstances can be given if required), "three times over, on the public Highway; shot "at him, tied him to a horse's tail, and dragged him along "with them; so that he is now lying ill, in danger of his life. "On the whole, it is our beloved Pastors, Clergymen most of "all, that have been plundered of everything they had.

"Balgart and Zschieplitz, both Villages half a league "from this, have likewise been heavily plundered; they have "even left the Parson nothing but what he wore on his back. "Gröst," another Rossbach place, "which belongs to the "Kammerjunker Heldorf, has likewise" * * *Ohe, satis!* — "All this happened between the 23d and 31st October; "consequently before the Battle." * * "In many Vil- "lages, you see the trees and fields sprinkled with feathers "from the beds that have been slit up.

"In several Villages belonging to the Royal Electoral "Privy Councillor von Brühl" (who is properly the fountain of all this and of much other misery to us, if we knew it!), "the plundering likewise had begun; and a quantity of about "a hundred swine" (so ho!) "had been cut in pieces: but in "the midst of their work, the Allies heard that these were "Brühl estates, and ceased their havoc of them. These ac- "cordingly are the only lands in all this region whose fate has "been tolerable.

"The appellation, every moment renewed, of 'Heretic!' "was the courteous address from these people to our fellow "Christians; 'heretic dogs *(ketzerische Hunde)*' was a *Prä- "dicat* always in their mouth.

"In Weischütz," a mile or two from us, up the Unstrut, "a "French Colonel who wanted to ride out upon the works, "made the there Pastor, Magister Schren, stoop down by "way of horse-block, and mounted into the saddle from his "back." (Messieurs, you will kindle the wrath of mankind some day, and get a terrible plucking, with those high ways of yours!)

"Churches are all smashed; obscene songs were sung, in "form of litany, from the pulpits and altars; what was done "with the communion-vessels, when they were not worth "stealing," — is hideous to the religious sense, and shall not be mentioned in human speech.

3º. *The Broglio Reinforcement coming across to join Soubise, and perform at Rossbach* (Humble Petition from the Magistrates of Sangerhausen, To the King of Poland's Majesty):

Sangerhausen, 23d October 1757. — "Scarcely had we, " with profound submission *(allerunterthänigst)*, under date of

"the 13th current, represented to your Royal Majesty and
"Electoral Translucency how heavily we were pressed down
"by the forage-requisitions and transits of troops, and the
"consequent expenditure in food, drinking, in oats and hay,
"which no one pays, — when directly thereafter, on the 14th
"of October, a new French party, of the Fischer Corps," —
Fischer is a mighty Hussar, scarcely inferior to Turpin; and
stands in astonishing authority with Richelieu, and an Army
whose object is plunder,* — "new party of the Fischer
"Corps, of some sixty men and horse, arrived in the Town;
"demanded meat, drink, oats and hay, and all things necessary;
"which they received from us; — and not only paid not one
"farthing for all this, but furthermore some of them, instead
"of thanks to their Landlord, Rossold, forcibly broke up his
"press, drank his brandy, and carried off a *Toute* (gather-all)
"with money in it. From a Tanner, Lindauer by name, they
"bargained for a buckskin; and having taken, would not pay
"it. In the *Rathskeller* (Town Public-house) they drank much
"wine, and gave nothing for it: nay on marching off, — be-
"cause no mounted guide *(reitender Bote)* was at hand, and
"though they had before expressly said none such would be
"needed, — they rushed about like distracted persons *(wie
"rasende Leute)* in the market-place and in the streets; beat
"the people, tumbled them about, and lugged them along, in
"a violent manner; using abusive language to a frightful
"extent, and threatening every misfortune.

"Hardly were we rid of this confusion and astonishment,
"when, on October 21st, a whole swarm of horses, men,
"women, children and wagons, which likewise all belonged
"to the Fischer Corps, and were commanded by First-
"Lieutenant Schmidt, came into our Town. This troop con-
"sisted of 80 men, part infantry, part cavalry; with some
"80 work-horses, 10 baggage-wagons, and about 100 persons,
"women, sick people and the like. They staid the whole
"night here; made meat, drink, corn, hay and whatever they
"needed be brought them; and went off next day without
"paying anything.

"Our Inns were now almost quite exhausted of forage in
"corn or hay; and we knew not how we were to pay what had
"been spent, — when the thirty French Light Cavalry, of

* Ferdinand's Correspondents, *assyies (Westphalen,* 1. 40-127); &c. &c.

"whom we, with profound submission, on the 13th *hujus* gave
"your Royal Majesty and Electoral Translucency account,
"renewed their visit upon us; came, under the command of
"Rittmeister de Mocu, on the 22d of October" (while the
baggage-wagons, work-horses, women, sick, and so forth
were hardly gone), "towards evening, into the Town; con-
"sumed in meat and drink, oats and hay, and the like, what
"they could lay hold of; and next morning early marched
"away, paying, as their custom is, nothing.

"Not enough that, — besides the great forage contribu-
"tion (*Lieferung*), which we already, with profound submis-
"sion, notified to your Royal Majesty and Electoral Trans-
"lucency as having been laid upon us; and that, by order of
"the Duc de Broglio, a new requisition is now laid on us, and
"we have had to engage for sixty-four more sacks of wheat,
"and thirty-two of rye (as is noted under head A, in the
"enclosed copy), — there has farther come on us, on the part
"of the Reichs Army, from Kreis-Commissarius Heldorf"
(whose Schloss of Gröst, we perceive, they have since burnt,
by way of thanks to him),* "the simultaneous Order for in-
"stant delivery of Forage (as under head B, here enclosed)!
"Thus are we, at the appointed places, all at once to furnish
"such quantities, more than we can raise; and know not when
"or where we shall, either for what has been already fur-
"nished, or for what is still to be, receive one penny of money:
"nay, over and above, we are to sustain the many marchings
"of troops, and provide to the same what meat, drink, oats,
"hay and so on they require, without the least return of pay-
"ment!

"So unendurable, and taken all together, so hard (*sic*)
"begins the conduct of these troops, that profess being come
"as friends and helpers, to appear to us. And Heaven alone
"knows how long, under a continuance of such things, the
"subjects (whom the Hailstorm of last year had at any rate
"impoverished) shall be able to support the same. We would,
"were a reasonable delivery of forage laid upon us even at a
"low price, and the board and billet of the marching troops
"paid to us even in part, lay out our whole strength in helping
"to bear the burdens of the Fatherland; but, if such things
"go on, which will soon leave us only bare life and empty

* Suprà, No. 1.

"huts, we can look forward to nothing but our ruin and de-
"struction. But, as it is not your Royal Majesty's and Elec-
"toral Translucency's most gracious will that we, your Most
"Supreme Self's most faithful subjects, should entirely perish,
"therefore we repeat our former most submissive prayer once
"again with hot (sic) sorrow of mind to Highest-the-Same;
"and sob most submissively for that help which your Most
"Supreme Self, through most gracious mediation with the
"Duc de Richelieu, with the Reichs Army or wherever else,
"might perhaps most graciously procure for us. Who, in
"deepest longing thitherwards, with the most deepest devo-
"tion, remain —"* (*Names*, unfortunately, not given).

How many Saxons and Germans generally, — alas, how many men universally, — cry towards celestial luminaries of the governing kind with the most deepest devotion, in their extreme need, under their unsufferable injuries; and are truly like dogs in the backyard barking at the Moon. The Moon won't come down to them, and be eaten as green cheese; the Moon can't! —

40. *Dauphiness after Rossbach.* "Excise-Inspector Neitsche, at Bebra, near Weissenfels" (Bebra is well ahead from Freiburg and the burnt Bridge, and a good twenty-five miles west of Weissenfels), "writes To the King of Poland's Majesty, *9th November 1757:*

"May it please your Royal Majesty and Electoral Trans-
"lucency, out of your highest grace, to take knowledge, from
"the accompanying Registers *sub signo Martis*"(sign unknown
"to readers here), "of the things which, in the name of this
"Township of Bebra, the Bürgermeister Johann Adam, with
"the Raths and others concerned, have laid before the Excise-
"Inspection here. As follows:

"'It will be already well known to the Excise-Inspection
"'that on the 7th of November (a.c.) of the current year' (day
"'before yesterday, in fact!) 'the French Army so handled
"'this place as to have not only taken from the inhabitants,
"'by open force, all bread and articles of food, but likewise
"'all clothes, beds, linens (*Wäsche*), and other portable

---

* *Helden-Geschichte,* IV. 688-691.

"'goods; that it has broken, split to pieces, and emptied out,
"'all chests, boxes, presses, drawers; has shot dead, in the
"'backyards and on the thatch-roofs, all manner of feathered-
"'stock, as hens, geese, pigeons; also carried forth with it all
"'swine, cow, sheep, and horse cattle; laid violent hands on
"'the inhabitants, clapped guns, swords, pistols to their
"'breast, and threatened to kill them unless they showed
"'and brought out whatever goods they had; or else has
"'hunted them wholly out of their houses, shooting at them,
"'cutting, sticking, and at last driving them away, thereby to
"'have the freer room to rob and plunder: flung out hay and
"'other harvest-stock from the barns into the mud and dung,
"'and had it trampled to ruin under the horses' feet; nay, in
"'fact, has dealt with this place in so unpermitted a way as
"'even to the most hard-hearted man must seem compassion-
"'able.'"—— Poor fellows: *cetera desunt;* but that is enough!
What can a Polish Majesty and Electoral Translucency do?
Here too is a sorrowful howling to the Moon."*

* * "For a hundred miles round," writes St. Germain,
"the Country is plundered and harried as if fire from Heaven
"had fallen on it; scarcely have our plunderers and marauders
"left the houses standing."—"I lead a band of robbers, of
"assassins, fit for breaking on the wheel; they would turn
"tail at the first gunshot, and are always ready to mutiny.
"If the Government (*la Cour*), with its Pompadour presiding,
very unlikely for such an enterprise!) "cannot lay the
"knife to the root of all this, we may give up the notion of
"War."† * *

Such a pitch have French Armies sunk to. When
was there seen such a Bellona as Dauphiness before?
Nay, in fact, she is the same devil-serving Army that
Maréchal de Saxe commanded with such triumph, —
Maréchal de Saxe in better luck for opponents; Army
then in a younger stage of its development. Foaming
then as sweet must, as new wine, in the hands of a

---
* *Helden-Geschichte,* iv. 692.
† St. Germain, after Rossbach and before (in Preuss, *ubi suprà*).

skilful vintner, poisonous but brisk; not run, as now, to the vinegar state, intolerable to all mortals. She can now announce from her camp-theatres, the reverse of the Roucoux program, "Tomorrow, Messieurs, you are going to fight; our Manager foresees" — you will be beaten; and we cannot say what or where the next Piece will be! Impious, licentious, high-flaring efflorescence of all the Vices is not to be redeemed by the one Quasi-Virtue of readiness to be shot; — sweet of that kind, and sour of this, are the same substance, if you only wait. How kind was the Devil to his Saxe; and flew away with him in rosepink, while it was still time!

CHAPTER IX.

FRIEDRICH MARCHES FOR SILESIA.

The fame of Friedrich is high enough again in the Gazetteer world; all people, and the French themselves, laughing at their grandiloquent Dauphiness-Bellona, and writing epigrams on Soubise. But Friedrich's difficulties are still enormous. One enemy coming with open mouth, you plunge in upon, and ruin, on this hand; and it only gives you room to attempt upon another bigger one on that. Soubise he has finished handsomely, for this season; but now he must try conclusions with Prince Karl. Quick, towards Silesia, after this glorious Victory which the Gazetteers are celebrating.

The news out of Silesia are ominously doubtful, bad at the best. Duke Bevern, once Winterfeld was gone, had, as we observed, felt himself free to act; unchecked, but also unsupported, by counsel of the due heroism; and had acted unwisely. Made direct for Silesia, namely, where are meal-magazines and strong places. Prince Karl, they say, was also unwise; took no thought beforehand, or he might have gained marches, disputed rivers, Bober, Queiss, with Bevern, and as good as hindered him from ever getting to Silesia. So say critics, Retzow and others; perhaps looking too fixedly on one side of the question. Certain it is, Bevern marched in peace to Silesia; found it by no means the better place it had promised to be.

Prince Karl, — Daun there as second, but Karl now the dominant hand, — was on the heels of Bevern, march after march. Prince Karl cut athwart him by one cunning march, in Liegnitz Country; barring him from Schweidnitz, the chief stronghold of Silesia, and to appearance from Breslau, the chief city, too. Bevern, who did not want for soldiership, when reduced to his shifts, now made a beautiful manœuvre, say the critics; struck out leftwards, namely, and crossed the Oder, as if making for Glogau, quite beyond Prince Karl's sphere of possibility, — but turned to right, not to left, when across, and got in upon Breslau from the other or east side of the River. Cunning manœuvre, if you will, and followed by cunning manœuvres: but the result is, Prince Karl has got Schweidnitz to rear, stands between Breslau and it; can besiege Schweidnitz when he likes, and no relief to it possible that will not cost a battle. A battle, thinks Friedrich, is what Bevern ought to have tried at first; a well-fought battle might have settled everything, and there was no other good likelihood in such an expedition: but now, by detaching reinforcements to this garrison and that, he has weakened himself beyond right power of fighting.* Schweidnitz is liable to siege; Breslau, with its poor walls and multitudinous population, can stand no siege worth mentioning; the Silesian strong places, not to speak of meal-magazines, are like to go a bad road. Quite dominant, this Prince Karl; placarding and proclaiming in all places, according to the new "Imperial Patent,"** That Silesia is her Imperial Majesty's again!

* *Œuvres de Frédéric,* iv. 141, 159.
** In *Helden-Geschichte* (iv. 832, 833), Copy of It: "Absolved from all prior Treaties by Prussian Majesty's attack on us, Wo" &c. &c. ("21st Sept. 1757").

Which seems to be fast becoming the fact; — unless contradicted better. Quick!

Bevern has now, October 1st, no manœuvre left but to draw out of Breslau; post himself on the southern side of it, in a safe angle there, marshy Lohe in front, broad Oder to rear, Breslau at his right-hand with bread; and there entrenching himself by the best methods, wait slowly, in a sitting posture, events which are extensively on the gallop at present. One fancies, Had Winterfeld been still there! It is as brave an Army, 30,000 or more, as ever wore steel. Surely something could have been done with it; — something better than sit watching the events on full gallop all round! Bevern was a loyal, considerably skilful and valiant man; in the Battle of Lobositz, and elsewhere, we have seen him brave as a lion; but perhaps in the other kind of bravery wanted here, he — Well, his case was horribly difficult; full of intricacy. And he sat, no doubt in a very wretched state, consulting the oracles, with events (which are themselves oracular) going at such a pace.

Schweidnitz was besieged, October 26th. Nadasti, with 20,000, was set to do it; Prince Karl, with 60,000, ready to protect him; Prince Bevern asking the oracles: — what a bit of news for Friedrich; breaking suddenly the effulgency of Rossbach with a bar of ominous black! Friedrich, still in the thick of pure Saxon business, makes instant arrangement for Silesia as well: Prince Henri with such and such corps, to maintain the Saale, and guard Saxony; Marshal Keith, with such and such, to step over into Bohemia, and raise contributions at least, and tread on the tail of the big Silesian snake: all this Friedrich settles within a week; takes certain corps of his own, effective about 13,000; and on November 13th, marches from Leipzig. Round by Torgau, by Mühlberg, Grossenhayn; by Bautzen, Weissenberg, across the Queiss, across the Bober; and so, with long marches, strides continually forward, all hearts willing, and all limbs, though in this sad winter weather, towards relief of Schweidnitz.

At Grossenhayn, fifth day of the march, Friedrich learns that Schweidnitz is gone. November 12th-14th, Schweidnitz went by capitulation; contrary to everybody's hope or fear; certainly a very short defence for such a fortress. Fault of the Commandant, was everybody's first thought. Not probably the best of Commandants, said others gradually; but his garrison had Saxons in it; — one day "180 of them in a lump "threw down their arms, in the trenches, and went over "to the Enemy." Owing to whatsoever, the place is gone. Such towers, such curtains, star-ramparts; such an opulence of cannons, stores, munitions, a 30,000*L* of hard cash, one item. All is gone, after a fortnight's siege. What a piece of news, as heard by Friedrich, coming at his utmost towards the scene itself! As seen by Bevern, too, in his questioning mood, it was an event of very oracular nature.

On Tuesday 14th, Schweidnitz fell; Karl, with Nadasti reunited to him, was now 80,000 odd; and lost no time. On Thursday next, *November* 22*d*, 1757, "at three in the morning," long hours before daybreak, Karl, with his 60,000, all learnedly arranged, comes rolling over upon hapless Bevern: with no end of cannonading and storm of war: *Battle of Breslau*, they call it; ruinous to Bevern. Of which we shall attempt no description; except to say, that Karl had five bridges on the Lohe, came across the Lohe by five Bridges; and that Bevern stood to his arms, steady as the rocks, to prevent his getting over, and to entertain him when over; that there were five principal attacks, renewed and re-renewed as long as needful, with torrents of shot, of death, and tumult; over six or eight miles of country, for the space of fifteen hours. Battle comparable only to Malplaquet, said the Austrians; such a hurricane of artillery, strongly entrenched enemy, and loud doomsday of war. Did not end till nine at night; Austrians victorious, more or less, in four of their attacks or separate enterprises: that is to say, masters of the Lohe, and of the outmost Prussian villages and posts in front of the Prussian centre and right wing; victorious in that northern part; — but plainly unvictorious in the south-east or Prussian left wing, — farthest off from Breslau, and under Ziethen's command, — where they were driven across the Lohe again, and lost prisoners and cannons, or a cannon.*

Some of Bevern's people, grounding on this latter circumstance, and that they still held the Battlefield, or most part of it, wrote themselves victorious; — though in a dim brief manner, as if conscious of the contrary. Which indeed was the fact. At the council of war, which he summoned that evening, there were proposals of night-attack, and other fierce measures: but Bevern, rejecting the plan for a night-attack on the Austrian camp as too dubious, did, in the dark hours, through the silent streets of Breslau, withdraw himself across the Oder, instead; leaving 80 cannon, and 6,000 killed and wounded; an evidently beaten

---

* In Seyfarth, Three Accounts; *Beylagen*, II. 196, 221, 234 et seq.

man and Army. And indeed did straightway disappear personally altogether, as no longer equal to events. Rode out, namely, to reconnoitre in the gray of his second sad morning, on this new Bank of the Oder; saw little except gray mist; but rode into a Croat outpost, only one poor groom attending him; and was there made prisoner: — intentionally, thought mankind; intentionally, thinks Friedrich, who was very angry with the poor man.*

The poor man was carried to Vienna, if readers care to know; but being a near Cousin there (second-cousin, no less, to the late Empress-Mother), was by the high now-reigning Empress-Queen received in a charmingly gracious manner, and sent home again without ransom. "To Stettin!" beckoned Friedrich sternly from the distance, and would not see him at all: "To Stettin, I say, your official post in time of peace! Command me the invalid Garrison there; you are fit for nothing better!" — I will add one other thing, which unhappily will seem strange to readers: that there came no whisper of complaint from Bevern; mere silence, and loyal industry with his poor means, from Bevern; and that he proved heroically useful in Stettin two years hence, against the Swedes, against the Russians in the Siege-of-Colberg time; and gained Friedrich's favour again, with other good results. Which I observe was a common method with Prussian Generals and soldiers, when, unjustly or justly, they fell into trouble of this kind; and a much better one than that of complaining in the Newspapers, and demanding Commis-

---

* Preuss, II. 102. More exact in Kutzen, *Der Tag von Leuthen* (Breslau, 1857, — an excellent exact little Compilation, from manifold sources well studied), pp. 166-169, date "24th November."

sions of Inquiry, presided over by Chaos and the Fourth-Estate, now is.

Bevern being with the Croats, the Prussian Army falls to General Kyau, as next in rank, who (directly in the teeth of fierce orders that are speeding hither for Bevern and him) marches away, leaving Breslau to its fate; and making towards Glogau, as the one sure point in this wreck of things. And Prince Karl, that same day, goes upon Breslau; which is in no case to resist and be bombarded: so that poor old General Lestwitz, the Prussian Commandant, — always thought to be a valiant old gentleman, but who had been wounded in the late Action, and was blamably discouraged, — took the terms offered, and surrendered without firing a gun. Garrison and he to march out, in "Free Withdrawal;" these are the terms: Garrison was 4,000 and odd, mostly Silesian recruits; but there marched hardly 500 out with poor Lestwitz; the Silesian recruits, — persuaded by conceivable methods, that they were to be prisoners of war, and that, in short, Austria was now come to be king again, and might make inquiry into men's conduct, — found it safer to take service with Austria, to vanish into holes in Breslau or where they could; and, for instance, one regiment (or battalion, let us hide the name of it), on marching through the Gate, consisted only of nine chief officers and four men.*

There were lost 98 pieces of cannon; endless magazines, and stores of war. A Breslau scandalously gone; — a Breslau preaching next day (26th, which was

* Müllor, *Schlacht bei Leuthen* (Berlin, 1857, — professedly a mere abridgment and shadow of *Kaisen*; unindexed like it), p. 12 (with name and particulars).

Sunday), in certain of its churches, especially Cardinal Schaffgotsch in the Dom Insel doing it, Thanksgiving Sermons, as per order, with unction real or official, "That our ancient sovereigns are restored to us:" which Sermons, — except in the Schaffgotsch case, Prince Karl and the high Catholic world all there in gala, — were "sparsely attended," say my authors. The Austrians are at the top of their pride; and consider full surely that Silesia is theirs, though Friedrich were here twice over. "What is Friedrich? We beat him at Kolin. His Prussians at Zittau, at Moys, at Breslau in the new Malplaquet, were we beaten by them? Hnh!" — and snort (in the Austrian messrooms), and snap their fingers at Friedrich and his coming.

It was at Görlitz (scene of poor Winterfeld's death) that Friedrich, "on November 23d, the tenth day of his march," first got rumour of the Breslau Malplaquet: "endless cannonading heard thereabouts all yesterday!" said rumour from the east, — more and more steadily, as Friedrich hastened forward; — and that it was "a victory for Bevern." Till, at Naumburg on the Queiss, he gets the actual tidings: Bevern gone to the Croats, Breslau going, Kyau marching vague; and what kind of victory it was.

Ever from Grossenhayn onwards there had been message on message, more and more rigorous, precise, and indignant, "Do this, do that; your Dilection shall answer it with your head!" — not one message of which reached his Dilection, till Dilection and Fate (such the gallop of events) had done the contrary: and now Dilection and his head have made a finish of it. "No," answers Friedrich to himself; "not till we are all finished!" — and pushes on, he too, like a kind of

Fate. "What does or can he mean, then?" say the Austrians, with scornful astonishment, and think his head must be turning: "Will he beat us out of Silesia with his Potsdam Guard-Parade, then?" "*Potsdamsche Wacht-Parade;*"— so they denominate his small Army; and are very mirthful in their messrooms. "I will attack them, if they stood on the Zobtenberg, if they stood on the steeples of Breslau!" said Friedrich; and tramped diligently forward. Day after day, as the real tidings arrive, his outlook in Silesia is becoming darker and darker: a sternly dark march this altogether. Prince Karl has thrown a garrison into Liegnitz on Friedrich's road; Prince Karl lies encamped with Breslau at his back; has above 80,000 when fully gathered; and reigns supreme in those parts. Darker march there seldom was: all black save a light that burns in one heart, refusing to be quenched till death.

Friedrich sends orders that Kyau shall be put in arrest; that Ziethen shall be general of the Bevern wreck, shall bring it round by Glogau, and rendezvous with Friedrich at a place and day, — Parchwitz, 2d of December coming; — and be steady, my old Ziethen. Friedrich brushes past the Liegnitz Garrison, leaves Liegnitz and it a trifle to the right; arrives at Parchwitz, November 28th; and there rests, or at least his weary troops do, till Ziethen come up; the King not very restful, with so many things to prearrange; a life or death crisis now nigh. Well, it is but death; and death has been fronted before now! We who are after the event, on the safe sunny side of it, can form small image of the horrors, and the inward dubieties, to him who is passing through it; — and how Hope is needed to shine heroically eternal in some hearts. Fire of Hope, that does not issue in mere blazings, mad audacities and chaotic despair, but advances with its eyes open, measuredly, counting its steps, to the wrestling-place, — this is a godlike thing; much available to mankind in all the battles they have; battles with steel, or of whatever sort.

Friedrich, at Parchwitz, assembled his Captains, and spoke to them; it was the night after Ziethen came in, night of December 3d, 1757; and Ziethen, no doubt, was there: for it is an authentic meeting, this at Parchwitz, and the words were taken down.

Friedrich's Speech to his Generals (Parchwitz, 3d December 1757).*

"It is not unknown to you, *Meine Herren*, what "disasters have befallen here, while we were busy with "the French and Reichs Army. Schweidnitz is gone; "Duke of Bevern beaten; Breslau gone, and all our "war-stores there; good part of Silesia gone: and, in "fact, my embarrassments would be at the insuperable "pitch, had not I boundless trust in you, and your "qualities, which have been so often manifested, as "soldiers and sons of your Country. Hardly one among "you but has distinguished himself by some nobly me"morable action: all these services to the State and me "I know well, and will never forget.

"I flatter myself, therefore, that, in this case too, "nothing will be wanting which the State has a right "to expect of your valour. The hour is at hand. I "should think I had done nothing, if I left the Austri"ans in possession of Silesia. Let me apprise you,

---

* From *Retzow*, I. 240-242 (slightly abridged).

"then: I intend, in spite of the Rules of Art, to attack
"Prince Karl's Army, which is nearly thrice our
"strength, wherever I find it. The question is not of
"his numbers, or the strength of his position: all this,
"by courage, by the skill of our methods, we will try
"to make good. This step I must risk, or everything
"is lost. We must beat the enemy, or perish all of us
"before his batteries. So I read the case; so I will
"act in it.

"Make this my determination known to all Officers
"of the Army; prepare the men for what work is now
"to ensue, and say that I hold myself entitled to de-
"mand exact fulfilment of orders. For you, when I
"reflect that you are Prussians, can I think that you
"will act unworthily? But if there should be one
"or another who dreads to share all dangers with me,
"he,"— continued his Majesty, with an interrogative
look, and then pausing for answer, "can have his Dis-
"charge this evening, and shall not suffer the least re-
"proach from me." — Modest strong bass murmur;
meaning "No, by the Eternal!" if you looked into the
eyes and faces of the group. Never will Retzow Junior
forget that scene, and how effulgently eloquent the
veteran physiognomies were.

"Hah, I knew it," said the King, with his most
radiant smile, "none of you would desert me! I depend
"on your help, then; and on victory as sure." — The
speech winds up with a specific passage: "The Cavalry
"regiment that does not on the instant, on order given,
"dash full plunge into the enemy, I will, directly after
"the Battle, unhorse, and make it a Garrison regiment.
"The Infantry battalion which, meet with what it may,
"shows the least signs of hesitating, loses its colours

"and its sabres, and I cut the trimmings from its uni-"form! Now good night, Gentlemen: shortly we have "either beaten the Enemy, or we never see one another "again."

An excellent temper in this Army; a rough vein of heroism in it, steady to the death; — and plenty of hope in it too, hope in Vater Fritz. "Never mind," the soldiers used to say, in John Duke of Marlborough's time, "Corporal John will get us through it!" — That same evening Friedrich rode into the Camp, where the regiments he had were now all gathered, out of their cantonments, to march on the morrow. First regiment he came upon was the Life-Guard Cuirassiers: the men, in their accustomed way, gave him good evening, which he cheerily returned. Some of the more veteran sort asked, ruggedly confidential, as well as loyal: "What is thy news, then, so late?" "Good news, children (*Kinder*): tomorrow you will beat the Austrians tightly!" "That we will, by—!" answered they. — "But think only where they stand yonder, and how they have entrenched themselves?" said Friedrich. "And if they had the Devil in front and all round them, we will knock them out; only thou lead us on!" — "Well, I will see what you can do: now lay you down, and sleep sound; and good sleep to you." "Good night, Fritz!" answer all;* as Fritz ambles on to the next regiment, to which, as to every one, he will have some word.

Was it the famous Pommern regiment, this that he next spoke to, — who answered London's summons to them once (as shall be noticed by and by) in a way ineffable, though unforgettable? Manteuffel of Foot;

* Müller, p. 34.

yes, no other!* They have their own opinion of their capacities against an enemy, and do not want for a good conceit of themselves. "Well, children, how think you it will be tomorrow? They are twice as strong as we." "Never thou mind that; there are no Pommerners among them; thou knowest what the Pommerners can do!" — *Friedrich:* "Yea, truly, that do I; otherwise I durst not risk the battle. Now good sleep to you; tomorrow, then, we shall either have beaten the Enemy or else be all dead." "Yea," answered the whole regiment; "dead, or else the Enemy beaten:" and so went to deep sleep, preface to a deeper for many of them, — as beseems brave men. In this world it much beseems the brave man, uncertain about so many things, to be certain of himself for one thing.

These snatches of Camp Dialogue, much more the Speech preserved to us by Retzow Junior, appear to be true; though as to the dates, the circumstances, there has been debating.** Other Anecdotes, dubious or more, still float about in quantity; — of which let us give only one; that of the Deserter (which has merit as a myth). "What made thee desert, then?" "Hm, alas, your Majesty, we were got so down in the world, and had such a time of it!" — "Well, try it one day more; and if we cannot mend matters, thou and I will both desert."

A learned Doctor, one of the most recent on these matters, is astonished why the Histories of Friedrich should be such dreary reading, and Friedrich himself so prosaic, barren an object; and lays the blame upon the Age, insensible to real greatness: led away by claptrap Napoleonisms, regardless of expense. Upon which Smelfungus takes him up, with a twitch:

* Archenholtz, n. 61; and Kutzen, p. 35.   ** Kutzen, pp. 175-181.

"To my sad mind, Herr Doctor, it seems ascribable rather to the Dryasdust of these Ages, especially to the Prussian Dryasdust, sitting comfortable in his Academies, waving sublimely his long ears as he tramples human Heroisms into unintelligible pipeclay and dreary continents of sand and cinders, with the Doctors all applauding.

"Had the sacred Poet, or man of real Human Genius, been at his work, for the thousand years last past, instead of idly fiddling far away from his work, — which surely is definable as being very mainly, That of *interpreting* human Heroisms; of painfully extricating, and extorting from the circumambient chaos of muddy babble, rumour and mendacity, some not inconceivable human and divine Image of them, more and more clear, complete and credible for mankind (poor mankind dumbly looking up to him for guidance, as to what it shall think of God and of Men in this Scene of Things); — I calculate, we should by this time have had a different Friedrich of it; O Heavens, a different world of it, in so many respects!

"My esteemed Herr Doctor, it is too painful a subject. Godlike fabulous Achilles, and the old Greek Kings of men, one perceives, after study, to be dim enough Grazier Sovereigns, 'living among infinite dung,' till their sacred Poet extricated them. And our *unsacred* all-desecrating Dryasdust. — Herr Doctor, I must say, it fills me with despair! Authentic human Heroisms, not fabulous a whit, but true to the bone, and by all appearance very much nobler than those of godlike Achilles and pious Æneas ever could have been, — left in this manner, trodden under foot of man and beast; man and beast alike insensible that there is anything but common mud under foot, and grateful to anybody that will assure them there is nothing. Oh Doctor, oh Doctor! And the results of it — You need not go exclusively 'to France' to look at them. They are too visible in the so-called 'Social Hierarchies,' and sublime gilt Doggeries, sacred and secular, of all Modern Countries! Let us be silent, my friend." —

"Prussian Dryasdust," he says elsewhere, "does make a terrible job of it; especially when he attempts to weep through his pipe-clay, or rise with his long ears into the moral sublime. As to the German People, I find that they dimly have not wanted sensibility to Friedrich; that their

"multitudes of Anecdotes, still circulating among them in
"print and *vivâ voce*, are proof of this. Thereby they have at
"least made a *Myth* of Friedrich's History, and given some
"rhythmus, life and cheerful human substantiality to his work
"and him. Accept these Anecdotes as the Epic *they* could
"not write of him, but were longing to hear from somebody
"who could. Who has not yet appeared among mankind,
"nor will for some time. Alas, my friend, on piercing through
"the bewildering nimbus of babble, malignity, mendacity,
"which veils sevenfold the Face of Friedrich from us, and
"getting to see some glimpses of the Face itself, one is sorrow-
"fully struck dumb once more. What a suicidal set of
"creatures; commanding as with one voice, That there shall
"be no Heroism more among them; that all shall be Doggery
"and Commonplace henceforth. '*Ach, mein lieber Sulzer*, you
"'don't know that damned brood!'—— Well, well. 'Solo-
"mon's Temple,' the Moslem say, 'had to be built under the
"chirping of ten thousand Sparrows.' Ten thousand of them;
"committee of the whole house, unanimously of the opposite
"view;—and could not quite hinder it. That too is some-
"thing!"—

More to our immediate purpose is this other thing:
That the Austrians have been in Council of War; and,
on deliberation, have decided to come out of their defences; to quit their strong Camp, which lies so eligibly,
ahead of Breslau and arear of Lissa and of Schweidnitz
Water yonder; to cross Schweidnitz Water, leave Lissa
behind them; and meet this offensively aggressive
Friedrich in pitched fight. Several had voted, No,
why stir?— Daun especially, and others with emphasis.
"No need of fighting at all," said Daun: "we can defend Schweidnitz Water; ruin him before he ever get
across." "Defend? Be assaulted by an Army like
his?" urges Lucchesi, the other Chief General: "It is
totally unworthy of us! We have gained the game;
all the honours ours; let us have done with it. Give
him battle, since he fortunately wishes it; we finish

him, and gloriously finish the War too!" So argued Lucchesi, with vivacity, persistency, — to his own ill luck, but evidently with approval from Prince Karl. Everybody sees, this is the way to Prince Karl's favour at present. "Have not I reconquered Silesia?" thinks Prince Karl to himself; and beams applause on the high course, not the low prudent one.* In a word, the Austrians decide on stepping out to meet Friedrich in open battle: it was the first time they ever did so; and it was likewise the last.

Sunday, December 4th, at four in the morning, Friedrich has marched from Parchwitz, straight towards the Austrian Camp;** he hears, one can fancy with what pleasure, that the Austrians are advancing towards him, and will not need to be forced in their strong position. His march is in four columns, Friedrich in the vanguard; quarters to be Neumarkt, a little Town about fourteen miles off. Within some miles of Neumarkt, early in the afternoon, he learns that there are a thousand Croats in the place, the Austrian Bakery at work there, and engineer people marking out an Austrian Camp. "On the Height beyond Neumarkt, that will be?" thinks Friedrich; for he knows this ground, having often done reviews here; to Breslau all the way on both hands, not a rood of it but is familiar to him. Which was a singular advantage, say the critics; and a point the Austrian Council of War should have taken more thought of.

Friedrich, before entering Neumarkt, sends a regiment to ride quietly round it on both sides, and to seise that Height he knows of. Height once seised, or ready

* Kutzen, pp. 45-48.   ** Müller, p. 26.

for seizing, he bursts the barrier of Neumarkt; dashes in upon the thousand Croats; flings out the Croats in extreme hurry, musketry and sabre acting on them; they find their Height beset, their retreat cut off, and that they must vanish. Of the 1,000 Croats, "569 were taken prisoners, and 120 slain," in this unexpected sweeping out of Neumarkt. Better still, in Neumarkt is found the Austrian Bakery, set up and in full work; — delivers you 80,000 bread-rations hot and hot, which little expected to go such a road. On the Height, the Austrian stakes and engineer-tools were found sticking in the ground; so hasty had the flight been.

How Prince Karl came to expose his Bakery, his staff of life so far ahead of him? Prince Karl, it is clear, was a little puffed up with high thoughts at this time. The capture of Schweidnitz, the late "Malplaquet" (poorish Anti-Bevern Malplaquet), capture of Breslau, and the low and lost condition of Friedrich's Silesian affairs, had more or less turned everybody's head, — everybody's except Feldmarschall Daun's alone: — and witty mess-tables, we already said, were in the daily habit of mocking at Friedrich's march towards them with aggressive views, and called his insignificant little Army the "Potsdam Guard-Parade."* That was the common triumphant humour; naturally shared in by Prince Karl; the ready way to flatter him being to sing in that tune. Nobody otherwise can explain, and nobody in anywise can justify, Prince Karl's ignorance of Friedrich's advance, his almost voluntary losing of his staff of life in that manner.

Prince Karl's soldiers have each (in the cold form) three-days provision in their haversacks: they have

* Cogniazo, ii. 417-418.

come across the Weistritz River (more commonly called Schweidnitz Water), which was also the height of contemptuous imprudence; and lie encamped, this night, — in long line, not ill chosen (once the River *is* behind), — perpendicular to Friedrich's march, some ten miles ahead of him. Since crossing, they had learned with surprise, How their Bakery and Croats had been snapt up; that Friedrich was not at a distance, but near; — and that arrangements could not be made too soon! Their position intersects the Great Road at right angles, as we hint; and has villages, swamps, woody knolls; especially, on each wing, good defences. Their right wing leans on Nypern and its impassable peatbogs, a Village two or three miles north from the Great Road; their centre is close behind another Village called Leuthen, about as far south from it: length of their bivouac is about five miles; which will become six or so, had Nadasti once taken post, who is to form the left wing, and go down as far as Sagschütz, southward of Leuthen. Seven battalions are in this Village of Leuthen, eight in Nypern, all the Villages secured; woods, scraggy abatis, redoubts, not forgotten: their cannon are numerous, though of light calibre. Friedrich has at least 71 heavy pieces; and 10 of them are formidably heavy, — brought from the walls of Glogau, with terrible labour to Ziethen; but with excellent effect, on this occasion and henceforth. They got the name of "Boomers, Bellowers (*Die Brummer*)," those Ten. Friedrich was in great straits about artillery; and Retzow Senior recommended this hauling up of the Ten Bellowers, which became celebrated in the years coming. And now we are on the Battle-ground, and must look into the Battle itself, if we can.

CHAPTER X.

BATTLE OF LEUTHEN.

From Neumarkt, on Monday, long before day, the Prussians, all but a small party left there to guard the Bakery and Army Properties, are out again; in four columns; towards what may lie ahead. Friedrich, as usual in such cases, for obvious reasons, rides with the vanguard. To Borne, the first Village on the Highway, is some seven or eight miles. The air is damp, the dim incipiences of dawn struggling among haze; a little way on this side Borne, we come on ranks of cavalry drawn across the Highway, stretching right and left into the dim void: Austrian Army this, then? Push up to it; see what it is, at least.

It proves to be poor General Nostitz, with his three Saxon regiments of dragoons, famous since Kolin day, and a couple of Hussar regiments, standing here as outpost; — who ought to have been more alert; but they could not see through the dark, and so, instead of catching, are caught. The Prussians fall upon them, front and flank, tumble them into immediate wreck; drive the whole outpost at full gallop home, through Borne, upon Nypern and the right wing, — without news except of this symbolical sort. Saxon regiments are quite ruined, "540 of them prisoners" (poor Nostitz himself not prisoner, but wounded to death*); and the ground clear in this quarter.

* Died in Breslau, the twelfth day after (Seyfarth, II. 562).

Friedrich, on the farther side of Borne, calls halt, till the main body arrive; rides forward, himself and staff, to the highest of a range or suite of knolls, some furlongs ahead; sees there in full view, far and wide, the Austrians drawn up before him. From Nypern to Sagschütz yonder; miles in length; and so distinct, while the light mended and the hazes faded, "that you could have counted them" (through your glasses), "man by man." A highly interesting sight to Friedrich; who continues there in the profoundest study, and calls up some horse regiments of the vanguard to maintain this Height and the range of Heights running south from it. And there, I think, the King is mainly to be found, looking now at the Austrians, now at his own people, for some three hours to come. His plan of Battle is soon clear to him: Nypern, with its bogs and scrags, on the Austrian right wing, is tortuous impossible ground, as he well remembers, no good prospect for us there: better ground for us on their left yonder, at Leuthen, even at Sagschütz farther south, whither they are stretching themselves. Attempt their left wing; try our "Oblique Order" upon that, with all the skill that is in us; perhaps we can do it rightly this time, and prosper accordingly! That is Friedrich's plan of action. The four columns once got to Borne, shall fall into two; turn to the right, and go southward, ever southward: — they are to become our two Lines of Battle, were they once got to the right point southward. Well opposite Sagschütz, that will be the point for facing to left, and marching up, — in "Oblique Order," with the utmost faculty they have!

"The Oblique Order, *Schräge Stellung*," let the hasty reader pause to understand, "is an old plan practised by

"Epaminondas, and revived by Friedrich, — who has tried it "in almost all his Battles more or less, from Hohenfriedberg "forward to Prag, Kolin, Rossbach; but never could, in all "points, get it rightly done till now, at Leuthen, in the highest "time of need. 'It is a particular manœuvre,' says Archen- "holtz, rather sergeant-wise, 'which indeed other troops are "'now' (1793) 'in the habit of imitating; but which, up to this "' 'present time, none but Prussian troops can execute with the "'precision and velocity indispensable to it. You divide your "'line into many pieces; you can push these forward stair- "'wise, so that they shall halt close to one another,' obliquely, "to either hand; 'and so, on a minimum of ground, bring "'your mass of men to the required point at the required "'angle. Friedrich invented this mode of getting into posi- "'tion; by its close ranking, by its depth, and the manner of "'movement used, it had some resemblance to the Macedo- "'nian Phalanx,'— chiefly in the latter point, I should guess; "for when arrived at its place, it is no deeper than common. "' 'Forming itself in this way, a mass of troops takes up in pro- "'portion'very little ground; and it shows in the distance, by "'reason of the mixed uniforms and standards, a totally "'chaotic mass of men heaped on one another,' going in rapid "mazes this way and that. 'But it needs only that the Com- "'mander lift his finger; instantly this living coil of knotted "'intricacies develops itself in perfect order, and with a speed "'like that of mountain rivers, when the ice breaks,'— is "upon its Enemy."*

"Your Enemy is ranked as here, in long line, three or two "to one. You march towards him, but keep him uncertain "as to how you will attack; then do on a sudden march up, "not parallel to him, but oblique, at an angle of 45^0, — swift, "vehement, in over-powering numbers, on the wing you have "chosen. Roll that wing together, ruined, in upon its own "line, you may roll the whole five miles of line into disorder "and ruin, and always be in overpowering number at the "point of dispute. Provided, only, you are swift enough "about it, sharp enough! But extraordinary swiftness, sharp- "ness, precision is the indispensable condition; — by no "means try it otherwise; none but Prussians, drilled by an "Old Dessauer, capable of doing it. This is the *Schräge Ord-*

* Archenholtz, I. 209.

"*nung*, about which there has been such commentating and "controversying among military people: whether Friedrich "invented it, whether Cæsar did it, how Epaminondas, how "Alexander at Arbela; how"— Which shall not in the least concern us on this occasion.

The four columns rustled themselves into two, and turned southward on the two sides of Borne; — southward henceforth, for about two hours; as if straight towards the Magic Mountain, the Zobtenberg, far off, which is conspicuous over all that region. Their steadiness, their swiftness and exactitude were unsurpassable. "It was a beautiful sight," says Tempelhof, an Eyewitness: "The heads of the columns were "constantly on the same level, and at the distance "necessary for forming; all flowed on exact, as if in a "review. And you could read in the eyes of our brave "troops the noble temper they were in."* I know not at what point of their course, or for how long, but it was from the column nearest him, which is to be first line, that the King heard, borne on the winds amid their field-music, as they marched there, the sound of Psalms, — many-voiced melody of a Church Hymn, well known to him; which had broken out, band accompanying, among those otherwise silent men. The fact is very certain, very strange to me: details not very precise, except that here, as specimen, is a verse of their Hymn:

"Grant that with zeal and skill, this day, I do
"What me to do behoves, what thou command'st me to;
"Grant that I do it sharp, at point of moment fit,
"And when I do it, grant me good success in it."

"*Gieb dass ich thu' mit Fleiss was mir zu thun gebühret,*
"*Wozu mich dein Befehl in meinem Stande führet,*
"*Gieb' dass ich's thue bald, zu der Zeit da ich's soll;*
"*Und wenn ich's thu', so gieb dass es gerathe wohl.*"**

* Tempelhof, I. 286, 287.
** "Hymn-Book of Porst" (Prussian Sternhold-and-Hopkins), "p. 689;" cited in Preuss, II. 107.

One has heard the voice of waters, one has paused in the mountains at the voice of far-off Covenanter psalms; but a voice like this, breaking the commanded silences, one has not heard. "Shall we order that to cease, your Majesty?" "By no means," said the King; whose hard heart seems to have been touched by it, as might well be. Indeed there is in him, in those grim days, a tone as of trust in the Eternal, as of real religious piety and faith, scarcely noticeable elsewhere in his History. His religion, and he had in withered forms a good deal of it, if we will look well, being almost always in a strictly voiceless state, — nay, ultra-voiceless, or voiced the wrong way, as is too well known. "By no means!" answered he; and a moment after, said to some one, Ziethen probably: "With men like these, don't you think I shall have victory this day!"

The loss of their Saxon Forepost proved more important to the Austrians than it seemed; — not computable in prisoners, or killed and wounded. The Height named Scheuberg, — "Borne Rise" (so we might call it, which has got its Pillar of memorial since, with gilt Victory atop[*]); — where Friedrich now is and where the Austrians are not, is at once a screen and a point of vision to Friedrich. By loss of their Nostitz Forepost, they had lost view of Friedrich, and never could recover view of him; could not for hours learn distinctly what he was about; and when he did come in sight again, it was in a most unexpected place! On the farther side of Borne, edge of the big expanse of open country there, Friedrich has halted; ridden with his adjutants to the top of "the Scheuberg (Shy-*hill*),"

[* Not till 1854 (Kutzen, pp. 194, 195).]

as the Books call it, though it is more properly a blunt Knoll or "Rise," — the nearest of a Chain of Knolls, or swells in the ground, which runs from north to south on that part.

Except the Zobtenberg, rising blue and massive, on the southern horizon (famous mythologic Mountain, reminding you of an *Arthur's Seat* in shape too, only bigger and solitary), this Country, for many miles round, has nothing that could be called a Hill; it is definable as a bare wide-waving champaign, with slight bumps on it, or slow heavings and sinkings. Country mostly under culture, though it is of sandy quality; one or two sluggish brooks in it; and reedy meres or mires, drained in our day. It is dotted with Hamlets of the usual kind; and has patches of scraggy fir. Your horizon, even where bare, is limited, owing to the wavy heavings of the ground; windmills and church-belfries are your only resource, and even these, from about Leuthen and the Austrian position, leave the Borne quarter mostly invisible to you. Leuthen Belfry, the same which may have stood a hundred years before this Battle, ends in a small tile-roof, open only at the gables: — "Leuthen Belfry," says a recent Tourist, "is "of small resource for a view. To south you can see "some distance, Sagschütz, Lobetintz, and other Ham- "lets, amid scraggy fir-patches, and meadows, once "miry pools; but to north, you are soon shut in by a "swell or slow rise, with two windmills upon it" (important to readers at present); "and to eastward" (Breslau side and Lissa side), "or to westward" (Friedrich's side), "one has no view, except of the old warped "rafters and their old mouldy tiles within few inches; "or, if by audacious efforts at each end, to the risk of "your neck, you get a transient peep, it is stopt, far "short of Borne, by the slow irregular heavings, with "or without fir about them."*

In short, Friedrich keeps possession of that Borne ridge of Knolls, escorted by Cavalry in good numbers; twinkling about in an enigmatic way: — "Prussian right wing yonder," think the Austrians; "whitherward, or what can they mean?" — and keeps his own columns and the Austrian lines in view; himself and his movements invisible, or worse, to the Austrian Generals from any spyglass or conjecture they can employ.

The Austrian Generals are in windmills, on church-belfries, here, there; diligently scanning the abstruse phenomenon, of which so little can be seen. Daun, who had always been against this adventure, thinks it probable the vanished Prussians are retiring southward: for Bohemia and our Magazines probably. "These good people are smuggling off (*Die guten Leute paschen ab*)," said he: "let them go in peace." ** Daun, that morning, in his reconnoiterings, had asked of a peasant, "What is that, then?" (meaning the top of a Village-steeple in the distance, but thought by the peasant to be meaning something nearer hand). "That is the Hill our King chases the Austrians over, when he is reviewing here!" Which Daun reported at head-quarters with a grin.***

Lucchesi, on the other hand, scanning those Borne Hills, and the Cavalry of Friedrich's escort twinkling hither and thither on them, becomes convinced to a moral certainty, That yonder is the Prussian Vanguard, probable extremity of left wing; and that he, Lucchesi, here at Nypern, is to be attacked. "Attacked, you?"

---

* Tourist's Note, *penes me.*
** Müller, p. 36. *** Nicolai, Anekdoten, iv. 34.

said one Montazet, French Agent or Emissary here: "unless they were snipes, it is impossible!" But Lucchesi saw it too well.

He sends to say that such is the evident fact, and that he, Lucchesi, is not equal to it, but must have large reinforcement of Horse to his right wing. "Tush!" answer Prince Karl and Daun; and return only argument, verbal consolation, to distressed Lucchesi. Lucchesi sends a second message, more passionately pressing, to the like effect; also with the like return. Upon which he sends a third message, quite passionate: "If Cavalry do not come, I will not be responsible for the issue!" And now Daun does collect the required reinforcement; "all the reserve of Horse, and a great many from the left wing;" — and, Daun himself heading them, goes off at a swift trot; to look into Lucchesi and his distresses, three or four miles to right, five or six from where the danger lies. Now is Friedrich's golden moment.

Wending always south, on their western or invisible side of those Knolls, Friedrich's people have got to about the level, or *latitude* as we might call it, of Nadasti's left. To Radaxdorf, namely, to Lobetintz, or still farther south, and perhaps a mile to west of Nadasti. Friedrich has mounted to Lobetintz Windmill; and judges that the time is come. Daun and Cavalry once gone to support their right wing, and our south latitude being now sufficient, Friedrich, swift as Prussian manœuvering can do it, falls with all his strength upon their left wing. Forms in oblique order, — horse, foot, artillery, all perfect in their paces; and comes streaming over the Knolls at Sagschütz, suddenly like a fire-deluge on Nadasti, who had charge there, and was expecting no such adventure! How Friedrich did the forming in oblique order was at that time a mystery known only to Friedrich and his Prussians; but soldiers of all countries, gathering the secret from him, now understand it, and can learnedly explain it to such as are curious. Will readers take a touch more of the *Drill-Sergeant?*

"You go stair-wise (*en échelon*)," says he: "first "battalion starts, second stands immovable till the first "have done fifty steps; at the fifty-first, second bat- "talion also steps along; third waiting for *its* fifty-first "step. First battalion" (rightmost battalion or left- most, as the case may be; rightmost in this Leuthen case) "doing fifty steps before the next stirs, and each "battalion in succession punctually doing the same:" march along on these terms, — or halt at either end, while you advance at the other, — it is evident you will swing yourself out of the parallel position into any degree of obliquity. And furthermore, merely by halting and facing half-round at the due intervals, you shove yourself to right or to left as required (always to right in this Leuthen case): and so, — provided you *can* march as a pair of compasses would, — you will, in the given number of minutes, impinge upon your Enemy's extremity at the required angle, and overlap him to the required length: whereupon, At him, in flank, in front, and rear, and see if he can stand it! "A beautiful manœuvre," says Captain Archenholtz; "devised by Friedrich," by Friedrich inheriting Epa- minondas and the Old Dessauer; "and which, perhaps, "only Friedrich's men, to this day, could do with the "requisite perfection."

Nadasti, a skilful War-Captain, especially with Horse, was beautifully posted about Sagschütz; his extreme left folded up *en potence* there (elbow of it at Sagschütz, fore-arm of it running to Gohlau eastward); potence ending in firwood Knolls with Croat musketeers, in ditches, ponds, difficult ground, especially towards Gohlau. He has a strong battery, 14 pieces, on the Height to rear of him, at the angle or elbow of his potence; strong abatis, well manned in front to rightwards: upon this, and upon the Croats in the firwood, the Prussians intend their attack. General Wedell is there, Prince Moritz as chief, with six battalions, and their batteries, battery of 10 Brummers and another; Ziethen also and Horse: coming on, in swift fire-flood, and at an angle of forty-five degrees. Most unexpected, strange to behold! From south-west yonder; about one o'clock of the day.

Nadasti, though astonished at the Prussian fire-deluge, stands to his arms; makes, in front, vigorous defence; and even takes, in some sort, the initiative, — that is, dashes out his Cavalry on Ziethen, before Ziethen has charged. Ziethen's Horse, who are rightmost of the Prussians, and are bare to the right, — ground offering no bush, no brook there (though Ziethen, foreseeing such defect, has a clump of infantry near by to mend it), — reel back under this first shock, coming downhill upon them; and would have fared badly, had not the clump of infantry instantly opened fire on the Nadasti visitors, and poured it in such floods upon them, that they, in their turn, had to reel back. Back they, well out of range; — and leave Ziethen free for a counter-attack shortly, on easier terms, which was successful to him. For, during that first tussle of his, the Prussian Infantry, to left of Ziethen, has attacked the Sagschütz Firwood; clears that of Croats; attacks Nadasti's line, breaks it, their Brummer battery potently assisting, and the rage of Wedell and everybody being extreme. So that, in spite of the fine ground, Nadasty is in a bad way, on the extreme left or outmost point of his *potence*, or tactical *knee*. Round the kneepan or angle of his *potence*, where is the abatis, he fares still worse. Abatis, beswept by those ten Brummers and other Batteries, till bullet and bayonet can act on it, speedily gives way. "They "were mere Würtembergers, these; and could not stand!" cried the Austrians apologetically, at a great rate, afterwards; as if anybody could well have stood.

Indisputably the Würtembergers and the abatis are gone; and the Brandenburgers, storming after them, storm Nadasti's interior battery of 14 pieces; and Nadasti's affairs are rapidly getting desperate in this quarter. Figure Prince Karl's scouts, galloping madly to recal that Daun Cavalry! Austrian Battalions, plenty of them, rush down to help Nadasti; but they are met by the crowding fugitives, the chasing Prussians; are themselves thrown into disorder, and can do no good whatever. They arrive on the ground, flurried, blown; have not the least time to take breath and order: the fewest of them ever got fairly ranked, none of them ever stood above one push: all goes rolling wildly back upon the centre about Leuthen. Chaos come on us;— and all for mere lack of time: could Nadasti but once stretch out one minute into twenty! But he cannot. Nadasti does not himself lose head; skilfully covers the retreat, trying to rally once and again. Not for the first few furlongs, till the ditches, till the firwood, quagmires are all done, could Ziethen, now on the open ground, fairly hew in; "take whole battalions prisoners;" drive the crowd in an altogether stormy manner; and wholly confound the matter in this part.

Prince Karl, his messengers flying madly, has struggled as man seldom did to put himself in some posture about Leuthen, to get up some defences there. Leuthen itself, the churchyard of it especially, is on the defensive. Men are bringing cannon to the windmills, to the swelling ground on the north side of Leuthen; they dig ditches, build batteries, — could they but make Time halt, and Friedrich with him, for one quarter of an hour! But they cannot. By the extreme of diligence, the Austrians have in some measure swung themselves into a new position, or imperfect Line round Leuthen as a centre, — Lucchesi, voluntarily or by order, swinging southwards on the one hand; Nadasti swinging northwards by compulsion; — new Line at an angle say of 75° to the old one. And here, for an hour more, there was stiff fighting, the stiffest of the day; — of which, take one direct glimpse, from the Austrian side, furnished by a Young Gentleman famous afterwards:

Leuthen, let us premise, is a long Hamlet of the usual littery sort; with two rows, in some parts three, of farm-houses, barns, cattle-stalls; with Church, or even with two Churches, a Protestant and a Catholic; goes from east to west above a mile in length. With the wrecks of Nadasti tumbling into it pell-mell from the south-east, and Lucchesi desperately endeavouring to swing round from the north-west, not quite incoherently, and the Prussian fire-storm for accompaniment, Leuthen is probably the most chaotic place in the Planet

Earth, during that hour or so (from half-past two to half-past three) while the agony lasted. At one o'clock Nadasti was attacked; at two, he is tumbling in mid-career towards Leuthen: I guess the date of this Excerpt, or testimony by a Notable Eyewitness, may be half-past two; crisis of the agony just about to begin: and before four it was all finished again. Eye-witness is the young Prince de Ligne, now Captain in an Austrian regiment of Foot; and standing here in this perilous posture, having been called in as part of the Reserve. He says:

"Cry had risen for the Reserve," in which was my regiment, "that it must come on as fast as possible,"— to Leuthen, west of us yonder. "We ran what we could run. Our Lieutenant-"Colonel fell killed almost at the first; beyond this we lost "our Major, and indeed all the Officers but three,—three "only, and about eleven or twelve of the Volunteer or Cadet "kind. We had crossed two successive ditches, which lay in "an orchard to left of the first houses in Leuthen; and were "beginning to form in front of the Village. But there was no "standing of it. Besides a general cannonade such as can "hardly be imagined, there was a rain of case-shot upon this "Battalion, of which I, as there was no Colonel left, had to "take command; and a third Battalion of the Royal Prussian "Footguards, which had already made several of our regi-"ments pass that kind of muster, gave, at a distance of eighty "paces, the liveliest fire on us. It stood as if on the parade-"ground, that third Battalion, and waited for us, without "stirring.

"The Austrian regiment Andlau, at our right hand, could "not get itself formed properly by reason of the houses; it "was standing thirty deep, and sometimes its shot hit us on "the back. On my left the Austrian regiment Merci ran its "ways; and I was glad of that, in comparison. By no method "or effort could I get the dragoons of Batthyani, who stood "fifty yards in rear of me, to cut-in a little, and help me out," — no good cutting hereabouts, think the dragoons of Batthyani. "My soldiers, who were still tired with running, and "had no cannon (these either from necessity or choice they "had left behind), were got scattered, fewer in number, and "were fighting mainly out of sullenness. More our honour, "than the notion of doing good in the affair, prevented us "from running off. An Ensign of the regiment Arberg helped "me a while to form, from his and my own fragments, a kind "of line; but he was shot down. Two Officers of the Grena- "diers brought me what they still had. Some Hungarians, "too, were luckily got together. But at last, as, with all helps "and the remnants of my own brave Battalion, I had come "down to at most 200, I drew back to the Height where the "Windmill is,"* — where many have drawn back, and are standing in sheltered places, a hundred deep, say our Books.

Stiff fighting at Leuthen; especially furious till Leuthen Churchyard, a place with high stone walls, was got. Leuthen Village, we observe, was crammed with Austrians spitting fire from every coign of vantage; Church and Churchyard especially are a citadel of death. Cannon playing from the Windmill Heights, too; — moments are inestimable. The Prussian Commander (name charitably hidden), at Leuthen Churchyard, seems to hesitate in the murderous fire-deluge: Major Möllendorf, nameable from that day forward, growling, "No time this for study," dashes out himself, "*Ein andrer Mann* (Follow me whoever is a man)!" — smashes-in the Church Gate of the place, nine muskets blazing on him through it; smashes, after a desperate struggle, the Austrians clean out of it, and conquers the citadel.**

The Austrians, on confused terms, made stiff dispute in this second position, for about an hour. The Prussian Reserve was ordered up by Friedrich; the Prussian left wing, which had stood "refused," about Radaxdorf, till now: at one time nearly all the Prussians were in fire. Friedrich is here, is there, wherever

---

* Kutzen, p. 103 (from "Prince de Ligne's *Diary*, I. 63, German Translation").

** Müller, p. 42.

the press was greatest; "Prince Ferdinand," whom we now and then find named, as a diligent little fellow, and ascertain to be here in this and other Battles of Friedrich's, — "Prince Ferdinand at one time "pointed his cannon on the Bush or Fir Clump of Radax-"dorf; — an aide-de-camp came to him with message: "'You are firing on the King; the King is yonder!' "At which Ferdinand" (his dear little Brother) "*erschrack*," or almost fainted with terror.*

Stiff dispute; and had the Austrians possessed the Prussian dexterity in manœuvering, and a Friedrich been among them, — perhaps? But on their own terms, there was from the first little hope in it. "Behind the "Windmills they are a hundred men deep;" by and by, your Windmills, riddled to pieces, have to be abandoned; the Prussian left wing rushing on with bayonets, will not all of you have to go? Lucchesi, with his abundant Cavalry, seeing this latter movement and the Prussian flank bare in that part, will do a stroke upon them; — and this proved properly the finale of the matter, final to both Lucchesi and it.

The Prussian flank was to appearance bare in that leftward quarter; but only to appearance: Driesen with the left wing of Horse is in a Hollow hard by; strictly charged by Friedrich to protect said flank, and take nothing else in hand. Driesen lets Lucchesi gallop by, in this career of his; then emerges, ranked, and comes storming in upon Lucchesi's back, — entirely confounding his astonished Cavalry and their career. Astonished Cavalry bullet-storm on this side of them, edge of sword on that, take wing in all directions (or all except to west and south) quite over

* Kutzen, p. 110.

the horizon; Lucchesi himself gets killed, — crosses a still wider horizon, poor man. He began the ruin, and he ends it. For now Driesen takes the bared Austrians in flank, in rear; and all goes tumbling here too, and in few minutes is a general deluge rearward towards Saara and Lissa side.

At Saara the Austrians, sun just sinking, made a third attempt to stand; but it was hopelessly faint this time; went all asunder at the first push; and flowed then, torrent-wise, towards all its Bridges over the Schweidnitz Water, towards Breslau by every method. There are four Bridges, Stabelwitz below Lissa; Goldschmieden, Hermannsdorf, above; and the main one at Lissa itself, a standing Bridge on the Highroad (also of wood); and by this the chief torrent flows; Prussian horse pursuing vigorously; Prussian Infantry drawn up at Saara, resting some minutes after such a day's work.[*]

Truly a memorable bit of work; no finer done for a hundred years, or for hundreds of years; and the results of it manifold, immediate and remote. About 10,000 Austrians are left on the field, 3,000 of them slain; prisoners already 12,000, in a short time 21,000; flags 51, cannon 116; — "Conquest of Silesia" gone to water; Prince Karl and Austria fallen from their high hopes, in one day. The Prussians lost in killed 1,141, in wounded 5,118; 85 had been taken prisoners about Sagschütz and Gohlau, in the first struggle there.[**] There and at Leuthen Village had been the

---

[*] Archenholtz, i. 209; Seyfarth, Beylagen, ii. 243-253 (by an eyewitness, Intelligent succinct Account of the Battle and previous March; ib. 253-272, of the Sieges &c. following); Preuss, ii. 118, &c.; Tempelhof, i. 276.

[**] Kutzen, pp. 118, 125.

two tough passages; about an hour each; in three hours the Battle was done. "*Meine Herren*," said Friedrich, that night at parole, "after such a spell of work, you "deserve rest. This day will bring the renown of "your name, and of the Nation's, to the latest pos-"terity."

High and low had shone this day; especially these four: Ziethen, Driesen, Retzow, — and above all Moritz of Dessau. Riding up the line, as night fell, Friedrich, in passing Moritz and the right wing, drew bridle for an instant: "I congratulate you on the Vic-"tory, Herr Feldmarschall!" cried he cheerily, and with emphasis on the last word. Moritz, still very busy, answered slightly; and Friedrich repeated louder, "Don't you hear that I congratulate you, Herr *Feld-*"*marschall!*" — a glad sound to Moritz, who ever since Kolin had stood rather in the shadow. "You "have helped me, and performed every order, as none "ever did before in any battle," added the grateful King.

Riding up the line, all now grown dusky, Friedrich asks, "Any battalion a mind to follow me to Lissa?" Three battalions volunteering, follow him; three are plenty. At Saara, on the Great Road, things are fallen utterly dark. "Landlord, bring a lantern, and "escort." Landlord of the poor Tavern at Saara escorts obediently; lantern in his right hand, left hand holding by the King's stirrup-leather, — King (Excellency or General, as the Landlord thinks him) wishing to speak with the man. Will the reader consent to their Dialogue, which is dullish, but singular to have in an authentic form, with Nicolai as voucher?*

* *Anekdoten*, DL 281-285.

Like some poor old horse-shoe, ploughed-up on the field. Two farthings worth of rusty old iron; now little other than a curve of brown rust: but it galloped at the Battle of Leuthen; that is something! —

King. "Come near; catch me by the stirrup-leather" (Landlord with lantern does so). "We are on the Breslau "Great Road, that goes through Lissa, aren't we?"
Landlord. "Yea, Excellenz."
King. "Who are you?"
Landlord. "Your Excellenz, I am the *Krätschmer*" (Silesian for Landlord) "at Saara."
King. "You have had a great deal to suffer, I suppose."
Landlord. "Ach, your Excellenz, had not I! For the last "eight-and-forty hours, since the Austrians came across "Schweidnitz Water, my poor house has been crammed to the "door with them, so many servants they have; and such a "bullying and tumbling:—they have driven me half mad; and "I am clean plundered out."
King. "I am sorry indeed to hear that! — Were there "Generals too in your house? What said they? Tell me, "then."
Landlord. "With pleasure, your Excellenz. Well; yester-"day noon, I had Prince Karl in my parlour, and his Adju-"tants and people all crowding about. Such a questioning "and bothering! Hundreds came dashing in, and other "hundreds were sent out: in and out they went all night; no "sooner was one gone, than ten came. I had to keep a roar-"ing fire in the kitchen all night; so many officers crowding "to it to warm themselves. And they talked and babbled this "and that. One would say, 'That our King was coming on, "then, 'with his Potsdam Guard-Parade.' Another answers, "'*Oach*, he daren't come! He will run for it; we will let him "'run.' But now my delight is, our King has paid them their "fooleries so prettily this afternoon!"
King. "When got you rid of your high guests?"
Landlord. "About nine this morning the Prince got to "horse; and not long after three, he came past again, with a "swarm of officers; all going full speed for Lissa. So full of "bragging when they came; and now they were off, wrong

"side foremost! I saw how it was. And ever after him, the "flood of them ran, High-road not broad enough, — an hour "and more before it ended. Such a pellmell, such a welter, "cavalry and musketeers all jumbled: our King must have "given them a dreadful lathering. That is what they have got "by their bragging and their lying, — for, your Excellenz, "these people said, too, 'Our King was forsaken by his own "Generals, all his first people had gone and left him:' what I "never in this world will believe."

King (not liking even rumour of that kind). "There you "are right; never can such a thing be believed of my Army."

Landlord (whom this "*my*" has transfixed). "*Mein Gott*, "you are our *gnädigster König* (most gracious King) yourself! "Pardon, pardon, if, in my stupidity, I have"—

King. "No, you are an honest man:— probably, a Pro- "testant?"

Landlord. "*Joa, joa, Ihr Majestät*, I am of your Majesty's "creed!"

Crack-crack! At this point the Dialogue is cut short by sudden musket-shots from the woody fields to right; crackle of about twelve shots in all; which hurt nothing but some horse's feet, — had been aimed at the light, and too low. Instantly the light is blown out, and there is a hunting out of Croats; Lissa or environs not evacuated yet, it seems; and the King's Entrance takes place under volleyings and cannonadings.

King rides directly to the Schloss, which is still a fine handsome house, off the one street of that poor Village, — north side of street; well railed off, and its old fences now trimmed into flower-plots. The Schloss is full of Austrian Officers, bustling about, intending to quarter, when the King enters. They, and the force they still had in Lissa, could easily have taken him: but how could they know? Friedrich was surprised; but had to put the best face on it.* "*Bon soir, Messieurs!*" said he, with a gay tone, stepping in: "Is there still room left, think you?" The Austrians, bowing to the dust, make way reverently to the divinity that hedges a King of this sort; mutely escort him to the best room (such the popular account); and for certain, make off, they and theirs, towards the Bridge, which lies a little farther east, at the end of the Village.

Weistritz or Schweidnitz Water is a biggish muddy stream in that part; gushing and eddying; not voiceless, vexed by mills and their weirs. Some firing there was from Croats in the lower houses of the Village, and they had a cannon at the farther Bridge-end; but they were glad to get away, and vanish in the Night; muddy Weistritz singing hoarse adieu to their cannon and them. Prussian grenadiers plunged indignant into the houses; made short work of the musketries there. In few minutes, every Croat and Austrian was across, or silenced otherwise too well; Prussian cannon now going in the rear of them, and continuing to go, — such had been the order, "till the powder you have is done." Fire of musketry and occasional cannon lasts, all night, from the Lissa or Prussian side of the River, — "lest they burn this Bridge, or attempt some mischief." A thing far from their thoughts, in present circumstances.

The Prussian Host at Saara, hearing these noises, took to its arms again; and marched after the King. Thick darkness; silence; tramp, tramp: — a Prussian grenadier broke out, with solemn tenor voice again, into Church-Music; a known Church-Hymn, of the

---

* In Kutzen (pp. 121, 209 et seq.), explanation of the true circumstances, and source of the mistake.

homely *Te-Deum* kind; in which five-and-twenty thousand other voices, and all the regimental bands, soon join:

"*Nun danket alle Gott*	"Now thank God, one and all,
"*Mit Herzen, Mund und Händen,*	"With heart, with voice, with hands-a,
"*Der grosse Dinge thut*	"Who wonders great hath done,
"*An uns und allen Enden,*" *	"To us and to all lands-a."

And thus they advance; melodious, far-sounding, through the hollow Night, once more in a highly remarkable manner. A pious people, of right Teutsch stuff, tender though stout; and, except perhaps Oliver Cromwell's handful of Ironsides, probably the most perfect soldiers ever seen hitherto. Arriving at the end of Lissa, and finding all safe as it should be there, they make their bivouac, their parallelogram of two lines, miles long across the fields, left wing resting on Lissa, right on Guckerwitz; and, — having, I should think, at least tobacco to depend on, and healthy joyful hearts, — pass the night in a thankful, comfortable manner.

Leuthen was the most complete of all Friedrich's victories; two hours more of daylight, as Friedrich himself says, and it would have been the most decisive of this century.** As it was, the ruin of this big Army, 80,000 against 30,000,*** was as good as total; and a world of Austrian hopes suddenly collapsed; and all their Silesian Apparatus, making sure of Silesia beyond an *if*, was tumbled into wreck, — by this one stroke it had got, smiting the corner-stone of it as if with un-

---

* Müller, p. 48.
** *Œuvres de Frédéric,* iv. 167.
*** "89,000 was the Austrian strength before the Battle" (deduct the Garrisons of Schweidnitz and Liegnitz); Preuss, II. 109 (from the *Staff-Officers*).

expected lightning. On the morrow after Leuthen, Friedrich laid siege to Breslau; Karl had left a garrison of 17,000 in it, and a stout Captain, one Sprecher, determined on defence: such interests hung on Breslau, such immensities of stores were in it, had there been nothing else. Friedrich, pushing with all his strength, in spite of bad weather and of Sprecher's industrious defence, got it in twelve days.* Sprecher had posted placards on the gallows and up and down, terrifically proclaiming that any man convicted of mentioning surrender should be instantly hanged: but Friedrich's bombardment was strong, his assaults continual: and the ditches were threatening to freeze. On the seventh day of the siege, a Laboratorium blew up; on the ninth, a Powder-magazine, carrying a lump of the rampart away with it. Sprecher had to capitulate: Prisoners of War, we 17,000; our cannons, ammunitions (most opulent, including what we took from Bevern lately); these, we, and Breslau altogether; alas, it is all yours again.

Liegnitz Garrison, seeing no hope, consented to withdraw on leave.** Schweidnitz cannot be besieged till Spring come: except Schweidnitz, Maria Theresa, the high Kaiserinn, has no foot of ground in Silesia, which she thought to be hers again. Gone utterly, Patents and all; Schweidnitz alone waiting till Spring. To the lively joy of Silesia in general; to the thrice-lively sorrow, and alarm of certain individuals, leading Catholic Ecclesiastics mainly, who had misread the signs of the times in late months! There is one Schaff-

---

* 7th-19th December: *Diarium &c.* of it in *Helden-Geschichte*, IV. 955-961.
** 20th December: *Helden-Geschichte*, IV. 1016.

gotsch, Archbishop or head-man of them, especially, who is now in a bad way. Never was such royal favour; never such ingratitude, say the Books at wearisome length. Schaffgotsch was a showy man of quality, nephew of the quondam Austrian Governor, whom Friedrich, across a good deal of Papal and other opposition, got pushed into the Catholic Primacy, and took some pains to make comfortable there, — Order of the Black Eagle, guest at Potsdam, and the like; — having a kind of fancy for the airy Schaffgotsch, as well as judging him suitable for this Silesian High-Priesthood, with his moderate ideas and quality ways, — which I have heard were a little dissolute withal. To the whole of which Schaffgotsch proved signally traitorous and ingrate; and had plucked off the Black Eagle (say the Books, nearly breathless over such a sacrilege) on some public occasion, prior to Leuthen, and trampled it under his feet, the unworthy fellow. Schaffgotsch's pathetic Letter to Friedrich, in the new days posterior to Leuthen, and Friedrich's contemptuous inexorable answer, we could give, but do not: why should we? Oh King, I know your difficulties, and what epoch it is. But, of a truth, your airy dissolute Schaffgotsch, as a grateful "Archbishop and Grand-Vicar," is almost uglier to me than as a Traitor ungrateful for it; and shall go to the Devil in his own way! They would not have him in Austria; he was not well received at Rome; happily died before long.* Friedrich was not cruel to Schaffgotsch or the others, contemptuously mild rather; but he knew henceforth what to expect of them, and slightly changed this and that in his Silesian methods in consequence.

* Preuss, ii. 113, 114; Kutzen, pp. 12, 155-160, for the real particulars.

Of Prince Karl let us add a word. On the morrow after Leuthen, Captain Prince de Ligne and old Papa D'Ahremberg could find little or no Army; they stept across to Gräbschen, a village on the safe side of the Lohe, and there found Karl and Daun: "rather silent, "both; one of them looking, 'Who would have thought "'it!' the other, 'Didn't I tell you?'"—and knowing nothing, they either, where the Army was. Army was, in fact, as yet nowhere. "Croat fellows, in this Farm- "stead of ours," says De Ligne, "had fallen to shooting "pigeons." The night had been unusually dark; the Austrian Army had squatted into woods, into office-houses, farm-villages, over a wide space of country; and only as the day rose, began to dribble in. By count, they are still 50,000; but heart-broken, beaten as men seldom were. "What sound is that?" men asked yesterday at Brieg, forty miles off; and nobody could say, except that it was some huge Battle, fateful of Silesia and world. Breslau had it louder; Breslau was still more anxious. "What *is* all that?" asked somebody (might be Deblin the Shoemaker, for anything I know) of an Austrian sentry there: "That? That is the Prussians giving us such a beating as we never had." What news for Deblin the Shoemaker, if he is still above ground! —

"Prince Karl, gathering his distracted fragments, put "17,000 into Breslau by way of ample garrison there; and "with the rest made off circuitously for Schweidnitz; thence "for Landshut, and down the Mountains, home to Königs-"gratz, — self and Army in the most wrecked condition. "Chased by Ziethen; Ziethen 'sticking always to the hocks "of them,' as Friedrich eagerly enjoins on him; or some-"times it is, 'sitting on the breeches of them:' for about a

"fortnight to come.* Ziethen took 2,000 prisoners; no end
"of baggages, of wagons left in the difficult places: wild
"weather even for Ziethen, still more for Karl, among the
"Silesian-Bohemian Hill-roads: heavy rains, deep muds,
"then sudden glass, with cutting snowblasts: 'An Army not
"a little dilapidated,' writes Prince Karl, almost with tears
"in his eyes; 'Army without linens, without clothes; in con-
"'dition truly sad and pitiable; and has always, so close
"'are the enemy, to encamp, though without tents.'** Did
"not get to Königsgratz, and safe shelter, for ten days
"more. Counted, at Königsgratz in the Christmas time,
"37,000 rank and file, — '22,000 of whom are gone to hos-
"pital,' by the Doctor's report.

"Universal astonishment, indignation, even incredulity,
"is the humour at Vienna: the high Kaiserinn herself, kept
"in the dark for some time, becomes dimly aware; and by
"Kaiser Franz's own advice, she relieves Prince Karl from
"his military employments, and appoints Daun instead.
"Prince Karl withdrew to his Government of the Nether-
"lands; and with the aid of generous liquors, and what
"natural magnanimity he had, spent a noiseless life thence-
"forth; Sword laid entirely on the shelf; and immortal
"Glory, as of Alexander and the like, quite making its exit
"from the scene, convivial or other. 'The first General in
"the world,' so he used to be ten years ago, in Austria, in
"England, Holland, the thrice-greatest of Generals: but
"now he has tried Friedrich in Five pitched Battles (Czaslau,
"Hohenfriedberg, Sohr, then Prag, then Leuthen); — been
"beaten every time, under every form of circumstance; and
"now, at Leuthen, the fifth beating is such, no public,
"however ignorant, can stand it farther. The ignorant
"public changes its long-eared eulogies into contumeliously
"horrid shrieks of condemnation; in which one is still farther
"from joining. 'That crossing of the Rhine,' says Friedrich,
"'was a *belle chose;* but flatterers blew him into dangerous
"'self-conceit; besides he was ill-obeyed, as others of us
"'have been.'*** Adieu to him, poor redfaced soul; — and

* Eleven Royal Autographs: in Blumenthal, *Life of De Ziethen* (n. 94-111), a feeble incorrect Translation of them.
** Kutzen, p. 134 ("Prince Karl to the Kaiser, December 14th").
*** "Prince de Ligne, *Mémoires sur Frédéric* (Berlin, 1780), p. 58" (Preuss, ii. 113).

"good liquor to him, — at least if he can take it in mo-
"deration!"

The astonishment of all men, wise and simple, at
this sudden oversetting of the scene of things, and
turning of the gazetteer-diplomatic theatre bottom
uppermost, was naturally extreme, especially in gazetteer and diplomatic circles; and the admiration, willing
or unwilling, of Friedrich, in some most essential
points of him, rose to a high pitch. Better soldier, it
is clear, has not been heard of in the modern ages.
Heroic constancy, courage superior to fate: several
clear features of a hero; — pity he were such a liar
withal, and ignorant of common honesty; thought the
simple sort, in a bewildered manner, endeavouring to
forget the latter features, or think them *not* irreconcilable.
Military judges, of most various quality, down to this
day, pronounce Leuthen to be essentially the finest
Battle of the century; and indeed one of the prettiest
feats ever done by man in his Fighting Capacity. Napoleon, for instance, who had run over these Battles of
Friedrich (apparently somewhat in haste, but always
with a word upon them which is worth gathering from
such a source), speaks thus of Leuthen: "This Battle
"is a masterpiece of movements, of manœuvres, and of
"resolution; enough to immortalise Friedrich, and rank
"him among the greatest Generals. Manifests, in the
"highest degree, both his moral qualities and his mili-
"tary." *

How the English Walpoles, in Parliament and out

---

* Montholon, *Mémoires &c. de Napoléon*, vii. 211. This Napoleon Summary *of Friedrich's Campaigns*, and these brief Bits of Criticism, are pleasant reading, though the fruit evidently of slight study, and do credit to
Napoleon perhaps still more than to Friedrich.

of it; how the Prussian Sulzers, D'Argenses, the gazetteer and vague public, may have spoken and written at that time, when the matter was fresh and on everybody's tongue, — judge still by two small symptoms which we have to show:

1º. *A Letter of Friedrich's to D'Argens* (Dürgoy, near Breslau, 19th December 1757). — "Your friendship seduces "you, *mon cher;* I am but a paltry knave *(polisson)* in com- "parison with 'Alexander,' and not worthy to tie the shoe- "latchets of 'Cæsar!' Necessity, who is the mother of in- "dustry, has made me act, and have recourse to desperate "remedies in evils of a like nature.

"We have got here" (this day, by capitulation of Breslau) "from fourteen to fifteen thousand prisoners: so that, in all, "I have above twenty-three thousand of the Queen's troops "in my hands, fifteen Generals, and above seven hundred "Officers. 'Tis a plaster on my wounds, but it is far enough "from healing them.

"I am now about marching to the Mountain region, to "settle the chain of quarters there; and if you will come, "you will find the roads free and safe. I was sorry at the "Abbé's treason," — paltry De Prades, of whom we heard enough already.*

2º. *A Pottery-Apotheosis of Friedrich.* — "There stands "on this mantelpiece," says one of my Correspondents, the amiable Smelfungus, in short, whom readers are acquainted with, "a small China Mug, not of bad shape; declaring "itself, in one obscure corner, to be made at Worcester, "'R. I., Worcester, 1757' (late in the season, I presume, "demand being brisk); which exhibits, all round it, a diligent " Potter's-Apotheosis of Friedrich, hastily got up to meet the "general enthusiasm of English mankind. Worth, while it "lasts unbroken, a moment's inspection from you in hurrying "along.

"Front side, when you take our Mug by the handle for "drinking from it, offers a poor well-meant China Portrait; "labelled KING OF PRUSSIA: copy of Friedrich's Portrait, by

* *Œuvres de Frédéric,* XIX. 47.

"Pesne, twenty years too young for the time, smiling out
"nobly upon you; upon whom there descends with rapidity
" a small Genius (more like a Cupid who had hastily forgotten
"his bow, and goes headforemost on another errand) to drop
"a wreath on this deserving head; — wreath far too small for
"ever getting on (owing to distance, let us hope), though
"the artless Painter makes no sign; and indeed both Genius
"and wreath, as he gives them, look almost like a big insect,
"which the King will be apt to treat harshly if he notice it.
"On the opposite side, again, separated from Friedrich's
"back by the handle, is an enormous image of Fame, with
"wings filling half the Mug, with two trumpets going at once
"(a bass, probably, and a treble), who flies with great ease;
"and between her eager face and the unexpectant one of
"Friedrich (who is 180° off, and knows nothing of it) stands
"a circular Trophy, or Imbroglio of drums, pikes, muskets,
"cannons, field-flags and the like; very slightly tied
"together, — the knot, if there is one, being hidden by
"some fantastic bit of scroll or escutcheon, with a Fame and
"*one* trumpet scratched on it; — and high out of the Im-
"broglio rise three standards inscribed with Names, which
"we perceive are intended to be names of Friedrich's
"Victories; standards notable at this day, with Names which
"I will punctually give you.

"Standard first, which flies to the westward or leftward,
"has 'Reisberg' (no such place on this distracted globe;
"meaning Bevern's *Reichenberg*, perhaps), — 'Reisberg,'
"'Prague,' 'Collin.' Middle standard curves beautifully
"round its staff, and gives us to read, 'Welham' (non-
"extant, too; may mean *Welmina* or Lobositz), 'Rossbach'
"(very good), 'Breslau' (poor Bevern's, thought a *victory* in
"Worcester, at this time!). Standard third, which flies to
"eastward or right hand, has 'Neumark' (that is, *Neumarkt*
"and the Austrian Bread-ovens, 4th December); 'Lissa' (not
"yet *Leuthen* in English nomenclature); and 'Breslau' again,
"which means the capture of Breslau *City* this time, and is a
"real success, 7th-19th December; — giving us the ap-
"proximate date, Christmas 1757, to this hasty Mug. A Mug
"got up for temporary English enthusiasm, and the ac-
"cidental instruction of posterity. It is of tolerable China;
"holds a good pint, 'To the Protestant Hero, with all the

"honours;' — and offers, in little, a curious eyehole into
"the then England, with its then lights and notions, which
"is now so deep hidden from us, under volcanic ashes, French
"Revolutions, and the wrecks of a Hundred very decadent
"Years."

CHAPTER XI.

WINTER IN BRESLAU: THIRD CAMPAIGN OPENS.

FRIEDRICH during those grand victories, is suffering sadly in health, "*colique depuis huit jours*, neither sleep nor appetite;" "eight months of mere anguishes and agitations do wear one down." He is tired too, he says, of the mere business talk, coarse and rugged, which has been his allotment lately; longs for some humanly roofed kind of lodging, and a little talk that shall have flavour in it.* The troops once all in their Winter-quarters, he sits down in Breslau as his own wintering place: place of relaxation, — of rest, or at least of changed labour, — no man needing it more. There for some three months he had a tolerable time; perhaps, by contrast, almost a delightful. Readers must imagine it; we have no details allowed us, nor any time for them even if we had.

There come various visitors, various gaieties, — King's Birthday (January 24th); quality Balls, "at which Royal Majesty sometimes deigned to show himself." A lively Breslau, in comparison. Sister Amelia paid a beautiful visit of a fortnight or more: Sister Amelia, and along with her, two married Cousins (once Margravines of Schwedt), whose Husbands, little Brother Ferdinand, and Eugene of Würtemberg, are wintering here. The Marquis D'Argens, how exquisitely treated

---

* Letters of his to Prince Henri (December 26th &c.: *Œuvres*, xxvi. 167, 169; Stenzel, v. 153).

we shall see, is a principal figure; Excellency Mitchell, deep in very important business just now, is another. Reader de Catt (he who once, in a Dutch River-Boat, got into conversation with the snuffy gentleman in black wig) made his new appearance, this Winter,— needed now, since De Prades is off. "Should you have known me again?" asked Friedrich. "Hardly, in that dress; besides, your Majesty looks thinner." "That I can believe, with the cursed life I have been leading!"* There came also, day not given, a Captain Guichard ("Major Quintus Icilius" that is to be) with his new Book on the Art Military of the Ancients, *Mémoires Militaires sur les Grecs et les Romains*;** which cannot but be welcome to Friedrich. A solid account of that matter, by the first man who had ever understood both War and Greek. Far preferable to Folard's, a man without Greek at all, and with military ideas not a little fantastic here and there. Of Captain Guichard, were his Book once read, and himself a little known, there will be more to say. For the present, fancy him retained as supernumerary: — and in regard to Friedrich's Winter generally, accept the following small hints, small but direct:

Friedrich to D'Argens (three different times).

1º. *On the road to Leuthen* "(Torgau, 15th November 1757). * * I have been obliged to have the Abbé arrested" (De Prades, of whom enough, long since); "he has been playing "the spy, and I have many evident proofs of it. That is very "infamous and very ungrateful. — I have made a prodigious "quantity of verses (*prodigieusement de vers*). If I live, I will "show them you in Winter-quarters: if I perish, they are

* Rödenbeck, i. 285.
** La Haye, 2 tomes, 4to, 1757 (Nicolai, *Anekdoten*, vi. 134).

"bequeathed to you, and I have ordered that they be put "into your hand."

"Adieu, my dear Marquis. I fancy you to be in bed: "don't rot there; — and remember you have promised to "join me in Winter-quarters:"— on this latter point Friedrich is very urgent, amiably eager; prepared to wrap the poor Marquis in cotton, and carry him and lodge him, like glass with care.* For example:

2°. *While settling the Winter-quarters* ("Striegau, 26th "December 1757:" Siege of Breslau done ten days ago). * * "What a pleasure to hear you are coming! Your travelling "you can do in your own way. I have chosen a party of "Light Horse (*Jäger*), who will appear at Berlin to conduct "you. You can make short journeys: the first to Frankfurt, "the second to Crossen, the third to Grünberg, fourth to "Glogau, fifth to Parchwitz, sixth to Breslau. I have "directed that horses be ordered for you, that your rooms "be warmed everywhere, and good fowls ready on all roads. "Your apartment in this House" (Royal House in Breslau, which the King has built for himself years ago) "is carpeted, "hermetically shut. You shall suffer nothing from draughts "or from noise."**—Lucky Marquis; what a landlord! Came accordingly; staid till deep in April, — waiting latterly for weather, I perceive; long after the King himself was off. Thus:

3°. *Friedrich on the field again for five weeks past* ("Münster-"berg, 23d April, 1758"). "Adieu, dear Marquis; I fancy "you are now in Berlin again. Go to Charlottenburg when-"ever and how you like; take care of yourself; and be ready "for the beginning of October next! — As to me, *mon cher*, "I am off to fight windmills and ostriches (*Autruches*), that "is Russians and Austrians (*Autrichiens*). Adieu, *mon* "*cher*.***

There circulated in the Newspapers, this Winter, something of what was called a *Letter* from Friedrich to Maria Theresa, formally proposing Peace, after these magnificent successes. And certainly, of all things in the Earth, Friedrich would have best liked Peace, this

---

* *Œuvres de Frédéric,* xix. 43.   ** Ib. xix. 48.   *** Ib. xix. 49.

year, last year, and for the next five years: "Go home, then, good neighbours; don't break into my house, don't cut my poor throat, and we will be friends again!" Friedrich, it appears, had actually, finding or making opportunity, sent some polite Letter, of pacific tenor, in his light clever way, to that address;—not without momentary hopes of perhaps getting good from it.* And the Kaiserinn herself, Austria's high Mother, did, they say, after such a Leuthen coming on the back of such a Rossbach, feel discouraged; but the Pompadour (not France's Mother, whatever she might be to France) was of far other mind: "Do not speak of it, *ma Reine!* Double or quits, that is our game: can we yield for a little ill-luck? Never!"

France dismisses its D'Argenson, "What Armies are these of his; flying home on us, like draggled poultry, across the Rhine!"— summons the famed Belleisle to be War-Minister, and give things an eagle-quality:** France engages to pay its subsidies better (France now the general paying party, Austria, Sweden, Russia itself, all looking to France,—would she were as punctual as England used to be!),— in a word, engages to be magnanimous extremely, and will hear of nothing but persistence. "Shall not we reap, then, where there is such a harvest standing white to us?" Kaunitz admits that there never will again be such a chance. — Peace, it is clear enough, will not be got of these people by any Letter, or human device whatever, except simply by uttermost, more or less miraculous fighting for it. Friedrich is profoundly aware

---

* In *Preuss*, II. 150 (Friedrich's Letter mostly given;—bearer a Prince von Lobkowitz, prisoner at Leuthen, now going home on handsome terms): Stenzel, v. 124 (for the *per-contra* feeling).

** "26th February 1758" (*Barbier*, IV. 258).

of this fact; — is busy completing his Army: 145,000 for the field, this Year, 53,000 the Silesian part, "a good many of them Austrian deserters;"* and is closing an important Subsidy Treaty with England, — of which more anon.

And if this is the mood in France and Austria, think what Russia's will be! The Czarina is not dead of dropsy, as some had expected, but, on the contrary, alive, and fiercer than ever; furious against Apraxin, and determined that Fermor, his successor, shall defy Winter, and begin work at once. She has indignantly dismissed Apraxin (to be tried by Court Martial, he); dismisses Bestuchef the Chancellor; appoints a new General, Fermor by name; orders Fermor to go and lose not a moment, now in the depth of Winter since it was not done in the crown of Summer, and take possession of East Preussen in her name.

Which Fermor does; 16th January, crosses the border again, 31,000 in all, without opposition except from the frost; plants himself up and down, — only two poor Prussian battalions there; who retire with their effects, especially "with seven wagons of money." January 22d, Fermor enters Königsberg; publishes no end of proclamations, manifestoes, rescripts, to inform the poor people, trembling at the Cossack atrocities of last Year, "That his august Sovereign Elizabeth of All the Russias has now become Proprietress of East Preussen, which shall be perfectly protected and exquisitely well governed henceforth; and that all men of official or social position have, accordingly, to come and take the oath to her, with the due alacrity and punctuality, at their peril."

* Stenzel, v. 135.

Jan. — April 1758.

No man is willing for the operation, most men shudder at it; but who can help them? Surely it was an unblessed operation. Poor souls, one pities them; for at heart they were, and continued, loyal to their own King; thoroughly abhorrent of becoming Russian, as Czarish Majesty has thoroughly resolved they shall. Some few absconded, leaving their property as spoil; the rest swore, with mental reservation, with shifts, such as they could devise: — for example, some were observed to swear with gloves on; the right hand, which they held up, was a mere right *fist* with a stuffed glove at the end of it, — *so* help me Beelzebub (or whoever is the recording Angel here)!* And thus does Preussen, with astonishment, as by the spell of a Czarina Circe, find itself changed suddenly to Russian: and does not recover the old human form till four years hence, — when, again suddenly, as we shall see, the Circe and her wand chance to get broken.

Friedrich could not mend or prevent this bad Business; but was so disgusted with it, he never set foot in East Preussen again, — never could bear to behold it, after such a transformation into temporary Russian shape. I cannot say he abhorred this constrained Oath as I should have done: on the contrary, in the first spurt of indignation, he not only protested aloud, but made reprisals, — "Swear *me* those Saxons, then!" said he; and some poor magistrates of towns, and official people, had to make a figure of swearing (if not allegiance altogether, allegiance for the time being), in the same sad fashion, till one's humour cooled again.** East Preussen, lost in this way, held by its King as

---

* *Helden-Geschichte*, v. 147-9; Preuss, II. 145, III. 578, IV. 477, &c.
** Preuss, II. 163: Oath given in *Helden-Geschichte*, v. 631.

before, or more passionately now than ever; still loved Friedrich, say the Books; but it is Russia's for the present, and the mischief is done. East Preussen itself, Circe Czarina cherishing it as her own, had a much peaceabler time: in secret it even sent moneys, recruits, numerous young volunteers to Friedrich; much more, hopes and prayers. But his disgust with the late transformation by enchantment was inexpiable.

It was May or June, as had been anticipated, before the Russian main Army made its practical appearance in those parts. Fermor had, in the interim, seized Thorn, seized Elbing ("No offence, magnanimous Polacks, it is only for a time!"), — and would fain have had Dantzig too, but Dantzig wouldn't. Not till June 16th did the unwieldly mass (on paper 104,000, and in effect, and exclusive of Cossack rabble, about 75,000) get on way; and begin slowly staggering westward. Very slowly, and amid incendiary fire and horrid cruelty, as heretofore; — and in August coming we shall be sure to hear of it.

Lehwald was just finishing with the Swedes, — had got them all bottled up in Stralsund again, about New-year's time, when these Russians crossed into Preussen. We said nothing of the Swedish so-called Campaign of last Year; — and indeed are bound to be nearly silent of that and of all the others. Five Campaigns of them, or at least Four and a half; such Campaigns as were never made before or since. Of Campaign 1757, the memorable feature is that of the whole "Swedish Division," as the laughing Newspapers called it, which was "put to flight by Five Berlin Postillions;" — substantially a truth, as follows:

"Night of September 12th-13th, the Swedes, 22,000 "strong, did at last begin business; crossed Peene River, "the boundary between their Pommern and ours; and, "having nothing but some fractions of Militia to oppose them, "soon captured the Redoubts there; spread over Prussian "Pommern, and on into the Uckermark; diligently raising "contributions, to a heavy amount. No less than 90,000*l.* in "all for this poor Province; though, by a strange accident, "60,000*l.* proved to be the actual sum.

"Towards the end of October they had got as much as "60,000*l.* from the northern parts of Uckermark, Prentzlow "being their headquarter during that operation; and they "now sent out a Detachment of 200 grenadiers and 100 "dragoons towards Zehdenick, another little Town, some "forty miles farther south, there to wring out the remaining "sum. The Detachment marched by night, not courting "notice; but people had heard of its coming, and five Prussian "Postillions, — shifty fellows, old hussars it may be, at any "rate skilful on the trumpet, and furnished with hussar "jackets and an old pistol each, determined to do something "for their Country. The Swedish Detachment had not "marched many miles, when, — after or before some "flourishes of martial trumpeting, — there verily fell on the "Swedish flank, out of a clump of dark wood, five shots, "and wounded one man. To the astonishment and panic of "the other Two hundred and ninety-nine; who made instant "retreat, under new shots and trumpet-tones, as if it were "from five whole hussar regiments; — retreat, double-quick, "to Prentzlow; alarm waxing by the speed; alarm spreading "at Prentzlow itself: so that the whole Division got to its "feet, recrossed the Peene; and Uckermark had nothing "more to pay, for that bout! This is not a fable, such as go "in the Newspapers," adds my Authority, "but an accurate "fact:" * — probably, in our day, the alone memorable one of that "Swedish War."

"The French," says another of my Notes, "who did "the subsidying all round (who paid even the Russian "Subsidy, though in Austria's name), had always an "idea that the Swedes, — 22,000 stout men, this year, 4,000 "of them cavalry, — might be made to cooperate with the

* *Helden-Geschichte*, iv. 764, 807; Archenholtz, i. 160.

"Russians; with them or with somebody; and do some-
"thing effective in the way of destroying Friedrich. And
"besides their subsidies and bribings, the French took
"incredible pains with this view; incessantly contriving,
"correspondencing, and running to and fro between the
"parties;* but had not, even from the Russians and Czarish
"Majesty, much of a result, and from the Swedes had ab-
"solutely none at all. By French industry and flagitation,
"the Swedish Army was generally kept up to about 20,000:
"the soldiers were expert with their fighting-tools, knew
"their field-exercise well; had fine artillery, and were stout
"hardy fellows: but the guidance of them was wonderful.
"'They had no field-commissariat,' says one Observer, 'no
"'field-bakery, no magazines, no pontoons, no light troops;
"'and,' among the Higher Officers, 'no subordination.'**
"Were, in short, commanded by nobody in particular. Com-
"manded by Senator Committee-men in Stockholm; and,
"on the field, by Generals anxious to avoid responsibility;
"who, instead of acting, held continual Councils of War.
"The history of their Campaigns, year after year, is, in
"summary, this:

"Late in the season (always late, War-Offices at home,
"and Captaincies here, being in such a state), they emerge
"from Stralsund, an impregnable place of their own, —
"where the men, I observe, have had to live on dried fishy
"substances, instead of natural boiled oatmeal;*** and have
"died extensively in consequence: — they march from Stral-
"sund, a forty or thirty miles, till they reach the Swedish-
"Pommern boundary, Peone River; a muddy sullen stream,
"flowing through quagmire meadows, which are miles broad,

* For example: M. le Marquis de Montalembert, *Correspondance avec
&c., étant employé par le Roi de France à l'Armée Suédoise*, 1757-1761 (" with
the Swedish Army," yes, and sometimes with the Russian, — and sometimes on the French Coasts, ardently fortifying against Pitt and his Descents there: — a very intelligent, industrious, observant man; still amusing
to read, if one were idler), *à Londres* (evidently Paris), 1777, 3 soll., small
8vo. Then, likewise very intelligent, there is a Montazet, a Mortaigne, a
Caulaincourt; a *Campagne des Russes en 1757*; &c. &c. — In short, a great
deal of fine faculty employed there in spinning ropes from sand.
** Archenholtz, i. 158.
*** Montalembert, i. 32-37, 335, 394 &c. (that of the demand for Norse
porridge, which interested me, I cannot find again).

"on each shore: River unfordable everywhere; only to be
"crossed in four or five places, where paved causeways are.
"The Swedes, with deliberation, cross Peene; after some
"time, capture the bits of Redoubts, and the one or two
"poor Prussian Towns upon it; Anklam Redoubt, *Peene-*
"*münde* (Peene-mouth) Redoubt; and rove forward into
"Prussian Pommern, or over into the Uckermark, for fifty,
"for a hundred miles; exacting contributions; foraging what
"they can; making the poor country people very miserable,
"and themselves not happy,—their soldiers 'growing yearly
"'more plunderous,' says Archenholtz, 'till at length they
"'got, though much shyer of murder, to resemble Cossacks,'
"in regard to other pleas of the crown.

"There is generally some fractional regiment or so of
"Prussian force, left under some select General Manteuffel,
"Colonel Belling; who hangs diligently on the skirts of
"them, exploding by all opportunities. There have been
"Country Militias voluntarily got on foot, for the occasion;
"five or six small regiments of them; officered by Prussian
"Veterans of the Squirearchy in those parts; who do ex-
"cellent service. The Governor of Stettin, Bevern, our old
"Silesian friend, strikes out now and then, always vigilant,
"prompt and effective, on a chance offering. This, through
"Summer, is what opposition can be made: and the Swedes,
"without magazines, scout-service, or the like military ap-
"pliances, but willing enough to fight' (when they can *see*),
"and living on their shifts, will rove inward, perhaps 100
"miles; say south-westward, say south-eastward' (towards
Ruppin, which we used to know),—"they love to keep
"Mecklenburg usually on their flank, which is a friendly
"Country. Small fights befal them, usually beatings; never
"anything considerable. That is their success through
"Summer.

"Then, in Autumn, some remnant more of Prussian
"regulars arrive, disposable now for that service; upon which
"the Swedes are driven over Peene again (quite sure to be
"driven, when the River with its quagmires freezes); lose
"Anklam Redoubt, Peenemünde Redoubt; lose Demmin,
"Wollin; are followed into Swedish Pommern, oftenest to
"the gates of Stralsund, and are locked up there, there and
"in Rügen adjoining, till a new season arrive."—This year

(1757-8), Lehwald, on turning the key of Stralsund, might have done a fine feat; frost having come suddenly, and welded Rügen to the mainland. "What is to hinder you from starving them into surrender?" signifies Friedrich, hastily: "Besiege me Stralsund!" Which Lehwald did; but should have been quicker about it; or the thaw came too soon, and admitted ships with provision again. Upon which Lehwald resigned, to a General Graf von Dohna; and went home, as grown too old: and Dohna kept them bottled there till the usual Russian Advent (deep in June); by which time, what with limited stockfish diet, what with sore labour (breaking of the ice, whenever frost reappeared) and other hardship, more than half of them had died. — "Every new "season, there was a new General tried; but without the "least improvement. There was mockery enough, complaint "enough; indignant laughter in Stockholm itself; and the "Dalecarlians thought of revolting: the Senator Committee- "men held firm, ballasted by French gold, for four years.

"The Prussian Militias are a fine trait of the matter; "about fifteen regiments in different parts; — about five in "Pommern, which set the example; which were suddenly "raised last Autumn by the *Stände* themselves, drilled in "Stettin continually, while the Swedes were under way, and "which stood ready for some action, under veterans of the "squirearchy, when the Swedes arrived. They were kept "up through the War. The *Stände* even raised a little fleet,* "river fleet and coast fleet, twelve gunboats, with a powerful "carronade in each, and effective men and captain; a great "check on plundering and coast-mischief, till the Swedes, "who are naval, at last made an effort and destroyed them "all."

Friedrich was very sensible of these procedures on the part of his *Stände;* and perhaps readers are not prepared for such, or for others of the like, which we could produce elsewhere, in a Country without Constitution to speak of. Friedrich raises no new taxes, — except upon himself exclusively, and these to the very

* Archenholtz, i. 110.

blood; — Friedrich gets no Life-and-Fortune Addresses of the vocal or printed sort, but only of the acted. Very much the preferable kind, where possible, to all parties concerned. These poor militias and flotillas one cheerfully puts on record; cheerfully nothing else, in regard to such a Swedish War; — nor shall we henceforth insult the human memory by another word upon it that is not indispensable.

Of the English Subsidy.

One of Friedrich's most important affairs, at present, — vitally connected with his Army and its furnishings, which is the all-important, — was his Subsidy Treaty with England. It is the third treaty he has signed with England in regard to this War; the second in regard to subsidy for it; and it is the first that takes real practical effect. It had cost difficulty in adjusting, not a little correspondence and management from Mitchell; for the King is very shy about subsidy, though grim necessity prescribes it as inevitable; and his pride, and his reflections on the last Subsidy Treaty, "One Million sterling, Army of Observation, and Fleet in the Baltic," instead of which came Zero and Kloster-Zeven, have made him very sensitive. However, all difficulties are got over; Plenipotentiary Knyphausen, Pitt, Britannic Majesty and everybody striving to be rational and practical; and at London, 11th April 1758, Subsidy Treaty, admirably brief and to the point, is finished:* "That Friedrich shall have Four Million Thalers, that is, 670,000 *l.*; payable in London to his order, in October, this Year; which sum Friedrich

---

* In four short Articles; given in *Helden-Geschichte*, v. 16-17.

engages to spend wholly in maintenance and increase of his Army for behoof of the common object; — neither party to dream of making the least shadow of peace or truce without the other." Of Baltic Fleet, there is nothing said; nor, in regard to that, was anything done, this year or afterwards; highly important as it would have been to Friedrich, with the Navies so-called of both Sweden and Russia doing their worst upon him. "Why not spare me a small English squadron, and blow these away?" Nor was the why ever made clear to him; the private why being, that Czarish Majesty had, last year, intimated to Britannic, "Any such step on your part will annihilate the now old friendship of Russia and England, and be taken as a direct declaration of War!" — which Britannic Majesty, for commercial and miscellaneous reasons, hoped always might be avoided. Be silent, therefore, on that of Baltic Fleet.

In all the spoken or covenanted points, the Treaty was accurately kept: 670,000 *l.*, two-thirds of a million very nearly, will, in punctual promptitude, come to Friedrich's hand, were October here. And in regard to Ferdinand (a point left silent, this too) Friedrich's expectations were exceeded, not the contrary, so long as Pitt endured. This is the Third English-Prussian Treaty of the Seven-Years War, as we said above; and it is the First that took practical effect: this was followed by three others, year after year, of precisely the same tenor, which were likewise practical and punctually kept, — the last of them, "12th December 1760," had reference to Subsidy for 1761: — and before another came, Pitt was out. So that, in all, Friedrich had Four Subsidies; $670,000\ l. + 4 = 2,680,000\ l.$ of English money altogether: — and it is computed by some, there was never as much good fighting otherwise had out of all the 800,000,000 *l.* we have funded in that peculiar line of enterprise.*

Pitt had no difficulty with his Parliament, or with his Public, in regard to this Subsidy; the contrary rather. Seldom, if ever, was England in such a heat of enthusiasm about any Foreign Man as about Friedrich, in these months since Rossbach and what had followed. Celebrating this "Protestant Hero," authentic new Champion of Christendom; toasting him, with all the honours, out of its Worcester and other Mugs, very high indeed. Take these Three Clippings from the old Newspapers, omitting all else; and rekindle these, by good inspection and consideration, into feeble symbolic lamps of an old illumination, now fallen so extinct.

No. 1. *Reverend Mr. Whitfield and the Protestant Hero.* "Monday, January 2d," 1758, "was observed as a Day of "Thanksgiving, at the Chapel in Tottenham-Court Road" (brand-new Chapel, still standing and acting, though now in a dingier manner), "by Mr. Whitfield's people, for the signal "Victories gained by the King of Prussia over his Enemies.** "'Why rage the Heathen; why do the people imagine a vain "thing? Sinful beings we, perilously sunk in sin against the "Most High: — but they, do they think that, by earthly "propping and hoisting, their unblessed Chimera, with his "Three Hats, can sweep away the Eternal Stars!'" — In this

---

* First Treaty, 16th January 1756 (is in *Helden-Geschichte,* III. 681), "We will oppose by arms any foreign Armament entering Germany;" Second Treaty, 11th January 1757 (never published till 1809), is in Scholl, III. 30-33: "one million subsidy, a Fleet &c." (not *kept* at all); after which, Third Treaty (the *first* really issuing in subsidy and performance) is 11th April 1758 (given in *Helden-Geschichte,* v. 17); Fourth (really second), 7th December 1758 (Ib. v. 752); Fifth (*third*), 9th November 1759; Sixth (*fourth*), 12th December 1760. See *Preuss,* II. 124 n.

** *Gentleman's Magazine,* XXVIII. (for 1758), p. 41.

strain, I suppose: Protestant Hero and Heaven's long-suffering Patiences and Mercies in raising up such a one for a backsliding generation; doubtless with much unction by Mr. Whitfield.

No 2. *King of Prussia's Birthday* (Tuesday, January 24th). "This being the Birthday of the King of Prussia, who then "entered into the forty-seventh year of his age, the same was "observed with illuminations and other demonstrations of "joy;"— throughout the Cities of London and Westminster, "great rejoicings and illuminations," it appears,* now shining so feebly at a century's distance! — No. 3 is still more curious; and has deserved from us a little special inquiring into.

No. 3. *Miss Barbara Wyndham's Subsidy.* "March 13th, "1758,"— while Pitt and Knyphausen are busy on the Subsidy Treaty, still not out with it, the Newspapers suddenly announce, —
"Miss Bab. Wyndham, of Salisbury, sister of Henry "Wyndham, Esq., of that City, a maiden lady of ample for-"tune, has ordered her banker to prepare the sum of 1,000l. to "be immediately remitted, in her own name, as a present to "the King of Prussia."** Doubtless to the King of Prussia's surprise, and that of London Society, which would not want for commentaries on such a thing!
Before long, the Subsidy Treaty being now out, and the Wyndham topic new again, London Society reads, in the same Newspaper, a Documentary Piece, calculated to help in its commentaries. There is good likelihood of guess, though no certainty now attainable, that the "English Lady" referred to may be Miss Bab. herself; — of whose long-vanished biography, and brisk, airy, nomadic ways, we catch hereby a faint shadow, momentary, but conceivable, and sufficient for us:

---

* *Gentleman's Magazine*, XXVIII. (for 1758), p. 45; and vol. XXIX. p. 42, for next year's birthday, and p. 61 for another kind of celebration.
** *London Chronicle*, March 14th-16th, 1758; *Lloyd's Evening Post*; &c. &c.

"*To the Authors of the London Chronicle.* *

"The following Account, which is a real fact, will serve to "show with what punctuality and exactness the King of "Prussia attends to the most minute affairs, and how open he "is to applications from all persons.

"An English Lady being possessed of actions" (shares) "in "the Embden Company, and having occasion to raise money "on them, repaired to Antwerp" (some two years ago, as will be seen), "and made application for that purpose to a Director "of the Company, established there by the King of Prussia "for the managing all affairs relative thereto. This person," Van Erthorn the name of him, "very willingly entered into "treaty with her; but the sum he offered to lend being far "short of what the actions would bring, and he also insisting "on forfeiture of her right in them, if not redeemed in twelve "months, — she broke off with him, and had recourse to some "merchants at Antwerp, who were inclinable to treat with her "on much more equitable terms. The proceeding necessarily "brought the parties before this Director for receiving his "sanction, which was essential to the solidity of the agree-"ment; and he, finding he was like to lose the advantage he "had flattered himself with, disputed the authenticity of the "actions, and thereby threw her into such discredit, as to "render all attempts to raise money on them ineffectual. "Upon this the Lady wrote a Letter by the common post to "his Majesty of Prussia, accompanied with a Memorial com-"plaining of the treatment she had received from the Director; "and she likewise enclosed the actions themselves in another "letter to a friend at Berlin. By the return of the post, his "Majesty condescended to answer her Letter; and the actions "were returned authenticated; which so restored her credit, "that in a few hours all difficulties were removed relating to "the transaction she had in hand; and it is more than probable "the Director has felt his Majesty's resentment for his ill be-"haviour. — The Lady's Letter was as follows:

'Antwerp, 19th February 1756.

'Sir, — Having had the happiness to pay my court to your 'Majesty during a pretty long residence at Berlin' (say in

* *London Chronicle,* of 13th-15th April 1758.

Voltaire's time; Miss Barbara's "Embden Company," I observe, was the first of the two, date 1750; that of 1753 is not hers), 'and to receive such marks of favour from their Majesties the 'Queens' (a Barbara capable of shining in the Royal soirées at Monbijou, of talking to, or of, your Voltaires and lions, and investing moneys in the new Embden Company) 'as I shall 'ever retain a grateful sense of, — I presume to flatter myself 'that your Majesty will not be offended at the respectful 'liberty I have taken in laying before you my complaints 'against one Van Erthorn, a Director of the Embden China 'Company, whose bad behaviour to me, as set forth in my 'Memorial, hath forced me to make a very long and expensive 'stay at this place; and, as the considerable interest I have in 'that Company may further subject me to his caprices, I 'cannot forbear laying my grievances at the foot of your 'Majesty's throne; most respectfully supplicating your Ma-'jesty that you would be graciously pleased to give orders 'that this Director shall not act towards me for the future as 'he hath done hitherto.

'I hope for this favour from your Majesty's sovereign 'equity; and I shall never cease offering up my ardent prayers 'for the prosperity of your glorious reign; having the honour 'to be, with the most respectful zeal, Sir, your Majesty's 'most humble, most obedient, and most devoted servant,

* * *'

'*The King of Prussia's Answer.*

'Potsdam, 26th February 1756.

'Madam, — I received the Letter of the 19th instant, which 'you thought proper to write to me, and was not a little dis-'pleased to hear of the bad behaviour of one of the Directors 'of the Asiatic Company of Embden towards you, of which 'you were forced to complain. I shall direct your grievances 'to be examined, and have just now despatched my orders for 'that purpose to Lenz, my President of the Chamber of East 'Friesland,' Chief Judge in those parts.* 'You may assure 'yourself the strictest justice shall be done you that the 'case will admit. God keep you in his holy protection. — 'FREDERICK.'

Whether this refers to Miss Barbara or not, there is no

* Seyfarth, ii. 139.

affirming. But the interesting point is, Friedrich did receive and accept Miss Barbara's 1,000*l*. The Prussian account, which calls her "an English *Jungfrau*, *Lady Salisbury*, who "actually sent a sum of money,"* would not itself be satisfactory: but, by good chance, there is still living, in Salisbury City, a very aged Gentleman, well known for his worth, and intelligence on such matters, who, being inquired of, makes reply at once: That the First Earl of Malmesbury (who was of his acquaintance, and had many anecdotes and reminiscences of Friedrich, all noted down, it was understood, with diplomatic exactitude, but never yet published or become accessible) did, as "I well remember, among other things, "mention the King's telling him that he," the King, "had "received a Thousand Pounds from Miss Wyndham; with a "part of which he had bought the Flute then in his hand."** Which latter circumstance, too, is curious. For, at all times, however straitened Friedrich's Exchequer might be, it was his known habit, during this War, to have always, before the current year ended, the ways and means completely settled and provided for the year coming; so that everything could be at once paid in money (good money or bad, — good still up to this date); — and nothing was observed to fall short, so much as the customary liberality of his gifts to those about him. I infer, therefore: Friedrich had decided to lay out this 1,000*l*. in what he would call luxuries, chiefly gifts, — and, among other things, had said to himself, "I will have a new flute, "too!" Probably one of his last; for I understand he had by this time (Malmesbury's time, 1772), ceased much playing, and ceased altogether not long after.***

James Harris, First Earl of Malmesbury, was Resident at Berlin, 1772: that is all the date we have for the King's saying, "And with part of it I bought this Flute!" Date of Lord Malmesbury's mention of it at Salisbury, we have none, — like-

* Preuss, II. 124, whose reference is merely "*Gentleman's Magazine for* 1758." Both in the *Annual Register* of that Year (t. 85), and in the *Gentleman's Magazine*, pp. 149, 177, the above Paragraph and Letters are copied from the Newspapers, but without the smallest commentary (there or elsewhere), or any mention of a "Lady Salisbury."

** Letter from John Fowler, Esq., "Salisbury, 2d April 1860," to a Friend of mine (*penes eus*): of Barbara's identity, or otherwise, with the Antwerp-Embden Lady, Mr. F. can say nothing.

*** Preuss, I. 371-378.

liest there might be various dates; a thing mentioned more than once, and not improvable by dating. The Wyndhams still live in the Close of Salisbury; a respected and well-known Family; record of them (none of Barbara there, or elsewhere except here) to be found in the County Histories.* I only know farther, Barbara died, May 1765, "aged and wealthy," and "with the bulk of her fortune endowed a Charity, to "be called 'Wyndham College,'"** — which I hope still flourishes. Enough on this small Wyndham matter; which is nearly altogether English, but in which Friedrich too has his indefeasible property.

Friedrich, as indeed Pitt's People and Others have done, takes the Field uncommonly early: Friedrich goes upon Schweidnitz, as the Preface to whatever his Campaign may be.

While this Subsidy Treaty is getting settled in England, Duke Ferdinand has his French in full cackle of universal flight; and before the signing of it (April 11th), every feather of them is over the Rhine; Duke Ferdinand busy preparing to follow. Glorious news, day after day, coming in, for Miss Barbara and for all English souls, Royal Highness of Cumberland hardly excepted! The "Descent on Rochefort," last Autumn, had a good deal disappointed Pitt and England; — an expensively elaborate Expedition, military and naval; which could not "descend" at all, when it got to the point; but merely went groping about, on the muddy shores of the Charente, holding councils of war yonder; "cannonaded the Isle of Aix for two hours;" and returned home without result of any kind. Courts-martial following on it, as too usual. This was an unsuccess-

* Britton's *Beauties of England and Wales*, xv. part ii. p. 118; Hoare's *Salisbury* (mistaken, p. 815); &c.
** *Annual Register* (for 1765), viii. 86.

ful first-stroke for Pitt. Indeed, he never did much succeed in those Descents on the French Coast, though never again so ill as this time. Those are a kind of things that require an exactitude as of clockwork, in all their parts: and Pitt's Generalcies and War-Offices, — we know whether they were of the Prussian type or of the Swedish! A very grievous hindrance to Pitt; — which he will not believe to be quite incurable. Against which he, for his part, stands up, in grim earnest, and with his whole strength; and is now, and at all times, doing what in him lies to abate or remedy it: — successfully, to an unexpected degree, within the next four years. From America, he has decided to recal Lord Loudon, as a cunctatory haggling mortal, the reverse of a General; how very different from his Austrian Cousin!* "Abercrombie may be better," hopes he; — was better, still not good. But already in the gloomy imbroglio over yonder, Pitt discerns that one Amherst (the son of people unimportant at the hustings) has military talent: and in this puddle of a Rochefort Futility, he has got his eye on a young Officer named Wolfe, who was Quartermaster of the Expedition; a young man likewise destitute of Parliamentary connection, but who may be worth something. Both of whom will be heard of! In a four-years determined effort of this kind, things do improve: and it was wonderful, to what amount, — out of these chaotic War-Offices little

---

* Cousins certainly enough: their Progenitors were Brothers, of that House, about 1563, — when Matthew, the cadet, went "into Livonia," into foreign Soldiering (Papa having fallen Prisoner "at the Battle of Langside," 1568, and the Family prospects being low); from this Matthew comes, through a series of Livonian Soldiers, the famed Austrian Loudon. Douglas, *Peerage of Scotland*, p. 425; &c. &c. *Vie de Loudon* (ill informed on that point and some others) says, the first Livonian Loudon came from Ayrshire, "in the fourteenth century!"

better than the Swedish, and ignorant Generalcies fully worse than the Swedish, — Pitt got heroic successes and work really done.

On Pitt, amid confused clouds, there is bright dawn rising; and Friedrich, too, for the last month, in Breslau, has a cheerful prospect on that Western side of his horizon. Here is one of his Postscripts, thrown off in Autograph, which Duke Ferdinand will read with pleasure: "I congratulate you, *mon cher*, with my "whole heart! May you *fleur-de-lys* every French skin "of them; cutting out on their" — what shall we say (*leur imprimant sur le cul*)! — "the Initials of the Peace "of Westphalia, and packing them across the Rhine," tattooed in that latest extremity of fashion!*

Friedrich, grounding partly on those Rhine aspects, has his own scheme laid for Campaign 1758. It is the old scheme tried twice already: to go home upon your Enemy swiftly, with your utmost collective strength, and try to strike into the heart of him before he is aware. Friedrich has twice tried this; the second time, with success, respectable though far short of complete. Weakened as now, but with Ferdinand likely to find the French in employment, he means to try it again; and is busy preparing at Neisse and elsewhere, though keeping it a dead secret for the time. There is, in fact, no other hopeful plan for him, if this prove feasible at all. Double your velocity, you double your momentum.

---

* Friedrich to Duke Ferdinand, "Grüssau, 19th March 1758:" in Knesebeck, *Herzog Ferdinand*, i, 64. *Herzog Ferdinand während des 7-jährigen Krieges* ("from the English and Prussian Archives") is the full Title of Knesebeck's Book: *Letters* altogether; not very intelligently edited, but well worth reading by every student, military and civil: 2 voll. 8vo Hannover, 1857.

One's weight is given, — weight growing less and less; — but not, or not in the same way and degree, one's velocity, one's rightness of aim. Weight given: it is only by doubling or trebling his velocity that a man can make his momentum double or treble, as needed! Friedrich means to try it, readers will see how, — were the Fort of Schweidnitz once had; for which object Friedrich watches the weather like a very D'Argens, eager that the frost would go. Recapture of Schweidnitz, the last speck of Austrianism wiped away there; that is evidently the preface to whatsoever dayswork may be ahead.

March 15th, frost being now off, Friedrich quits Breslau and D'Argens, — his Headquarter thenceforth Kloster-Grüssau, near Landshut, troops all getting cantoned thereabout, to keep Bohemia quiet, — and goes at once upon Schweidnitz. With the top of the morning, so to speak; means to have Schweidnitz before campaigning usually can begin, or common labourers take their tools in this trade. The Austrian Commandant has been greatly strengthening the works; he had, at first, some 8,000 of garrison; but the three-months blockade has been tight upon him and them; and it is hoped the thing can be done.

April 1*st*-2*d*, — Siege-material being got to the ground, and Siege Division and Covering Army all in their places, — in spite of the heavy rains, we open our first parallel, Austrian Commandant not noticing till it is nearly done. April 8th, we have our batteries built; and burst out, at our best rate, into cannonade; aiming a good deal at "Fort No. 1," called also "*Galgen* or Gallows Fort," which we esteem the principal. Cannonade continues day after day, prospers tolerably on

Gallows Fort, — though the wet weather, and hardship to the troops, are grievous circumstances, and make Friedrich doubly urgent. "Try it by storm!" counsels Balbi, who is Engineer. Night of *April* 15*th*-16*th*, storm takes place; with such vigour and much cunning, that the Gallows Fort is got for almost nothing (loss of ten men); — and few hours after, Austria beat the chamade.* Fifty-one new Austrian guns, for one item, and about 7,000*l.* of money. Prisoners of War the garrison, 8,000 gone to 4,900; with such stores as we can guess, of ours and theirs added: Balbi was Prussian Engineer-in-Chief, Treskau Captain of the Siege; — other particulars I spare the reader.

Unfortunate Schweidnitz underwent four Sieges, four captures or recaptures, in this War; — upon all of which we must be quite summary, only the results of them important to us. For the curious in sieges, especially for the scientifically curious, there is, by a Captain Tielcke, excellent account of all these Schweidnitz Sieges, and of others; — Artillery-Captain Tielcke, in the Saxon or Saxon-Russian service; whom perhaps we shall transiently fall in with, on a different field, in the course of this Year.

---

* Tempelhof, II. 21-25; *Helden-Geschichte*, v. 109-123: above all, Tielcke *Beyträge zur Kriegs-Kunst und zur Geschichte des Krieges von 1756 bis 1763* (6 voll. 4to, Freyberg, 1775-1786), iv. 43-76. Vol. iv. is wholly devoted to Schweidnitz and its successive Sieges.

CHAPTER XII.

SIEGE OF OLMÜTZ.

FOUQUET, on the first movement towards Schweidnitz, had been detached from Landshut to sweep certain Croat Parties out of Glatz; Ziethen, with a similar view, into Troppau Country; both which errands were at once perfectly done. Daun lies behind the Bohemian Frontier (betimes in the field, he too, "arrived at Königsgrätz, March 13th"); and is, with all diligence,. perfecting his new levies; entrenching himself on all points, as man seldom did; "felling whole forests," they say, building abatis within abatis; — not doubting, especially on these Ziethen-Fouquet symptoms, but Friedrich's Campaign is to be an Invasion of Bohemia again. "Which he shall not do gratis!" hopes Daun; and, indeed, judges say the entrance would hardly have been possible on that side, had Friedrich tried it; which he did not.

Schweidnitz being done, and Daun deep in the Bohemian problem, — Friedrich, in an unintelligible manner, breaks out from Grüssau and the Landshut region (April 19th—25th), not straight southward, as Daun had been expecting, but straight south-eastward through Neisse, Jägerndorf: all gone, or all but Ziethen and Fouquet gone, that way; — meaning who shall say what, when news of it comes to Daun? In two divisions, from 30 to 40,000 strong; through Jägerndorf, ever onward through Troppau, and not till *then* turning southward: indubitable march of that cunning Enemy; rapidly proceeding, his 40,000 and he, along those elevated upland countries, watershed of the Black Sea and the Baltic, bleakly illumined by the April sun; a march into the mists of the future tense, which do not yet clear themselves to Daun. Seeing the march turn southward at Troppau, a light breaks on Daun: "Ha! coming round upon Bohemia from the east, then?" That is Daun's opinion, for some time yet; and he immediately starts that way, to save a fine magazine he has at Leutomischl over there. Daun, from Skalitz near Königsgrätz where he is, has but some eighty miles to march, for the King's hundred-and-fifty; and arrives in those parts few days after the King; posts himself at Leutomischl, veiled in Pandours. Not for two weeks more does he ascertain it to have been a march upon the Olmütz Country, and the intricate forks of the Morawa River; with a view to besieging Olmütz, by this wily Enemy! Upon which Daun did strive to bestir himself thitherward, at last; and, though very slow and hesitative, his measures otherwise were unexceptionable, and turned out luckier than had been expected by some people.

Olmütz is an ancient pleasant little City, in the Plains of Mähren, romantic, indistinct to the English mind; with Domes, with Steeples eminent beyond its size, — population little above 10,000 souls; — has its Prince-Archbishop and ecclesiastic outfittings, with whom Friedrich has lodged in his time. City which trades in leather, and Russian and Moldavian droves of oxen. Memorable to the Slavic populations for its grand Czech Library, which was carried away by the

Swedes, happily into thick night;* also for that poor little Wenzel of theirs (last heir of the Bohemian Czech royalties, whom no reader has the least memory of) being killed on the streets here; — uncertain, to this day, by whom, though for whose benefit that dagger-stroke ended is certain enough:** — poor little Wenzel's dust lies under that highest Dome, of the old Cathedral yonder, if anybody thought of such a thing in hot practical times. Poor Lafayette, too, lodged here in prison, when the Austrians seized him. City trades in leather and live stock, we said; has much to do with artillery, much with ecclesiastry; — and Friedrich besieged it, for seven weeks, in the hot summer days of 1758, to no purpose. Friedrich has been in Olmütz more than once before; his Schwerin once took it in a single day, and it was his for months, in the old Moravian-Foray time: but the place is changed now; become an arsenal or military storehouse of Austria; strongly fortified, and with a Captain in it, who distinguishes himself by valiant skill and activity on this occasion.

Friedrich's Olmütz Enterprise, the rather as it was unsuccessful, has not wanted critics. And certainly, according to the ordinary rules of cautious prudence, could these have been Friedrich's in his present situation, it was not to be called a prudent Enterprise. But had Friedrich's arrangements been punctually fulfilled, and Olmütz been got in fair time, as was possible or probable, the thing might have been done very well. Duke Ferdinand, in these early May days, is practically making preparations to follow the French across the Rhine; no fear of French Armies interfering with

---

* To Stralsund (1645), "and has not since been heard of."
** Supra, vol. I. p. 169.

us this year. Dohna has the Swedes locked in Stralsund (capable of being starved, had not the thaw come); and in Hinter-Pommern he has General Platen, with a tolerable Detachment, watching Fermor and his Russians; Dohna, with Platen, may entertain the Russians for a little, when they get on way, — which we know will be at a slow pace, and late in the season. Prince Henri commands in Saxony, say with 30,000; — King's vicegerent and other self there, "Do *you* wisest and promptest; hold no councils of war!" Prince Henri, altogether on the aggressive as yet, is waiting what Reichs Army there may be; — has already had Mayer and Free Corps careering about in Franken Country once and again, tearing up the incipiences and preparations, with the usual emphasis; and is himself intending to follow thither, in a still more impressive manner. Friedrich's calculation is, Prince Henri will have his hands free for a good few weeks yet. Which proved true enough, so far as that went.

And now, supposing Olmütz ours, and Vienna itself open to our insults, does not, by rapid suction, every armed Austrian flow thitherward; Germany all drained of them: in which case, what is to hinder Prince Henri from stepping into Böhmen, by the Metal-Mountains; capturing Prag; getting into junction with us here, and tumbling Austria at a rate that will astonish her! Her, and her miscellaneous tagraggery of Confederates, one and all. Königsberg, Stralsund, Bamberg; Russians, Swedes, Reichsfolk, — here, in Mähren, will be the crown of the game for all these. Prosper in Mähren, all these are lamed; one right stroke at the heart, the limbs become manageable quantities! This was Friedrich's program; and had not imperfections of execution, beyond what was looked for, and also a good deal of plain ill-luck, intervened, this bold stroke for Mähren might have turned out far otherwise than it did.

The march thither (started from Neisse, April 27th) was beautiful: Friedrich with vanguard and first division; Keith with rearguard and second, always at a day's distance; split into proper columns, for convenience of road and quarter in the hungry countries; threading those silent mountain villages, and upper streamlets of Oder and Morawa: Ziethen waving intrusive Croateries far off; Fouquet, in thousands of wagons, shoving on from Neisse, "in four sections," with the due intervals, under the due escorts, the immensity of stores and siege-furniture, through Jägerndorf, through Troppau, and onwards;* — punctual everybody; besiegers and siege-materials ready on their ground by the set day. Daun too had made speed to save his Magazine. Daun was at Leutomischl, May 5th, — a forty miles to west of the Morawa, — few days after Friedrich had arrived in those countries by the eastern or left bank, by Troppau, Gibau, Littau, Aschmeritz, Prossnitz; and a week before Friedrich had finished his reconnoiterings, campings, and taken position to his mind. Camps, four or more (shrank in the end to three), on both banks of the River: a matter of abstruse study; so that it was May 12th before Friedrich first took view of Olmütz itself, and could fairly begin his Problem, — Daun, with his best Tolpatcheries, still unable to guess what it was.

Of the Siege I propose to say little, though the accounts of it are ample, useful to the Artillerist and

* Table of his routes and stages, in *Tempelhof*, ii. 46.

Engineer. If the reader can be made to conceive it as a blazing loud-sounding fact, on which, and on Friedrich in it, the eyes of all Europe were fixed for some weeks, it may rest now in impressive indistinctness to us. Keith is Captain of the Siege, whom all praise for his punctual firmness of progress; Balbi, as before, is Engineer, against whom goes the criticism, Keith's first of all, that he "opened his first parallel 800 yards too far off," — which much increased the labour, and the expenditure of useless gunpowder, shot having no effect at such a distance. There were various criticisms: some real, as this; some imaginary, as that Friedrich grudged gunpowder, the fact being that he had it not, except after carriage from Neisse, say a hundred and twenty miles off, — Troppau, his last Silesian Town, or safe place (*his* for the moment), is eighty miles; — and was obliged to waste none of it.

Friedrich is not thought to shine in the sieging line as he does in the fighting; which has some truth in it, though not very much. When Friedrich laid himself to engineering, I observe, he did it well: see Neisse, Graudenz, Magdeburg. His Balbi went wrong with the parallels, on this occasion; many things went wrong: but the truly grievous thing was his distance from Silesia and the supplies. A hundred and twenty miles of hill-carriage, eighty of them disputable, for every shot of ammunition, and for every loaf of bread; this was hard to stand: — and perhaps no War-apparatus but a Prussian, with a Friedrich for sole chief-manager, could have stood it so long. Friedrich did stand it, in a wonderfully tolerable manner; and was continuing to stand it, and make fair progress; and it is not doubted he would have got Olmütz, had not there another fact come on him, which proved to be of unmanageable nature. The actual loss, namely, of one Convoy, after so many had come safe, and when, as appears, there was now only one wanted and no more! — Let us attend to this a little.

Had Daun, at Olmütz, been as a Duke of Cumberland relieving Tournay, rushing into fight at Fontenoy, like a Hanover White-Horse, neck clothed with thunder, and head destitute of knowledge, — how lucky had it been for Friedrich! But Daun knows his trade better. Daun, though superior in strength, sits on his Magazine, clear not to fight. By no art of manœuvering, had Friedrich much tried it, or hoped it, this time, could Daun have been brought to give battle. As Fabius Cunctator he is here in his right place; taking impregnable positions, no man with better skill in that branch of business; pushing out parties on the Troppau road; and patiently waiting till this dangerous Enemy, with such endless shifts in him, come in sight perhaps of his last cartridge, or perhaps make some stumble on the way towards that consummation. Daun is aware of Friedrich's surprising qualities. Bos against Leo, Daun feels these procedures to be altogether feline *(felis-leonine)*; such stealthy glidings about, deceptive motions; appearances; then such a rapidity of spring upon you, and with such a set of claws, — destructive to bovine or rhinoceros nature: in regard to all which, Bos, if he will prosper, surely cannot be too cautious. It was remarked of Daun, that he was scrupulously careful; never, in the most impregnable situations, neglecting the least precaution, but punctiliously fortifying himself to the last item, even to a ridiculous extent, say Retzow and the critics. It was the one resource of

Daun: truly a solid stubborn patience is in the man; stubborn courage too, of bovine-rhinoceros type; — stupid, if you will, but doing at all times honestly his best and his wisest without flurry; which character is often of surprising value in War; capable of much mischief, now and then, to quicker people. Rhinoceros Daun did play his Leo a bad prank, more than once; and this of barring him out from Olmütz was one of them, perhaps the worst after Kolin.

Daun's management of this Olmütz business is by no means reckoned brilliant, even in the Fabius line; but, on the contrary, inert, dim-minded, inconclusive; and in reality, till almost the very last, he had been of little help to the besieged. For near three weeks (till May 23d) Daun sat at Leutomischl, immovable on his bread-basket there, forty or more miles from Olmütz; and did not see that a Siege was meant. May 27th-28th, Balbi opened his first parallel, in that mistaken way; four days before which, Daun does move inwards a march or so, to Zwittau, to Gewitsch (still thirty miles to west of Olmütz); still thinking of Bohemia, not of any siege; still hanging by the mountains and the bread-basket. And there, about Gewitsch, siege or no siege, Daun sits down again; pretty much immovable, through the five weeks of bombardment; and, — except that Loudon and the Light Horse are very diligent to do a mischief, "attempting our convoys, more than "once, to no purpose, and alarming some of our out- "posts almost every night, but every night beaten off," — does, in a manner, nothing; sits quiet, behind his impenetrable veil of Pandours, and lets the bombardment take its course. Had not express Order come from Vienna on him, it is thought Daun would have sat till Olmütz was taken; and would then have gone back to Loutomischl and impregnable posts in the Hills. On express order, he — But gather, first, these poor sparks in elucidation:

"The 'destructive sallies' and the like, at Olmütz, were "principally an affair of the gazetteers and the imagination: "but it is certain, Olmütz, this time, was excellently well "defended; the Commandant, a vigorous skilful man, prompt "to seize advantages; and Garrison and Townsfolk zealously "helping: so that Friedrich's progress was unusally slow. "Friedrich's feelings, all this while, and Balbi's (who 'spent "'his first 1220 shots entirely in vain,' beginning so far off), "may be judged of, — the sound of him to Balbi sometimes "stern enough! As when (June 9th) he personally visits "Balbi's parallels (top of the Tafelberg yonder); and inquires, "'When do you calculate to get done, then?' West side of "Olmütz and of the River (east side lies mostly under water), "there is the bombarding; seventy-one heavy guns; Keith, in "his expertest manner, doing all the captaincies: Keith has "about 8,000 of foot and horse, busy and vigilant, with their "faces to the east: in a ring of four camps, or principally three "(Prossnitz, Littau, and Neustadt, which is across the River), "all looking westward or north-westward, some ten or twenty "miles from Keith, Friedrich (headquarters oftenest Prossnitz, "the chief camp) stands facing Daun; who lies concentric to "him, at the distance of another ten or twenty miles, in good "part still thirty or forty miles from Olmütz, veiled mostly "under a cloud of Pandours.

"Of Friedrich's impatiences, we hear little, though they "must have been great. Prince Henri is ready for Prag; many "things are ready, were Olmütz but done! May 22d, Prince "Henri had followed Mayer in person, with a stronger corps, "to root out the Reichsfolk, — and is now in Bamberg City "and Country. And is even in Baireuth itself, where was "lately the Camp of the new Reichs General, Serene Highness "of Zweibrück, and his nascent Reichs Army; who are off "bodily to Bohemia, 'to Eger and the Circle of Saatz,' a week "before.* Fancy that visit of Henri's to a poor Wilhelmina;

* *Helden-Geschichte*, v. 206-209. Wilhelmina's pretty Letter to Friedrich

"the last sight she ever had of a Brother, or of the old Prussian
"uniforms, clearing her of Zweibrücks and sorrowful guests!
"Our poor Wilhelmina, alas she is sunk in sickness, this year
"more than ever; journeying towards death, in fact; and is
"probably the most pungent, sacredly tragic, of Friedrich's
"sorrows, now and onwards. June 12th, Friedrich's pouting
"Brother, the Prince of Prussia, died; this also he had to hear
"in Camp at Olmütz. 'What did he die of?' said Friedrich to
"the Messenger, a Major Something. 'Of chagrin,' said the
"Major, "*Aus Gram.*" Friedrich made no answer.

"On the last night of May, by beautiful management, mi-
"litary and other, Duke Ferdinand is across the Rhine; again
"chasing the French before him; who, as they are far the more
"numerous, cannot surely but make some stand: so that a
"Battle there may be expected soon,—let us hope, a Victory;
"as indeed it beautifully proved to be, three weeks after.*
"On the other hand, Fermor and his Russians are astir; con-
"tinually wending towards Brandenburg, in their voluminous
"manner, since June 16th, though at a slow rate. How desir-
"able the Siege of Olmütz were done!"

On express from Vienna, Daun did bestir himself;
cautiously got on foot again; detached, across the River,
an expert Hussar General ("Be busy all ye Loudons,
St. Ignons, Ziskowitzes, doubly now!"), — expert
Hussar General, one item of whose force is 1100
chosen grenadiers; — and himself cautiously stept
southward and eastward, nearer the Siege Lines. The
Hussar General's meaning seemed to be some mischief
on our Camp of Neustadt and the outposts there; but
in reality it was to throw his 1100 into Olmütz (useful to the Commandant); which, — by ingenious
manœuvering, and guidance from the peasants "through
bushy woods and bypaths" on that east side of the

("Baireuth, 10th May"); Friedrich's Answer ("Olmütz, June 1758"): in
Œuvres de Frédéric, xxvii. i. 313-315.
* Battle of Crefeld, 23d June.

River, — the expert Hussar General, though Ziethen was sent over to handle him, did perfectly manage, and would not quit for Ziethen till he saw it finished. Which done, Daun keeps stepping still farther southward, nearer the Siege Lines; and, at Prossnitz, morning of June 22d, Friedrich, with his own eyes, sees Daun taking post on the opposite heights; says to somebody near him, " *Voilà les Autrichiens, ils appren-* "*nent à marcher*, There are the Austrians; they are "learning to march, though!" — getting on their feet, like infants in a certain stage ("*marcher*" having that meaning too, though I know not that the King intended it); they have learned a great many things, since your Majesty first met them. Friedrich took Daun to be, now at last, meaning Battle for Olmütz, and made some slight arrangements accordingly; but that is not Daun's intention at all; as Friedrich will find to his cost, in few days. That very day, Daun has vanished again, still in the southerly direction, again under veil of Pandours.

Meanwhile, in spite of all things, the Siege makes progress; "June 22d, Balbi's sap had got to their glacis, "and was pushing forward there," — June 22d, day when Daun made momentary appearance, and the reinforcement stole in: — within a fortnight more, Balbi promises the thing shall be done. But supplies are indispensable: one other convoy from Troppau, and let it be a big one, "between 3 and 4,000 wagons," meal, money, iron, powder; Friedrich hopes this one, if he can get it home, will suffice. Colonel Mosel is to bring this Convoy; a resolute expert Officer, with perhaps 7,000 foot and horse: surely sufficient escort: but, as Daun is astir, and his Loudons, Ziskowitzes, and light people, are gliding about, Friedrich orders Ziethen to meet this important Convoy, with some thousands of new force, and take charge of bringing it in. Mosel was to leave Troppau, June 26th; Ziethen pushes out to meet him from the Olmütz end, on the second day after; and, one hopes, all is now safe on that head.

The driving of 3,000 four-horse wagons, under escort, ninety miles of road, is such an enterprise as cannot readily be conceived by sedentary pacific readers; — much more the attack of such! Military science, constraining chaos into the cosmic state, has nowhere such a problem. There are twelve thousand horses, for one thing, to be shod, geared, kept roadworthy and regular; say six thousand country wagoners, thicksoled peasants: then, hanging to the skirts of these, in miscellaneous crazy vehicles and weak teams, equine and asinine, are one or two thousand sutler people, male and female, not of select quality, though on them, too, we keep a sharp eye. The series covers many miles, as many as twenty English miles (says Tempelhof), unless in favourable points you compress them into five, going four wagons abreast for defence's sake. Defence, or escort, goes in three bulks or brigades; vanguard, middle, rearguard, with sparse pickets intervening; — wider than five miles, you cannot get the parts to support one another. An enemy breaking in upon you, at some difficult point of road, woody hollow or the like, and opening cannon, musketry and hussar exercise on such an object, must make a confused transaction of it! Some commanders, for the road has hitherto been mainly pacific, divide their train into parts, say four parts; moving with their partial escorts, with an interval of one day between each two:

this has its obvious advantages, but depends, of course,
on the road being little infested, so that your partial
escort will suffice to repel attacks. Tolling forward,
at their diligent slow rate, I find these trains from
Troppau take about six days (from Neisse to Olmütz
they take eleven, but the first five are peaceable*);
— can't be hurried beyond that pace, if you would
save your laggards, your irregulars, and prevent what
we may call *raggery* in your rearward parts; the skirts
of your procession get torn by the bushes if you go
faster. This time Colonel Mosel will have to mend his
pace, however, and to go in the lump withal; the case
being critical, as Mosel knows, and *more* than he yet
knows.

Daun, who has friends everywhere, and no lack of
spies in this country, generally hears of the convoys.
He has heard, in particular, of this important one, in
good time. Hitherto Daun had not attempted much
upon the convoys, nor anything with success: King's
posted corps and other precautions are of such a kind,
not even Loudon, when he tried his best, could do any
good; and common wandering hussar parties are as
likely to get a mischief as to do one, on such service.
Cautious Daun had been busy enough keeping his own
Camp safe, and flinging a word of news or encourage-
ment, at the most a trifle of reinforcement, into Olmütz
when possible. But now it becomes evident there must
be one of two things: this convoy seized, or else a
battle risked; — and that in defect of both these,
the inevitable third thing is, Olmütz will straightway
go.

Major-General Loudon, the best partisan soldier

* Tempelhof, ii. 48.

extant, and ripening for better things, has usually a force of perhaps 10,000 under him, four regiments of them regular grenadiers; and has been active on the convoys, though hitherto unsuccessful. Let an active Loudon, with increased force, try this, their vitally important convoy, from the west side of the River; an active Ziskowitz cooperating on the east side, where the road itself is; and do their uttermost! That is Daun's plan, — now in course of execution. Daun, instead of meaning battle, that day when Friedrich saw him, was cautiously stealing past, intending to cross the River farther down; and himself support the operation. Daun has crossed accordingly, and has doubled up northward again to the fit point; Ziskowitz is in the fit point, in the due force, on this east side too. Loudon, on the west side, goes by Muglitz, Hof; making a long deep bend far to westward and hillward of all the Prussian posted corps and precautions, and altogether hidden from them; Loudon aims to be in Troppau neighbourhood, "Güntersdorf, near Bautsch," by the proper day, and pay Mosel an unexpected visit in the passage there.

Colonel Mosel, marshalling his endless Trains with every excellent precaution, and the cleverest dispositions (say the Books), against the known and the unknown, had got upon the road, and creaked forward, many-wheeled, out of Troppau, Monday, 26th June.* The roads, worn by the much travelling and wet weather, were utterly bad; the pace was perhaps quicker than usual; the much-jolting Train got greatly into a jumble: — Mosel, to bring up the laggards, made the morrow a rest-day; did get about two-thirds of his laggards

* Tempelhof, II. 89-94.

marshalled again; ordered the others to return, as impossible. They say, had it not been for this rest-day, which seemed of no consequence, Loudon would not have been at Güntersdorf in time, nor have attempted as he did at Güntersdorf and afterwards. At break of day (Wednesday 28th), Mosel is again on the road, heavily jumbling forward from his quarters in Bautsch. Few miles on, towards Güntersdorf, he discovers Loudon posted ahead in the defiles. What a sight for Mosel, in his character of Wagoner up with the dawn! But Mosel managed the defiles and Loudon, this time; halted his train, dashed up into the woody heights and difficult grounds; stormed Loudon's cannon from him, smote Loudon in a valiant tempestuous manner; and sent him travelling again, for the present.

Loudon, I conjecture, would have struggled farther, had not he known that there would be a better chance again not very many miles ahead. Loudon has studied this Convoy; knows of Ziethen coming to it with so many; of Ziskowitz coming to him, Loudon, with so many; that Ziethen cannot send for more (roads being all beset by our industry yesterday), that Ziskowitz can, should it be needful; — and that at Domstädtl there is a defile, or confused woody hollow, of unequalled quality! Mosel jumbles on all day with his Train, none molesting; at night gets to his appointed quarters, Village of Neudörfl;[*] and there finds Ziethen: a glad meeting, we may fancy, but an anxious one, with Domstädtl ahead on the morrow. Loudon concerts with Ziskowitz this day; calls in all reinforcements possible, and takes his measures. Thursday morning,

[*] The *l*, or *el*, is a diminutive in these Names: "New-Thorp*let*," "Cathedral-Town*let*," and the like.

Ziethen finds the Train in such a state, hardly half of it come up, he has to spend the whole day, Mosel and he, in rearranging it: Friday morning, June 30th, they get under way again; — Friday, the catastrophe is waiting them.

The Pass of Domstädtl, lapped in the dim Moravian distance, is not known to me or to my readers; nor indeed could the human pen or intellect, aided by ocular inspection or whatever helps, give the least image of what now took place there, rendering Domstädtl a memorable locality ever since. Understand that Ziethen and Mosel, with their waste slow deluge of wagons, come jumbling in, with anxiety, with precautions, — precautions doubled, now that the woody intricacies about Domstädtl rise in sight. "Pooh, it is as we thought: there go Austrian cannon-salvoes, horse-charges; volleying musketries, as our first wagons enter the Pass; — and there will be a job!" Indecipherable to mankind, far off, or even near. Of which only this feature and that can be laid hold of, as discernible, by the most industrious man. Escort, in three main-bodies, vanguard, middle, rearguard, marches on each side; infantry on the left, cavalry on the right, as the ground is leveller there. Length of the Train in statute miles, as it jumbles along at this point, is not given; but we know it was many miles; that horses and wagoners were in panic hardly restrainable; and we dimly descry, here especially, human drill-sergeantcy doing the impossible to keep chaos plugged down. The poor wagoner, cannon playing ahead, whirls homeward with his vehicle, if your eye quit him, still better, and handier, cuts his traces, mounts in a good moment, and is off at heavy-footed gallop, leaving his wagon. Seldom had human drill-sergeantcy such a problem.

The Prussian Vanguard, one Krockow its commander, repulsed that first Austrian attack; swept the Pass clear for some minutes; got their section of the carriages, or some part of it, 250 in all, hurried through; then halted on the safe side, to wait what Ziethen would do with the remainder. Ziethen does his best and bravest, as everybody does; keeps his wagon chaos plugged down; ranks it in square mass, as a wagon-fortress (*Wagenburg*); ranks himself and everybody, his cannon, his platoon musketry, to the best advantage round it; furiously shoots out in all manner of ways, against the furious Loudon on this flank, and the furious Ziskowitz on that; takes hills, loses them; repels and is repelled (wagon chaos ever harder to keep plugged); finally perceives himself to be beaten; that the wagon chaos has got *unplugged* (fancy it!) — and that he, Ziethen, must retreat; back foremost if possible. He did retreat, fighting all the way to Troppau; and the Convoy is a ruin and a prey.

Krockow, with the 250, has got under way again, hearing the powder-wagons start into the air (fired by the enemy), and hearing the cannon and musketry take a northerly course, and die away in that ominous direction. These 250 were all the carriages that came in: — happily, by Ziethen's prudence, the money, a large sum, had been lodged in the vanmost of these. The rest of the Convoy, ball, powder, bread, was of little value to Loudon, but beyond value to Friedrich at this moment; and it has gone to annihilation and the belly of Chaos and the Croats. Among the tragic wrecks of this Convoy there is one that still goes to our heart. A longish, almost straight row of young Prussian recruits stretched among the slain, what are these? These were 700 recruits coming up from their cantons to the Wars; hardly six months in training: see how they have fought to the death, poor lads, and have honourably, on the sudden, got manumitted from the toils of life. Seven hundred of them stood to arms, this morning; some sixty-five will get back to Troppau; that is the invoice account. They lie there, with their blond young cheeks and light hair; beautiful in death; — could not have done better, though the sacred poet has said nothing of them hitherto, — nor need, till times mend with us and him. Adieu, my noble young Brothers; so brave, so modest, no Spartan nor no Roman more; may the silence be blessed to you!

Contrary to some current notions, it is comfortably evident that there was a considerable fire of loyalty in the Prussians towards their King, during this War; loyalty kept well under cover, not wasting itself in harangues or noisy froth; but coming out, among all ranks of men, in practical attempts to be of help in this high struggle, which was their own as well as his. The *Stände*, landed Gentry, of Pommern and other places, we heard of their poor little Navy of twelve gunboats, which were all taken by the Swedes. Militia Regiments too, which did good service at Colberg, as may transiently appear by and by: — in the gentry or upper classes, a respectable zeal for their King. Then, among the peasantry or lower class — Here are Seven Hundred who stood well where he planted them. And their Mothers — Be Spartan also, ye Mothers!

In peaceable times, Tempelhof tells us the Prussian Mother is usually proud of having her son in this King's service: a country wife will say to you: "I have three of them, all in the regiment," Billerbeck, Itzenplitz, or whatever be the Canton regiment; "the eldest is ten inches" (stands five feet ten), "the second is eleven, the third eight, for indeed he is yet young."

Daun, on the day of this Domstädtl business, and by way of masking it, feeling how vital it was, made various extensive movements, across the River by several Bridges; then hither, thither, on the farther side of Olmütz, mazing up and down: Friedrich observing him, till he should ripen to something definite, followed his bombarding the while; perhaps having hopes of wager of battle ensuing. Of the disaster at Domstädtl, Friedrich could know nothing, Loudon having closed the roads. Daun by no means ripens into battle: news of the disaster reached Friedrich early next day (Saturday, July 1st), — who "immediately assembled his Generals, and spoke a few "inspiring words to them," such as we may fancy. Friedrich perceives that Olmütz is over; that his Third Campaign, third lunge upon the Enemy's heart, has prospered worse, thus far, than either of the others; that he must straightway end this of Olmütz, without any success whatever, and try the remaining methods and resources. No word of complaint, they say, is heard from Friedrich in such cases; face always hopeful, tone cheery. A man in Friedrich's position needs a good deal of Stoicism, Greek or other.

That Saturday night the Prussian bombardment is quite uncommonly furious, long continuing; no night

yet like it: — the Prussians are shooting off their
superfluous ammunition this night; do not quite end
till Sunday is in. On Sunday itself, packings, preparations all completed; and "Keith, with above 4,000
"wagons, safe on the road since 2 A. M." — the Prussians softly vanish in long smooth streams, with music
playing, unmolested by Daun; and leaving nothing, it
is boasted, but five or three mortars, which kept playing to the last, and one cannon, to which something
had happened.

Of the retreat, there could be much said, instructive
to military men who were studious; extremely fine retreat, say all judges; — of which my readers crave
only the outlines, the results. Daun, it was thought,
should have ruined Friedrich in this retreat; but he
did nothing of harm to him. In fact, for a week he
could not comprehend the phenomenon at all, and did
not stir from his place, — which was on the other, or
wrong, side of the River. Daun had never doubted
but the retreat would be to Silesia; and he had made
his detachments, and laid himself out for doing something upon it, in that direction: but, lo, what roads
are these, what motions whitherward? In about a week
it becomes manifest that the retreat, which goes on
various roads, sometimes three at once, has converged
on Leutomischl; straight for Bohemia instead of Silesia;
and that Daun is fallen seven days behind it; incapable
now to do anything. Not even the Magazine at Leutomischl could be got away, nor could even the whole
of it be burnt.

Keith and the baggage once safe in Leutomischl
(July 8th), all goes in deliberate long column; Fried-

rich ahead to open the passages. July 14th, after five more marches, Friedrich bursts up Königsgrätz; scattering any opposition there is; and sits down there, in a position considered, he knows well how inexpugnable; to live on the Country, and survey events. The 4,000 baggage-wagons came in about entire. Fouquet had the first division of them, and a secondary charge of the whole; an extremely strict, almost pedantic man, and of very fiery temper: "*Ilé, d'où venez-vous?*" asked he sharply of Retzow senior, who had broken through his order, one day, to avert great mischief: "How come you here, *Mon Général?*" "By the Highway, your Excellency!" answered Retzow in a grave stiff tone.*

Keith himself takes the rear-guard, the most ticklish post of all, and manages it well, and with success, as his wont is. Under sickness at the time, but with his usual vigilance, prudence, energy; qualities apt to be successful in War. Some brushes of Croat fighting he had from Loudon; but they did not amount to anything. It was at Holitz, within a march of Königsgrätz, that Loudon made his chief attempt; a vehement, well-intended thing; which looked well at one time. But Keith heard the cannonading ahead; hurried up with new cavalry, new sagacity and fire of energy; dashed out horse charges, seized hill tops, of a vital nature; and quickly ended the affair. A man fiery enough, and prompt with his stroke when wanted, though commonly so quiet. "Tell Monsieur, —" some General who seemed too stupid or too languid on this occasion, — "Tell Monsieur from me," said Keith to his Aide-de-Camp, "he may be a very pretty

* Retzow, i. 302.

"thing, but he is not a man (*qu'il peut être une bonne* "*chose, mais qu'il n'est pas un homme*)!"* The excellent vernacular Keith; — still a fine breadth of accent in him, one perceives! He is now past sixty; troubled with asthma; and I doubt not may be, occasionally, thinking it near time to end his campaigns. And in fact, he is about ending them; sooner than he or anybody had expected.

Daun, picking his steps and positions, latterly with threefold precaution, got into Königsgrätz neighbourhood, a week after Friedrich; and looked down with enigmatic wonder upon Friedrich's new settlement there. Forage abundant all round, and the corn-harvest growing white — here, strange to say, has Friedrich got planted in the *in*side of those innumerable Daun redoubts, and "woods of abatis;" and might make a very pretty "Bohemian Campaign" of it, after all, were Daun the only adversary he had! Judges are of opinion, that Daun, with all his superiority of number, could not have disrooted Friedrich this season.** Daun did try him by the Pandour methods, "1,000 Croats stealing in upon Königsgrätz at one in the morning," and the like; but these availed nothing. By the one effectual method, that of beating him in battle, Daun never would have tried. What did disroot Friedrich, then? — Take the following dates, and small hints of phenomena in other parts of the big Theatre of War. "Konitz" is a little

---

* Varnhagen, *Leben des &c. Jakob von Keith*, p. 227.

** *Tempelhof*, II. 170-176, 185; — who, unluckily, in soldier fashion, here as too often elsewhere, does not give us the Arithmetical Numbers of each, but counts by "Battalions" and "Squadrons," which, except in time of Peace, are a totally uncertain quantity: — guess vaguely, 75,000 against 90,000.

Polish Town, midway between Dantzig and Friedrich's Dominions:

"*Konitz, 16th June 1758.* This day Feldmarschall Fermor "arrives in his principal Camp here. For many weeks past, "he has been dribbling across the Weichsel hitherward, into "various small camps, with Cossack Parties flying about, "under check of General Platen. But now, being all across, "and reunited, Fermor shoots out Cossack Parties of quite "other weight and atrocity; and is ready to begin business, "— still a little uncertain how. His Cossacks, under their "Demikows, Romanzows, capable of no good fighting, but of "endless incendiary mischief in the neighbourhood; — shoot "far ahead into Prussian territory: Platen, Hordt with his "Free-Corps, are beautifully sharp upon them; but many "beatings avail little. 'They burn the town of Driesen' "(Hordt having been hard upon them there); 'town of "Ratzebuhr, and nineteen villages around;' — burn poor old "women and men, one poor old clergyman especially, wind "him well in straw-roping, then set fire, and leave him; — "and are worse than fiends or hyænas. Not to be checked by "Platen's best diligence; not, in the end, by Platen and "Dohna together. Dohna (18th June) has risen from Stral- "sund in check of them, — leaving the unfortunate Swedes "to come out" (shrunk to about 7,000, so unsalutary their stockfish diet there), — "these hyæna Cossacks being the far "more pressing thing. Dohna is diligent, gives them many "slaps and checks; Dohna cannot cut the taproot of them in "two; that is to say, fight Fermor and beat him: other effec- "tual check there can be none. *

"*Tschopau (in Saxony), 21st June.* Prince Henri has quitted "Bamberg Country; and is home again, carefully posted, at "Tschopau and up and down, on the southern side of Saxony; "with his eye well on the Passes of the Metal-Mountains, — "— where now, in the turn things at Olmütz have taken, his "clear fate is to be invaded, *not* to invade. The Reichs Army "fairly afoot in the Circle of Saatz, counts itself 35,000; add "15,000 Austrians of a solid quality, there is a Reichs Army

---

* *Helden-Geschichte,* v. 149 et seq.; Tempelhof, ii. 135 &c.

"of 50,000 in all, this Year. And will certainly invade
"Saxony, — though it is in no hurry; does not stir till August
"come, and will find Prince Henri elaborately on his
"guard, and little to be made of him, though he is as one
"to two.
"*Crefeld* (Rhine-Country), *23d June.* Duke Ferdinand,
"after skilful shoving and advancing, some forty or fifty
"miles, on his new or French side of the Rhine, finds the
"French drawn up at Crefeld (June 23d); 47,000 of them
"*versus* 33,000: in altogether intricate ground; canal-
"ditches, osier-thickets, farm-villages, peat-bogs. Ground
"defensible against the world, had the 47,000 had a Captain;
"but reasonably safe to attack, with nothing but a Clermont
"acting that character. Ferdinand, I can perceive, knew his
"Clermont; and took liberties with him. Divided himself
"into three attacks: one in front, one on Clermont's right
"flank, both of which cannonaded, as if in earnest, but did
"not prevent Clermont going to dinner. One attack on front,
"one on right flank; then there was a third, seemingly on
"left flank, but which winded itself round (perilously im-
"prudent, had there been a Captain, instead of a Clermont
"deepish in wine by this time), and burst in upon Clermont's
"rear: jingling his wine-glasses and decanters, think at what
"a rate; — scattering his 47,000 and him to the road again,
"with a loss of men, which was counted to 4,000 (4,000
"against 1,700), and of honour — whatever was still to
"lose!" *

Ferdinand, it was hoped, would now be able to maintain
himself, and push forward, on this French side of the Rhine:
and had Wesel been his (as some of us know it is not!), perhaps he might. At any rate, veteran Belleisle took his
measures: — dismissal of Clermont Prince of the Blood, and
appointment of Contades, a man of some skill; recal of
Soubise and his 24,000 from their Austrian intentions; these
and other strenuous measures, — and prevented such consummation. A gallant young Comte de Gisors, only son of
Belleisle, perished in that disgraceful Crefeld : — unfortunate
old man, what a business that of "cutting Germany in four"
has been to you, first and last!

* Mauvillon, L 197-309; Westphalen, I. 588-604; Tempelhof; &c. &c.

"*Louisburg* (North America), *July 8th.* Landing of General
"Amherst's people, at Louisburg in Cape Breton; with a
"view of besieging that important place. Which has now
"become extremely difficult; the garrison, and their de-
"fences, military, naval, being in full readiness for such an
"event. Landing was done by Brigadier Wolfe; under the
"eye of Amherst and Admiral Boscawen from rearward, and
"under abundant fire of batteries and musketries playing on
"it ahead: in one of the surfiest seas (but we have waited
"four days, and it hardly mends), tossing us about like corks;
"— so that 'many of the boats were broken;' and Wolfe and
"people 'had to leap out, breast deep,' and make fight for
"themselves, the faster the better, under very intricate cir-
"cumstances! Which was victoriously done, by Wolfe and
"his people; really in a rather handsome manner, that
"morning. As were all the subsequent Siege-operations,
"on land and on water, by them and the others: — till
"(August 8th) the Siege ended: in complete surrender, —
"positively for the last time (Pitt fully intends); no Austrian
"Netherlands now to put one on revoking it!*

"These are pretty victories, cheering to Pitt and Fried-
"rich: but the difficult point still is that of Fermor. Whose
"Cossacks, and their devil-like ravagings, are hideous to
"think of: — unrestrainable by Dohna, unless he could cut
"the root of them; which he cannot. *June 27th*" (while
Colonel Mosel, with his 3,000 wagons, still only one stage from
Troppau, was so busy), "slow Fermor rose from Konitz;
"began hitching southward, southward gradually to Posen,
"— a considerably stronger Polish Town; on the edge both of
"Brandenburg and of Silesia; — and has been sitting there,
"almost ever since our entrance into Bohemia; his Cossacks
"burning and wasting to great distances in both Countries;
"no deciding which of them he meant to invade with his main
"Army. Sits there almost a month, enigmatic to Dohna,
"enigmatic to Friedrich: till Friedrich decides at last that he
"cannot be suffered longer, whichever of them he mean; and
"rises for Silesia (August 2d). Precisely about which day
"Fermor had decided for Brandenburg, and rolled over

* General Amherst's *Diary of the Siege* (in *Gentleman's Magazine*, xxviii.
384-89).

"thither, towards Cüstrin and the Frankfurt-on-Oder Coun-"try, heralded by fire and murder, as usual."

Friedrich's march to Landshut is again much admired. Daun had beset the three great roads, the two likeliest especially, with abundant Pandours, and his best Loudons and St. Ignons: Friedrich, making himself enigmatic to Daun, struck into the third road by Skalitz, Nachod; circuitous, steep, but lying Glatzward, handy for support of various kinds. He was attempted, once or more, by Pandours, but used them badly; fell in with Daun's old abatis (well wind-dried now), in different places, and burnt them in passing. And in five days, was in Kloster-Grüssau, safe on his own side of the Mountains again. One point only we will note, in these Pandour turmoilings. From Skalitz, the first stage of his march, he answers a Letter of Brother Henri's:

To Prince Henri (at Tschopau in Saxony). "What you "write to me of my Sister of Baireuth" (that she has been in extremity, cannot yet write, and must not be told of the Prince of Prussia's death lest it kill her) "makes me tremble! "Next to our Mother, she is what I have the most tenderly "loved in this world. She is a Sister who has my heart and "all my confidence; and whose character is of price beyond "all the crowns in this universe. From my tenderest years, I "was brought up with her: you can conceive how there reigns "between us that indissoluble bond of mutual affection and "attachment for life, which in all other cases, were it only "disparity of ages, is impossible. Would to Heaven I might "die before her; — and that this terror itself don't take away "my life without my actually losing her!"† * *

† *Œuvres de Frédéric,* xxvi. 179, "Klenny, near Skalitz, 3d August 1758; Henri's Letter is dated, "Camp of Tschopau, 28th July" (ib. 177).

At Grüssau (August 9th) he writes to his dear Wilhelmina herself: "Oh, you the dearest of my family, you whom I have "most at heart of all in this world, — for the sake of whatever "is most precious to you, preserve yourself, and let me have "at least the consolation of shedding my tears in your bosom! "Fear nothing for us, and" — O King, she is dying, and I believe knows it, though you will hope to the last! There is something piercingly tragical in those final Letters of Friedrich to his Wilhelmina, written from such scenes of wreck and storm, and in Wilhelmina's beautiful everloving quiet Answers, dictated when she could no longer write. *

Friedrich had last left Grüssau, April 18th; he has returned to it, August 8th: after sixteen weeks of a very eventful absence. In Grüssau he staid two whole days; — busy enough he, probably, though his people were resting! August 10th, he draws up, for Prince Henri, "under seal of the most absolute secrecy," and with admirable business-like strictness, brevity and clearness, forgetting nothing useful, remembering nothing useless, a Paper of Directions in case of a certain event: "I march tomorrow against the Russians: as "the events of war may lead to all sorts of accidents, "and it may easily happen to me to be killed, I have "thought it my duty to let you know what my plans "were," and what you are to do in that event, — "the rather as you are Guardian of our Nephew" (late Prince of Prussia's Son) "with an unlimited authority." Oath from all the armies the instant I am killed: rapid, active, as ever; the enemy not to notice that there is

---

* "July 18th" is the last by her hand, and "almost illegible;" — still extant, it seems, though withheld from us. Was received at Grüssau here, and answered at some length (*Œuvres*, XXVII. i. 316), according to the specimen just given. Two more of hers follow, and Four of the King's (ib. 317-323). Nearly meaningless, as printed there, without commentary for the unprepared reader.

any change in the command. I intend to "beat the "Russians utterly" (à plate couture, "splay-seam"), "if it be possible;" then to &c.: — gives you his "itinerary," too, or probable address, till "the 25th" (notably enough); in short, forgets nothing useful, nor remembers any thing that is not, in spite of his hurry.* For Minister Finck also there went a Paper; seal *not* needing to be opened, for the moment.

With Margraf Karl, and Fouquet under him, who are to guard Silesia, he leaves in two Divisions about Half the late Olmütz Army: — added to the other force, this will make about 40,000 for that service.** Keith has the chief command here; but is ordered to Breslau, in the mean time, for a little rest and recovery of health. Friday, 11th August, Friedrich himself, with the other Half, pushes off towards Fermor and the Cossack demons; through Liegnitz, through Hohenfriedberg Country, straight for Frankfurt, with his best speed.

---

* "*Disposition Testamentaire*" (so they have labelled it); given in *Œuvres*, IV. (*Appendice*) 261-262. Friedrich's *Testament* proper is already made, and all in order, years ago ("11th January 1752"); of this there followed Two new Redactions (new *editions* with slight improvements, "7th November 1768," and "8th January 1769" the *finally* valid one); and various Supplements, or summary Enforcements (as here), at different times of crisis: See *Preuss*, IV. 277, 401, and *Œuvres de Frédéric*, VI. p. 13 (of Preface), for some confused account of that matter.

** Stenzel, v. 163.

END OF VOL. X.

www.ingramcontent.com/pod-product-compliance
Lightning Source LLC
Chambersburg PA
CBHW031855220426
43663CB00006B/630